THE FATHERS
OF THE CHURCH

A NEW TRANSLATION

VOLUME 99

THE FATHERS OF THE CHURCH

A NEW TRANSLATION

EDITORIAL BOARD

Thomas P. Halton
The Catholic University of America
Editorial Director

Elizabeth Clark
Duke University

Robert D. Sider
Dickinson College

Joseph T. Lienhard, S.J.
Fordham University

Michael Slusser
Duquesne University

Frank A.C. Mantello
The Catholic University of America

Cynthia White
The University of Arizona

Kathleen McVey
Princeton Theological Seminary

Robin Darling Young
The Catholic University of America

David J. McGonagle
Director
The Catholic University of America Press

FORMER EDITORIAL DIRECTORS

Ludwig Schopp, Roy J. Deferrari, Bernard M. Peebles,
Hermigild Dressler, O.F.M.

Cornelia Horn
Staff Editor

IBERIAN FATHERS

VOLUME 3

PACIAN OF BARCELONA
OROSIUS OF BRAGA

Translated by

CRAIG L. HANSON
Muskingum College
New Concord, Ohio

THE CATHOLIC UNIVERSITY OF AMERICA PRESS
Washington, D.C.

Copyright © 1999
THE CATHOLIC UNIVERSITY OF AMERICA PRESS
All rights reserved
Printed in the United States of America

The paper used in this publication meets the minimum requirements of the American National Standards for Information Science— Permanence of Paper for Printed Library Materials, ANSI Z39.48–1984.
∞

LIBRARY OF CONGRESS CATALOGING-IN-PUBLICATION DATA

Iberian fathers : Pacian of Barcelona and Orosius of Braga :
  [writings] / translated by Craig L. Hanson.
      p. cm. — (The fathers of the church ; v. 99)
  Includes bibliographical references and Indexes.
  ISBN 0-8132-0099-7 (alk. paper)
  ISBN 978-0-8132-2631-6 (pbk.)
  1. Theology—Early works to 1800. 2. Apologetics—Early works to 1800. I. Pacian, Saint, Bishop of Barcelona, 4th cent.
II. Orosius, Paulus III. Hanson, Craig L. IV. Series.
BR60.F3127   1999
[BR65]
270 s—dc21
[270.2]
                                               98-16992

UXORI DILECTISSIMAE
ROBIN

CONTENTS

Preface ix

PACIAN OF BARCELONA

Introduction	3
Select Bibliography	14
Letter 1	17
Letter 2	27
Letter 3	38
On Penitents	71
On Baptism	87

OROSIUS OF BRAGA

Introduction	97
Select Bibliography	112
Book in Defense against the Pelagians	115
Inquiry or Memorandum to Augustine on the Error of the Priscillianists and Origenists	168

Indices

General Index	177
Index of Holy Scripture	187

PREFACE

This volume brings together writings from Pacian of Barcelona and Orosius of Braga, two leading Iberian Fathers of the late fourth and early fifth centuries. In the case of Pacian, bishop of Barcelona, this includes all of his extant works: a treatise on penance; a sermon on baptism; and his correspondence with the Novatianist Sympronian. For Orosius, priest of Braga, this comprises two short treatises written not long before his famous *Historiarum adversus paganos libri septem*:[1] a memorandum to Augustine of Hippo on Priscillianism and Origenism in Spain; and an apologetic tract directed against Pelagius and his supporters. As such, this book complements existing volumes in the "Fathers of the Church" series. It completes the *corpus* of Orosius's writings which began with the publication of Roy Deferrari's translation of the *Historia* in volume 50 (1964); and it adds the works of these two Iberian Fathers to those of Martin of Braga, Paschasius of Dumium, Leander of Seville, Braulio of Saragossa, and Fructuosus of Braga gathered in volumes 62 and 63 (1969, translated by Claude Barlow).

While today Orosius is a well-known figure in the history of Christianity, due in large part to his *Historia* and his prominent, if controversial, role in the Pelagian controversy, Pacian has received far less notice and recognition. Yet his writings reveal much about Spanish Christianity of his own time. In particular he furnishes valuable insights into the presence of the Novatianist movement in Spain and its distinctive doctrines, the Catholic modes of resistance, and contemporary orthodox theory and teachings on penance and baptism. Both authors were well-educated in classical pagan and Christian Latin literature, and accomplished in rhetorical technique. Orosius especially is fond

1. Hereafter, *Historia*.

of displaying his rhetorical knowledge and training. But it is Pacian who is the more effective stylist and writer. As Jerome noted long ago in his *De viris illustribus*, 106, Pacian is a man "of restrained eloquence."

The translation of these two authors' works is fairly literal. Readers will notice that, as a result, the use of inclusive language is somewhat restricted. As scholars before me have observed, there is no entirely consistent or satisfactory solution to this problem. The most a translator can do, in the words of a noted authority, is "to echo the original's true meaning in context, with its significant overtones, distinctive style, special individual use of words, and perceptible 'flavor.'"[2]

The biblical references in the notes accompanying the translations give the chapter and verse numbers of the New Revised Standard Version. But in quoting Pacian's and Orosius's own biblical texts I have, of course, faithfully translated their Latin. Also, it should be noted that there are indications for both men occasionally quoting biblical passages from memory. Finally, beyond such scriptural references, only a few important classical pagan and early Christian literary parallels have been cited in the notes; more extensive citations may be found in the editions themselves.

I am grateful to Thomas P. Halton and the other "Fathers of the Church" editors for their support of this project and for including the volume in the present series. Special thanks go to Cornelia Horn, who has been unfailing with her editorial advice and assistance.

2. Raymond V. Schoder, *The Art and Challenge of Translation* (Oak Park: Bolchazy-Carducci, 1987), vii.

PACIAN OF BARCELONA

INTRODUCTION

St. Jerome, in chapter 106 of his *De viris illustribus*, furnishes most of the meager biographical data which we possess concerning the bishop and theologian Pacian of Barcelona. It reads as follows: "Pacian, bishop of Barcelona in the foothills of the Pyrenean mountains, a man of restrained eloquence[1] and as distinguished for his life as for his words, wrote various short works among which are *The Stag* and *Against the Novatianists*, and died at an advanced age in the reign of the emperor Theodosius." Barcelona (ancient Barcino) in the Roman province of Tarraconensis was known early on for its Christian connections.[2] St. Cucuphas, celebrated by Prudentius as the "glory of Barcelona,"[3] as well as the martyrs Eulalia and Severus were noteworthy in the history of the early Church. The city eventually became the suffragan diocese of Tarragona, and the succession of bishops in the fourth century included Praetextatus, Pacian, and Lampius. Although neither Jerome nor any other source explicitly indicates Pacian's nationality, Lisardo Rubio Fernández makes the point that at this time prelates were chosen here, as in many locations, from among the local diocesan clergy.[4] Thus, he supposes that

---

1. *Castigatae eloquentiae.* A variant manuscript reading, accepted by some scholars, is *castitate et eloquentia.* In this case the passage should be translated as "Pacian . . . distinguished for his chastity and eloquence . . ." But since Pacian was married and had a son before his elevation to the see of Barcelona, this reading seems less appropriate and thus less likely to be authentic. Cf. Lisardo Rubio Fernández, *San Paciano. Obras* (Barcelona: Universidad de Barcelona, 1958), 5; and Ángel Anglada Anfruns, *Las obras de Paciano publicadas por V. Noguera y edición crítica del "Liber de paenitentibus"* (Valencia: Universidad de Valencia, 1982), 14.

2. Valuable background on the history of Christianity in the city is available in J. Mas, *Notes històriques del bisbat de Barcelona* (Barcelona: J. Vives y La Renaixensa, 1906) and Sebastián Puig y Puig, *Episcopologio de la sede Barcinonense* (Barcelona: Balmes, 1929).

3. *Peristephanon* 4.33–34.

4. *San Paciano*, 5. Cf. canon 24 from the Council of Elvira: *Omnes qui peregre*

Pacian, a "son of the diocese of Barcelona," was native to the region if not the city. On the matter of Pacian's dating, it can be noted that Jerome's catalog of Christian writers, *De viris illustribus*, was produced in 393. Since therein he speaks of Pacian as having died "at an advanced age" during Theodosius's reign (379–95), it appears that Pacian passed away sometime between 379 and 392 and may have been born in the first decade of the fourth century.

(2) Judging from his extant writings as well as Jerome's brief evaluation of his literary qualities, Pacian received a good education and solid literary training in his early life. Most likely such was provided by his parents who, in turn, were probably wealthy. Pacian himself admits his classical schooling in one of his letters to Sympronian.[5] Of his subsequent life before his consecration as bishop of Barcelona little is known, except that he was married and had a son who was to figure prominently in the later political and literary history of the Empire. Even the date of his elevation to the see of Barcelona is controversial. Certainly it was after 343 (when we know that Praetextatus still presided in Barcelona)[6] and probably before 377.[7] Some modern authorities have ventured that Pacian perhaps came to Christianity as a convert. They base their view upon a statement made by the bishop in his *De baptismo* where he seems to associate himself with paganism.[8] Rubio Fernández, for his part, raises some interesting

---

fuerint baptizati, eo quod eorum minime sit cognita vita, placuit ad clerum non esse promovendos in alienis provinciis.

5. *Ep.* 2.4: "And yet I had learned this verse [of Virgil] as a little child."
6. In that year sources indicate that he was present at the Council of Sardica.
7. In Pacian's initial letter to Sympronian (*Ep.* 1.3) he mentions the Apollinarians, among other heretical groups. Since they were not condemned until 377 in a church council convoked by Pope Damasus, this would seem to furnish the needed *ante quem*. Rubio Fernández, *San Paciano*, 14–16, prefers 380, based on the significance he attaches to Pacian's statements that only orthodox Christians had the right to be called the "Catholic" Church—something not officially recognized until Theodosius's edict of March 28, 380. Anglada Anfruns, *Las obras*, 16, rejects 377 for very different reasons. He argues that in *Ep.* 1.3 Pacian does not mention the Apollinarians, but the followers of Apelles. This is based on what he sees as the original, correct manuscript reading of *Apelliacos* (not *Apollinariaeos*).
8. *De baptismo* 6: "In other words, having put aside the errors of our former

questions about Pacian's marriage. Was Pacian a widower when he attained the episcopal throne? Or did he pass directly from a married state to that high position?[9] If his wife was living when Pacian was elevated, both were bound to renounce their marriage.[10] Typically, in such circumstances the former wife would become a deaconess in the local church. Concerning Pacian's son, Jerome once again in his *De viris illustribus* provides some detail. In chapter 132 he writes: "Dexter,[11] son of Pacian whom I mentioned above, distinguished in his generation and devoted to the Christian faith, has, I am told, written a *Universal History*[12] which I have not yet read." Scholars agree that it was this Dexter to whom Jerome dedicated his famous work.[13] In addition, Jerome notes in one of his polemical writings directed at Rufinus that his friend Dexter ultimately achieved the office of praetorian prefect.[14] He occupied this position under the emperor Honorius in 395 and previously had served as proconsul of Asia (379-87) and *comes rei privatae* (387) under Theodosius I.

(3) Pacian was the author of several writings well-known in his own time, including the *Cervus* and *Contra Novatianos* cited by Jerome. Unfortunately for the modern reader, only five works

---

life—namely, servitude to idols, cruelty, fornication, licentiousness and all the other vices of flesh and blood—we should, through the Spirit, follow new ways in Christ: faith, modesty, innocence, and chastity."

9. Rubio Fernández, *San Paciano*, 6. Cf. the situations of Gregory of Nyssa and Hilary of Poitiers.

10. The Spanish Council of Elvira, held in the first decade of the fourth century, in canon 33 imposed sexual continence on bishops (and the clergy in general), and this prescription was renewed in later years.

11. His full name was Nummius Aemilianus Dexter.

12. *Omnimoda historia*. Unfortunately, Dexter's work has not survived. The so-called *Chronicon Dextri* which is extant (*Patrologia Latina* 21.55–572) is a forgery by a Spanish Jesuit, Jeronimo Roman de la Higuera (1538–1611).

13. *De viris illustribus*, preface: "You have urged me, Dexter, to follow the example of [Gaius Suetonius] Tranquillus in giving a systematic account of ecclesiastical writers, and to do for our writers what he did for the illustrious men of letters among the pagans."

14. *Apologia adversus libros Rufini* 2.23: "It was thus that, when my friend Dexter, who held the office of praetorian prefect, asked me ten years ago to make a list for him of the writers of our faith, I placed among the various treatises assigned to various authors this book as composed by Pamphilus, supposing the matter to be as it had been brought before the public by you and your disciples."

6   INTRODUCTION

have been preserved. These include three letters addressed to a prominent Novatianist partisan from Spain named Sympronian,[15] a short treatise on penance, and a sermon on baptism. Pacian's correspondence with Sympronian, who is otherwise unknown in patristic literature, apparently began when the bishop received an unsolicited letter from the Novatianist requesting explanations of the use of the term "Catholic," of penitential practice, and of repentance generally. It is clear, as well, that he expressed several rather vehement objections to various theological and disciplinary positions held by Pacian's majority "party" of Christians. Pacian responds to his critic in this, his first letter, and the others with respect and Christian compassion,[16] but couples this with an unflagging determination to uphold the age-old prerogatives of the orthodox Church as he sees them. Indeed, the tone of his reply to Sympronian's initial inquiries is rather boastful. Pacian proudly asserts and justifies the application of the name "Catholic" to his co-religionists past and present, by use of biblical and historical arguments. It is in this context that his famous phrase "'Christian' is my first name, and 'Catholic' is my surname" appears.[17] The meaning of "Catholic" is supplied as well: "And if, lastly, we must give an explanation of the word 'Catholic' and extract it from the Greek by a Latin interpretation, 'Catholic' means 'one in every place' or perhaps, as our learned men think, it is said to mean 'obedience in all things'—that is, in all the commandments of God."[18] The unity of the Catholic Church is contrasted with the plurality of heresies, which take their names from their founders.[19] In addition, the possibility of reconcilia-

15. On Sympronian, see the helpful discussions by Rubio Fernández, *San Paciano*, 21–23, and Leo Wohleb, "Bischof Pacianus von Barcelona und sein Gegner, der Novatianer Sympronianus," *Spanische Forschungen der Görresgesellschaft* 2 (1930): 25–35.
16. For example, Sympronian is addressed throughout as "my brother" and "sir."
17. *Christianus mihi nomen est, catholicus vero cognomen* (*Ep.* 1.4).
18. *Ep.* 1.4.
19. In *Ep.* 1.1–3 the following apostolic and post-apostolic heretical groups are named: Ebionites, Marcionites, Valentinians, Apollinarians, Montanists (Cataphrygians / Phrygians), and Novatianists. Also mentioned are Dositheus the Samaritan, the Sadducees and Pharisees, Simon Magus, Menander, Nicolaus, Apelles, Blastus, Theodotus, Praxeas, Leucius, Proculus, Maximilla, and Priscilla.

tion and forgiveness for penitent sinners, as well as the right and power of the Church to grant such, is stoutly defended. This is contrasted with the Novatianists' excessive rigorism and refusal to grant forgiveness for sins committed after baptism. It is clear from Pacian's second letter that Sympronian did not react well to these arguments by the bishop, and perhaps it was at this point that Sympronian sent, attached to his own second epistle, a Novatianist treatise for which he wished Pacian's response.[20] Pacian, for his part, defends in the second letter his previous description of the heresies and their attributed names, but makes the point that he does not accuse the Novatianists because of their name, but because of their doctrines. Ironically, he follows this with a devastating personal attack on the eponymous founder of the Novatianists, Novatian himself.[21] Pacian's source here is Cyprian of Carthage and he appeals to the authority of the North African bishop both for this attack and subsequently in his critique of Novatianist teachings. The third and final missive to Sympronian may represent something more than a mere personal letter. Granting its essentially epistolary nature, it is also virtually a proper anti-Novatianist tract: lengthy, carefully constructed, and filled with elaborate arguments, biblical quotations, and metaphors, and point by point rebuttals of major arguments found in the treatise previously sent to him by Sympronian. Because of its resemblance to a proper anti-Novatianist tract, some modern scholars have attempted to identify it with the writing cited by Jerome: *Contra Novatianos*.[22] But without further proof, such an identification must be resisted. Pacian quotes extensively

20. Cf. *Ep.* 2.8: "But, seeing that you have argued rather extensively concerning penance, that it ought not to be done or that it should take place before baptism, and you have filled the pages with innumerable citations of examples from his [Novatian's] treatise, I will respond to each point, though this is more than is called for." Such a response by Pacian, however, does not occur later in this letter, but in his third and final letter to Sympronian.

21. This attack is developed further and also expanded in Pacian's last letter to Sympronian.

22. See, for example, Rubio Fernández, *San Paciano*, 12. But other scholars point to Pacian's own words at the end of his third letter: "I will add, when I shall have the time, another letter also, in which I will not refute your views, but rather, set forth ours." This, they argue, might well designate the treatise cited by Jerome.

and verbatim from the Novatianist treatise received from Sympronian, and from this it is possible to reconstruct its major arguments, if not the entire text. The bishop himself summarizes the Novatianists' main points opposing the Catholic Church's teachings and practices: (1) the performance of penance is not permitted after baptism, (2) the Church cannot remit mortal sin, and (3) the Church by admitting sinners condemns itself and perishes. (Chief among the biblical texts employed by the Novatianists are Mt 18.15, Jn 15.1, and 1 Cor 5.3–5.) Methodically, Pacian addresses and seeks to refute these major points and their implications, as well as many other arguments raised by Sympronian and the Novatianist treatise. His chief sources of authority are the Bible, Tertullian (whose early orthodoxy Pacian is careful to defend), and Cyprian. As each Novatianist position is discredited, Pacian puts in its place a Catholic teaching. His discussions are far-ranging and his argumentation is, for the most part, logical, hardhitting, and effective.[23] Only occasionally does his attack take on a personal nature, and even there it is directed against Novatian, not Sympronian.[24] From the three letters collectively, a fairly clear picture of Spanish Novatianist ideas emerges. According to their teachings, the Church, as the body of Christ, must maintain a complete freedom from impurity and stain. This, in turn, precludes its acceptance of sinners. All penance outside of and after baptism, accordingly, is not permitted to believers. If people were to believe that God allowed them to perform penance, they would take it as permission to sin continually, if not freely. Pacian counters that God himself wishes not the death, but the pardon of the sinner, and cites numerous biblical passages which support this viewpoint.

23. Especially telling, perhaps, is his argument that Novatian himself, before separating from the Catholics, had approved of the pardoning of the so-called *lapsi*. Pacian also focuses on the irregularity of Novatian's episcopal ordination.

24. Indeed, the ending of the third letter is indicative of Pacian's overall tone: "Meanwhile, in the present letter, I ask you to examine each and every part of it thoroughly. For all that is read in haste passes by unnoticed. If you desire the nobler spiritual gifts and possess a spirit which is open to good instruction, you will not easily disregard things so true. May the Lord see fit to guard and protect you forever, and cause you to live as a Christian in accordance with spiritual harmony."

INTRODUCTION 9

In particular, the very disciples of Jesus are pointed to as examples of sinners to whom Christ entrusted the very fabric and future of his Church.

(4) Perhaps the most famous of Pacian's extant writings is his *De paenitentibus*, a short work which complements his correspondence and takes his views on repentance and penance from the realm of theory to that of real world action, ritual, and ceremony.[25] Addressed especially to the public penitents but not excluding the catechumens, regular members, and attending worshippers within his own congregation,[26] this exhortation to penance was likely intended first as a sermon and later as a published, circulating work.[27] As scholars have noted, for a church such as Pacian's whose numbers were steadily increasing and were ever more liable to fall into sin, penitential practice was becoming increasingly crucial. In *De paenitentibus* Pacian discusses the many practical issues of penance, identifies its underlying justifications, and encourages his congregants to avail themselves of such a salutary institution. The tract is divided into roughly four major sections. The first deals with the various types of sins which individuals commit and establishes a classification scheme for such sins according to their seriousness. For Pacian only three sins require formal public penance: idolatry, murder, and fornication. All others may be compensated for by the exercise of opposite virtues. The second section treats sinners who, because of embarrassment or for other reasons, do not perform public penance and continue to participate in the life of the

---

25. For a thorough analysis of Pacian's theoretical and practical views on repentance and penance, see Clarence McAuliffe, "Absolution in the Early Church: The View of St. Pacianus," *Theological Studies* 6 (1945): 51–61.

26. *De paenitentibus* 2: "Furthermore, let no one imagine that this very sermon on the institution of penance is drawn up for penitents alone, lest for this reason whoever is not placed in that position scorn what will be said here as intended for others. Rather, the discipline of the entire Church is tied, as it were, into this clasp, since catechumens have to take care that they do not pass into such a state, and the faithful that they do not return to it; but the penitents themselves have to work hard that they arrive swiftly at the fruit of this labor."

27. Although most modern editions give the title as *Paraenesis sive exhortatorius libellus ad paenitentiam*, Anglada Anfruns, the most recent editor, is correct in asserting (*Las obras*, 19–20) that a better attested and more authentic title is simply *De paenitentibus*.

Church. This, says Pacian, clearly constitutes sacrilegious behavior and should not be tolerated. The third takes up the issue of sinners who, though admitting their sin, do not follow through with the formal process and public exercises of penance, either because of ignorance or, again, because of embarrassment or lack of courage. The last section depicts both the ultimate reward accorded those who complete the difficult process of penance and the final punishment reserved for those who reject the Church's offering. Few texts provide as much insight into the penitential life of a fourth-century Christian community as *De paenitentibus*.

(5) Pacian's sermon *De baptismo* is directed particularly to the catechumens in his congregation as they advanced as candidates for baptism. In it he reminds his listeners of the fall of Adam (and Eve) in the Garden of Eden and its attendant consequences for all of humanity,[28] the nature and domain of the devil, the struggle of the Immaculate One, Christ, against him, and the liberation of all people through faith. He emphasizes the efficacy of both the baptismal font and its accompaniment, ritual anointing, in cleansing humans of sin and conferring the gift of the Holy Spirit. By such means all can be assured of the redemption brought by Christ. Pacian concludes with an exhortation to his congregation to keep themselves apart from sin so that they might gain the ineffable prize on that final "day of the Lord."

(6) Of the known works of Pacian which have not been preserved,[29] the most intriguing is surely the *Cervus* (or *Cervulus*).[30]

---

28. An interesting and very clear exposition of the concept of original sin occurs in chapter 5.

29. Almost certainly Pacian produced still other writings, now lost, whose titles are not recorded in the extant contemporary literature.

30. Jerome, as noted above, cites the work as *The Stag* (*Cervus*). But Pacian, according to the manuscript tradition of *De paenitentibus* (where the writing is mentioned), offers the name *The Fawn* (*Cervulus*). To account for the discrepancy, Rubio Fernández (*San Paciano*, 10–11) concludes that the diminutive form is more in keeping with both the popular literary conventions of the fourth century and the stylistic preferences of Pacian himself, while in the more sophisticated genre of Jerome's *De viris illustribus* the basic term *cervus* was perhaps preferred. Finally, Fernández notes that popular festivals generally were often denoted with a diminutive form.

According to the author himself, his purpose in writing the tract is to dissuade the Christian faithful from attending or participating in the various pagan festivities which marked the beginning of the new year. Despite his best intentions, his treatise had just the opposite effect. As Pacian puts it, "For this, I think, has most recently been the effect of my treatise, *The Fawn*, to such a degree that the more earnestly this festival was branded with disgrace the more diligently it was practiced."[31] The popularity and staying power of such pagan celebrations in Roman Europe and the Mediterranean (amply attested in Christian sources, eastern and western, through the seventh century) are easily understandable in terms of the sizable non-Christian elements in society, the conservatism of social custom, and even the lure of the unusual and the forbidden. Unfortunately, we know little more either about Pacian's writing or about this particular festival, though it is perhaps similar to others described by such Christian authors as Caesarius of Arles.[32] Most modern authorities think, too, that the other work mentioned by Jerome, Pacian's *Contra Novatianos*, has not been preserved. But whether this view or that of scholars who identify this "lost" treatise with the bishop's third letter to Sympronian eventually gains scholarly consensus, there is no doubt as to the essential fact of Pacian's great concern over the existence of Novatianism in his diocese and homeland.

(7) In 1913 Dom G. Morin attributed to Pacian two previously known anti-Manichaean writings, one transmitted under the name Marius Victorinus (*Liber ad Iustinum Manichaeum*), the other anonymously (*De similitudine carnis*). These attributions were not based on extrinsic considerations, but rather on observations of style, in particular biblical usages, rhetorical figures, and distinctive vocabulary. Although Morin's thesis was initially accepted by many scholars, opposition grew and today most agree that neither work can be assigned to the bishop of Barcelona.

(8) Pacian, like such Christian intellectuals of late antiquity as

---

31. *De paenitentibus* 1.
32. See his *Sermo* 192. On this subject generally, see the definitive study by M. Meslin, *La fête des Kalendes de janvier dans l'empire romain. Étude d'un rituel de Nouvel An* (Brussels: Latomus, 1970), esp. 80–88.

Ambrose and Jerome, was in large part molded by his classical education. And like Tertullian, Cyprian, Arnobius, and Lactantius before him, he drew freely on his knowledge of both the style and content of the pagan authors he knew from childhood. But, unlike Tertullian and Jerome in particular, he does not publicly display the same tensions or qualms on the issue. Indeed, responding to Sympronian's criticism of his use of Virgil, Pacian says, "Has a bishop quoted a verse of poetry? What! Does the Apostle Paul feel ashamed when he quotes and accepts as true a particular Athenian verse?"[33] And later he asserts, "Nor are we rhetoricians; but whatever means of expression we use, we believe it to be of the resource given by God."[34] Pacian's writings are filled with quotations, paraphrases, and adaptations of (as well as allusions to) numerous pagan authors.[35] Virgil, Ovid, Horace, Lucretius, and Cicero all appear within his pages. There are also references to sayings by Hesiod and Solon.

(9) But, of course, the greatest literary influences on Pacian and his writings were Christian ones, notably the Bible, Tertullian, and Cyprian.[36] His easy familiarity with these sources is obvious throughout. The two individual authors were especially relevant and influential for his discussions of penance and Novatianism. It should be noted that in the case of Tertullian, Pacian is careful to differentiate his early works and teachings from those of his later, Montanist period. Pacian apparently felt a special affinity for Cyprian and speaks of him in the most respectful and affectionate terms. Finally, there are numerous references to other Latin Christian authors in Pacian's writings.

(10) As scholars beginning with Jerome have noted over the centuries, Pacian exhibits a style which manages to be both simple

33. *Ep.* 2.4. This is an allusion to Paul's quotation from the *Phaenomena* of Aratus in Acts 17.28–29.
34. *Ep.* 2.4.
35. An indicative sampling of these is provided by Rubio Fernández (*San Paciano*, 25–29). An exhaustive line-by-line listing is furnished by Philippe Henri Peyrot in the critical apparatus to his edition of Pacian's works, *Paciani Barcelonensis episcopi opuscula edita et illustrata* (Zwolle: Tijl Heredum, 1896).
36. It is interesting to note that the text of Pacian's Latin Bible closely parallels that of Cyprian. On this subject generally, see J. Vilar, "Les citacions bíbliques de Sant Pacià," *Estudis Universitaris Catalans* 17 (1932): 1–49.

and elegant. Although he can and occasionally does employ all of the sophisticated figures and embellishments of the high rhetorical style, for the most part he uses such techniques sparingly. When Pacian does, however, the reader is struck by his effective use of rhetorical questions, sarcasm, anaphoras, paronomasia, synonyms, etymological figures, hypallage, brachylogy, anacoluthon, prolepsis, redundancy, antithesis, litotes, alliteration and assonance, and hyperbole. Equally striking is Pacian's originality in terms of figurative language, symbolism, and metaphorical expression. Finally, there is to be noted the use of unusual vocabulary and provincialisms. His is an artistic prose, well-adapted to the needs of his topics and audience.[37]

(11) The *editio princeps* of Pacian's works was published by Jean du Tillet in Paris in 1538. Since that time numerous editions have appeared.[38] The planned critical edition by Robert Kauer for the Vienna series *Corpus scriptorum ecclesiasticorum latinorum* was never completed or published. The present translation of Pacian's letters and *De baptismo* is based on the critical text of Lisardo Rubio Fernández, published in 1958.[39] For *De paenitentibus*, the more recent edition of Ángel Anglada Anfruns, published in 1982, has been used.[40]

---

37. On Pacian's use of rhetorical techniques, see Anton Grüber, *Studien zu Pacianus von Barcelona* (Munich: Schuh, 1901). On his mastery of the rules of prose cadence, see Robert Kauer, *Studien zu Pacianus* (Vienna: Verlag des K. K. Staatgymnasiums, 1902).

38. For a convenient listing and evaluation of these, see Rubio Fernández, *San Paciano*, 40–43.

39. Lisardo Rubio Fernández, *San Paciano. Obras* (Barcelona: Universidad de Barcelona, 1958). The edition by Peyrot, cited above, is invaluable for its extensive philological and historical commentary and its citation of classical and patristic sources. Cf. E. Dekkers and A. Gaar, *Clavis Patrum Latinorum*, 3rd ed. (Turnhout: Brepols, 1995) [hereafter CPL], 196 (nos. 561, 563).

40. Ángel Anglada Anfruns, *Las obras de Paciano publicadas por V. Noguera y edición crítica del "Liber de paenitentibus"* (Valencia: Universidad de Valencia, 1982). Cf. CPL, 196 (no. 562).

SELECT BIBLIOGRAPHY

Akeley, T. C. *Christian Initiation in Spain c. 300–1100*. London: Darton, Longman and Todd, 1967.

Anglada Anfruns, Ángel. "*Christiano mihi nomen est, Catholico vero cognomen* a la luz de la doctrina gramatical." *Emerita* 32 (1964): 253–66.

———. "Le corruttele del membro *Aquarum in penitis ignibus fuerit* alla luce della metafora della febbre (Paciano, *Paen*. 11,5)." *Vetera Christianorum* 14 (1977): 253–72.

———. La fuente del catálogo heresiológico de Pacian." *Emerita* 33 (1965): 321–46.

———. *Las obras de Paciano publicadas por V. Noguera y edición crítica del "Liber de paenitentibus."* Valencia: Universidad de Valencia, 1982.

———. "La punctuación de ms Reginensis 331 en el texto de Paciano de Barcelona." *Vetera Christianorum* 12 (1975): 269–316.

———. "El texto de Paciano en la *Bibliotheca Patrum* de Margarin de la Bigne." In *Homenaje a Pedro Sainz Rodríguez*. 1: 309–37. Madrid: Fundacion Universitaria Espanola, 1986.

———. "La tradición manuscrita de Paciano de Barcelona." *Emerita* 35 (1967): 137–61.

———. "Unas notas críticas al texto de Paciano de Barcelona." *Emerita* 47 (1979): 11–34.

———. "Unas notas críticas al texto de Paciano de Barcelona." *Vetera Christianorum* 31 (1994): 279–313.

Borleffs, J. W. "Zwei neue Schriften Pacians?" *Mnemosyne* 3.7 (1939): 180–92.

Constanza, Salvatore. "La polemica di Paciano e Simproniano sull'uso di citare i poeti classici." *Vetera Christianorum* 15 (1978): 45–50.

Dalmau, J. M. "La doctrina del pecat original en Sant Pacià." *Analecta Sacra Tarraconensia* 4 (1928): 203–10.

Dominguez de Val, U. "Doctrina eclesiólogica de San Paciano de Barcelona." *The Hibbert Journal* 77 (1958): 83–90.

———. "Paciano de Barcelona. Escritor, teólogo y exégeta." *Salmanticensis* 9 (1962): 53–85.

SELECT BIBLIOGRAPHY 15

———. "La teología de San Paciano de Barcelona." *La Ciudad de Dios* 171 (1958): 5-28.
Fitzgerald, Allan. *Conversion through Penance in the Italian Church of the Fourth and Fifth Centuries: New Approaches to the Experience of Conversion from Sin.* Lewiston: Mellen, 1988.
Granado, Carmelo, S.J. *Pacien de Barcelone. Écrits.* Introduction, critical text, commentary, and index. Translated by Chantal Épitalon and Michel Lestienne. Sources chrétiennes 410, Paris: Les Éditions du Cerf, 1995.
Grüber, Anton. *Studien zu Pacianus von Barcelona.* Munich: Schuh, 1901.
Güzlow, Henneke. *Cyprian und Novatian.* Tübingen: Mohr, 1975.
Kauer, Robert. *Studien zu Pacianus.* Vienna: Verlag des K. K. Staatgymnasiums, 1902.
Martinez, M. "San Paciano, obispo de Barcelona." *Helmantica* 3 (1952): 221-38.
Martinez Sierra, A. "San Paciano, teólogo del pecado original." *Miscelánea Comillas* 49 (1968): 279-84.
———. "Teología penitencial de S. Paciano de Barcelona." *Miscelánea Comillas* 47/48 (1967): 75-94.
Mas, Joseph. *Notes historíques del bisbat de Barcelona.* Barcelona: J. Vives y La Renaixensa, 1906.
McAuliffe, Clarence. "Absolution in the Early Church: The View of St. Pacianus." *Theological Studies* 6 (1945): 51-61.
Meslin, Michel. *La fête des Kalendes de janvier dans l'empire romain. Étude d'un rituel de Nouvel An.* Brussels: Latomus, 1970.
Morin, Germain. "Un nouvel opuscule de Saint Pacien? Le *Ad Iustinum Manichaeum*." *Revue bénédictine* 30 (1913): 286-93.
———. "Un traité inédit du IV siècle: le *De similitudine carnis peccati* de l'évêque Saint Pacien de Barcelone." *Revue bénédictine* 29 (1912): 1-28.
Puig y Puig, Sebastían. *Episcopologio de la sede Barcinonense.* Barcelona: Balmes, 1929.
Peyrot, Philippe Henri. *Paciani Barcelonensis episcopi opuscula edita et illustrata.* Zwolle: Tijl Heredum, 1896.
Poschmann, Bernhard. *Penance and the Anointing of the Sick.* Translated by Francis Courtney. New York: Herder and Herder, 1964.
Rahner, Karl. *Penance in the Early Church.* Translated by Lionel Swain. New York: Crossroad, 1982.
Rubio Fernández, Lisardo. *San Paciano. Obras.* Barcelona: Universidad de Barcelona, 1958.
———. "El texto de San Paciano." *Emerita* 25 (1957): 327-67.
Salisbury, Joyce E. *Iberian Popular Religion 600 B.C. to 700 A.D.: Celts, Romans and Visigoths.* New York: Mellen, 1985.

Sullivan, Patrick A. "St. Pacian, Bishop of Barcelona." *Folia* 4 (1950): 43-44.
Vilar, J. "Les citacions bíbliques de Sant Pacià." *Estudis Universitaris Catalans* 17 (1932): 1-49.
Watkins, Oscar D. *A History of Penance: Being a Study of the Authorities*. 2 vols. London: Longmans and Green, 1920.
Wohleb, Leo. "Bischof Pacianus von Barcelona und sein Gegner, der Novatianer Sympronianus." *Spanische Forschungen der Görresgesellschaft* 2 (1930): 25-35.

LETTER 1

PACIAN TO SYMPRONIAN, his brother, [greeting].

1. Sir, if it is not an earthly purpose but, as I think, a spiritual calling that leads you to inquire of us regarding the faith of Catholic truth, you above all else, having begun your exposition so it appears from the vantage of a small stream far away and not holding to the fount and source of the original Church, should have shown what or how different the ideas are that you follow. You also should have revealed what cause more than any had detached your group from the unity of our body. For those parts for which a remedy is required should be exposed. Since now, if I may say, the refuge of correspondence has been closed, we do not see on what members especially we have to bestow our care. So numerous are the heresies which have arisen from the Christian headwaters that the roster of the mere names would be immense. For even if I were to neglect to mention the heretics of the Jews—Dositheus the Samaritan,[1] the Sadducees, and the Pharisees—it would take a very long time to recount how many emerged in the times of the apostles—Simon Magus, Menander, Nicolaus, and all the rest of them now hidden by a dark fame.[2] What again in later times were Ebion, Apelles, Marcion, Valentinus and Cerdo, and not long after them, the

---

1. For current scholarship on Dositheus and the other heretics and heretical groups named by Pacian in this and later sections, consult the pertinent entries in Angelo Di Berardino, ed., *Encyclopedia of the Early Church*, trans. Adrian Walford, with foreword and bibliographic amendments by W. H. C. Frend, 2 vols. (Oxford: Oxford University, 1992); Everett Ferguson, ed., *Encyclopedia of Early Christianity*, 2nd ed., 2 vols. (New York: Garland, 1997); and E. A. Livingstone and F. L. Cross, eds., *The Oxford Dictionary of the Christian Church*, 3rd ed. (Oxford: Oxford University, 1997). Also, on the classification of such heretics by Pacian, see Ángel Anglada Anfruns, "La fuente del catalogo heresiologico de Paciano," *Emerita* 33 (1965): 321–46.

2. Cf. Virgil, *Aeneis* 5.302.

Cataphrygians[3] and the Novatianists, not to mention any of the recent swarms?

(2) Who, therefore, must first be refuted through my letter? Even if you wish it, these pages will not be able to hold just the mere names of all of these heretics,[4] unless by your own writings, which in every way are condemnatory of penance, you declare that you have shared the views of the Phrygians.[5] But, dear Sir, so manifold and diverse is the error alone of these individuals that among them we have not only to strike against that belief which they hold against penance, but also to cut off the heads, as it were, of some Lernaean creature.[6]

2. First of all, they rely on several authorities, for, I think, Blastus the Greek is one of them; Theodotus also and Praxeas were once teachers of your group. They themselves, also Phrygians of some notoriety who falsely allege that they are inspired by Leucius, boast that they are instructed by Proculus. And having followed Montanus, Maximilla, and Priscilla, what numerous controversies have they roused concerning the day of Easter, the Paraclete, the apostles, the prophets, and many other things—as, for example, the appellation "Catholic" and the forgiveness of penance!

(2) Hence, if we should wish to discuss all of these matters, you would need to be present and ready to listen. And if my instruction should not be sufficient concerning only those points on which you write, nevertheless, since we ought to serve in whatever way we can those who are earnestly entreating us, we will now, for the sake of informing you, discuss in summary fashion those matters about which you have thought it appropriate

---

3. Another, earlier name for the Montanists. Such writers as Eusebius of Caesarea and Epiphanius of Salamis used the phrase "heresy of (*kata*) the *Phryges*" to designate this heretical movement; hence "Cataphrygians." Its birthplace was the region between Mysia and Phrygia in Asia Minor.

4. Peyrot here conjectures a gap in the text. Rubio Fernández notes such in his critical apparatus, but maintains the text. Either interpretation is possible.

5. Again, the Montanists are meant. Also, Pacian here as elsewhere in his letters purposely links Sympronian and his Novatianist colleagues with the Montanists.

6. A reference to the mythological Lernaean Hydra, a multi-headed serpentine monster disposed of by Heracles in the course of his Labors. The Hydra's mortal heads were believed to regenerate themselves and multiply when cut off.

to write. If you wish to have a more complete knowledge of our views, you ought to declare your own more frankly, lest by not seeking such information in rather plain terms, you leave us uncertain as to whether you are seeking information or challenging us.

(3) In the meantime—and this will pertain to our present correspondence—I wish above all to ask you not to borrow justification for your error from this very fact: that, as you say, throughout the entire world no one has been found who could convince or persuade you contrary to what you already believe. For although we are unskilled, most skillful is the spirit of God. And "even if we are faithless, faithful is God, who cannot deny himself."[7] When such happened in the distant past, the priests of God were not permitted to engage in dispute for long with one who resisted. "We," says the Apostle [Paul],[8] "have no such custom, nor does the church of God."[9] As you yourself know, "after a single admonition" the contentious individual is forsaken.[10] For who can persuade another person of anything against his will? Therefore, it is your own fault, my brother, and not theirs, if no one convinced you of what was best. On this day, too, it is in your power to scorn our writings also, if you would rather refute than approve of them. Moreover, a great number of people resisted both the Lord himself and his apostles; nor could the truth ever be convincingly told to anyone except to him who assented to it through his own religious feelings. Therefore, Sir, we have not written these things with a confidence that we could persuade you of anything if you resist, but rather, with the faith that we would not deny you access to a desirable harmony [with the Church][11] if you are willing. And with

---

7. Cf. 2 Tim 2.13.
8. Like many Latin patristic authors, Pacian in his writings identifies Paul solely by the word *apostolus* (i.e., the Apostle). Hereafter when this identification is intended by Pacian, *apostolus* will be rendered as "the Apostle."
9. 1 Cor 11.16.
10. Cf. Titus 3.10. The complete text, however, reads: *Hereticum hominem post unam et secundam correptionem devita* (Vulgate version).
11. *Volenti bonae pacis aditum non negemus.* On the special usage of *pax* to denote a harmony with or community of the Church, see L. R. Palmer, *The Latin Language* (London: Faber and Faber, 1961), 194.

such harmony, if it is dear to your own soul, there ought to be no dispute concerning the designation "Catholic." For if it is through God that our people obtain this designation, no question is to be raised, since divine authority takes precedence. If it is through human means, it must be disclosed when it was first taken. Then, if the name is estimable, it is not subject to hatred; if it is evil, it need not be envied.

3. The Novatianists, I am told, are named after Novatus or Novatian;[12] yet it is the sectarian teaching with which I find fault in them, not their name. Nor has anyone brought up against Montanus or the Phrygians their name [as ground for condemnation].

(2) But during the time of the apostles, you will say, no one used to be called "Catholic." So be it. It may have been so. I allow you even that. But when, after the apostles, heresies had appeared and were striving under various names to tear to pieces and split apart the Dove and the Queen of God, did not the apostolic people require a name of their own, by which they would mark the unity of an uncorrupted people, lest the error of some should tear limb from limb the undefiled virgin of God? Was it not right that the original [ecclesial] source[13] be designated by its own particular appellation?

(3) Suppose that this very day I entered a populous city. When I had found Marcionites, Apollinarians, Cataphrygians, Novatianists, and the rest of that kind who call themselves Christians, by what name should I recognize the congregation of my own people, unless it were called "Catholic"? Come now! Who has conferred so many names on these other groups? Why do so many cities, so many nations, each have their own defining designation? The same man who asks about the name "Catholic" will not himself be ignorant of the origin of his own name if I shall inquire about such. From where was the name "Catholic" bequeathed to me? Certainly that which has not fallen for so many ages was not borrowed from a man. This name "Catholic"

---

12. Novatus was a follower of Evaristus, the bishop who ordained Novatian. Later himself ordained priest by Evaristus, he opposed Cyprian's election and formed part of the Novatianist community at Carthage. Eusebius of Caesarea and various Greek patristic writers who follow him confuse Novatus with Novatian.

13. *Caput principale.* Cf. *Ep.* 1.1 above (*principalis ecclesiae*).

does not ring of Marcion, nor of Apelles, nor of Montanus; nor does it take heretics as its originators.

(4) Many things the Holy Spirit, whom God sent from heaven to the apostles as their comforter and guide, has taught us; many things reason teaches us, as Paul declares; and honesty, too, and, as he says, nature itself.[14] And what now? Does the authority of the disciples of the apostles, of the earliest priests, of the most blessed martyr and teacher Cyprian, carry so little weight with us? Do we wish to teach the teacher? Are we wiser than he was, and are we roused by the spirit of the flesh against this man, whom the noble shedding of his own blood and the crown of his most glorious suffering have presented as a witness of the eternal God? What about the great number of priests on this, our side, who throughout the entire world were united in a single ecclesial community[15] with this very same Cyprian? What about the great number of venerable bishops, of martyrs, of confessors? Come now, even if these were not adequate authorities for the use of this name, are we then adequate for its rejection? And shall the Fathers, instead, follow our authority; and the antiquity of the saints give way to our "corrections"; and our own times, which are already decaying through sin, scrape away the [wise] gray hair of apostolic antiquity?

4. And yet, my brother, do not be troubled. "Christian" is my first name, and "Catholic" is my surname. The former term designates me; the latter distinguishes me from others. By one I am given sanction; by the other I am signified. And if, lastly, we must give an explanation of the word "Catholic" and extract it from the Greek by a Latin interpretation, "Catholic" means "one in every place" or perhaps, as our learned men think, it is said to mean "obedience in all things"—that is, in all the commandments of God. Whence the Apostle states, "If you are obedient in all things."[16] And again, "For just as by the disobedience of one man many were made sinners, so, I declare, by the attention of one many will be made righteous."[17] Therefore the person who is a Catholic, this same one is obedient. And the person who is

---

14. Cf. 1 Cor 11.14.
16. 2 Cor 2.9.
15. *Pax una.* Cf. note 11 above.
17. Cf. Rom 5.19.

obedient, this same one is a Christian. Thus, the Catholic is a Christian. Wherefore, our people, when they are designated as Catholic, are separated by this appellation from any heretical name. But if the word "Catholic" also means "one in every place," as those who were mentioned above think it does, then David points out this very thing when he says, "The queen stood in clothing embroidered with gold and adorned with diverse colors"[18]—that is, she was one in the midst of all. And in the Song of Songs, the bridegroom speaks these words, "One is my dove, my perfect one; she is the only one for her mother; she is the chosen one for her that bore her."[19] And again, "The virgins shall be brought to the king after her."[20] And in addition to this, "young maidens without number."[21] Therefore, in the midst of all she is one, and one over all.

5. If you are seeking an explanation for this name, now it has been made clear. But as for penance, may God grant that it be necessary for no one among the faithful; that no one, after the assistance given in the sacred font [of baptism], plunge headlong into the pit of death; and that our priests not be compelled to inculcate or teach its late consolations, lest, while they soothe the sinner by [such] remedies, they open a path to sin. But we for our part reveal this kindness of our God to the wretched, not to the fortunate; and not before sin, but after sins. Nor do we proclaim this medicine to the healthy, but rather to those who are sick. If spiritual evils[22] have no power over the baptized, nor that trickery of the serpent which caused the downfall of the first man and which has stamped on his descendants so many marks of condemnation; if it [i.e., the serpent] has withdrawn from this world; if we [Christians] have already begun to reign; if no misdeed stealthily ensnares our eyes, or our hands, or our minds: then let this gift of God be cast aside, this assistance be rejected. Let no confession, no sorrowful groans [of penitence] be heard; let a disdainful righteousness scorn every remedy.

(2) But if the Lord himself has provided these things for man,

---

18. Cf. Ps 45.12.
19. Song 6.9.
20. Ps 45.14.
21. Song 6.8.
22. *Nequitiae spiritales*. On this interesting usage, cf. John Cassian, *De institutis coenobiorum* 5.16.1.

LETTER 1   23

his own creature, and if the same Lord who has bestowed such remedies upon those who lie helpless, has given rewards to those who stand firm, then cease from finding fault with divine goodness, from erasing so many marks of heavenly mercy by the interjection of your own rigor, or from banning the freely given bounties of the Lord by your relentless severity. We are not bestowing these things on the basis of our own authority. "Return to me," says the Lord, "and together with fasting and weeping and mourning, rend your hearts."[23] And again, "Let the impious man forsake his ways, and the vicious man his thoughts, and return to the Lord, and he shall obtain mercy."[24] And also in this manner the prophet proclaims, "For God is benevolent and merciful and patient, and he relents from the called-for punishment for such wicked acts."[25] Does the serpent have so long-lasting a venom, and Christ not a remedy? Does the devil go about killing in this world, and Christ not have the power to provide relief?

(3) May we by all means be filled with revulsion for sin, but not for repentance. May we be ashamed to put ourselves at risk, but not to be delivered. Who will snatch away the wooden plank from the shipwrecked so that he may not escape? Who will begrudge the curing of wounds? Does David not say, "Every single night I will bathe my bed, I will drench my couch in my tears"?[26] And again, "I acknowledge my sin, and my iniquity I have not concealed"?[27] And further, "I said, 'I will reveal against myself my sin to my God,' and you forgave the wickedness of my heart"?[28] Did not the prophet answer [David] as follows when, after the guilt of murder and adultery for the sake of Bathsheba, he was penitent? "The Lord has taken away from you your sin."[29] Did not confession deliver the king of the Babylonians when he had been condemned after so many sins of idolatry?[30] And what is it that the Lord says? "Shall he who has fallen not arise, and shall he who has turned away not return?"[31] What conclusion do the

---

23. Joel 2.12–13.   24. Isa 55.7; Prov 28.13.
25. Joel 2.13.   26. Ps 6.6.
27. Ps 32.5.   28. Ps 32.5.
29. 2 Sam 12.13.
30. The king referred to is Nebuchadnezzar. Cf. Dan 4.
31. Jer 8.4.

subjects of those many parables of our Lord provide? That the woman finds the silver coin and rejoices when she has found it?[32] That the shepherd carries back the sheep gone astray?[33] That when the son returned, after he had squandered all his goods in dissolute living[34] with harlots and whores, his indulgent father hurries to meet him and, explaining his reasons, reprimands the jealous older brother?[35] He says, "This son of mine was dead and has come to life again; he was lost, and has been found."[36] And what about the man who lay wounded in the road, whom the Levite and the priest passed by? Is he not cared for?[37]

(4) Think back upon what the Spirit indicates to the churches.[38] The Ephesians he accuses of having abandoned their love. To those of Thyatira he imputes fornication. The people of Sardis he blames for ceasing in their work. Those of Pergamum he indicts for teaching divergent views. Of the Laodiceans he brands their riches as disgraceful. And yet he calls all of them to satisfactory penance. What does the Apostle mean when he speaks to the Corinthians in the following manner, "Lest, when I come, I grieve over many among these who have sinned before and have not done penance for the fornication and impurities which they have committed previously"?[39] What does he mean when again he writes to the Galatians, "If anyone has been detected in some transgression," that is, in any place, "then you who are spiritual, instruct such a person in the spirit of gentleness, taking care that you yourself are not also tempted"?[40] Can it be said that the head of a family in a great house guards only the silver and golden vessels? Does he not deign to guard both the earthenware and the wooden vessels, as well as certain ones that are put back together and repaired? "Now I rejoice," says the Apostle, "because you have been saddened unto repentance."[41] And again, "Because sorrow in accordance with God produces penance, enduring unto salvation."[42]

32. Cf. Lk 15.8–9.
33. Cf. Lk 15.4–6.
34. *Nepotata*. Rubio Fernández prefers the reading *epotata*.
35. Cf. Lk 15.11–32.
36. Lk 15.32.
37. Cf. Lk 10.30–35.
38. Cf. Rev 2–3; Tertullian, *De paenitentia* 8.
39. 2 Cor 12.21.
40. Gal 6.1.
41. 2 Cor 7.9.
42. 2 Cor 7.10.

6. But to perform penance, you say, was not allowed. Yet no one commands an unprofitable labor. "For the laborer is worthy of his wage."[43] Never would God threaten the unrepentant unless he would pardon the penitent. This, you will say, God alone can do. True enough. But it is also true that what he does through his priests still represents his own power. For what else can it mean when he says to his apostles, "Whatsoever you shall bind on earth shall be bound in heaven; and whatsoever you shall loose on earth shall be loosed in heaven"?[44] Why was he saying this, if it were not lawful for men to bind and loose? Can it really be that this was permitted to the apostles only? Then it would likewise be permitted to them alone to baptize, to them alone to confer the Holy Spirit, and to them to cleanse the nations of their sins; for all of this was commissioned to no others but the apostles! But if both the loosing of bonds and the power of the sacrament is given to anyone in that place, either the whole has been passed on to us from the form and authority of the apostles, or else nothing of it is allowed to us by such decrees. "I," Paul says, "have laid the foundation, and another is building upon it."[45] Upon this, therefore, which the teaching of the apostles has laid as foundation, we build. And lastly, bishops are also called "apostles," as Paul relates concerning Epaphroditus. "My brother and fellow-soldier," he says, "but your apostle."[46]

(2) If, then, the power of both baptism and confirmation, which are far greater than charisms, is passed on in this way to the bishops, then, too, the right of binding and loosing was with them. Even though for us, because of our own sins it is presumptuous to claim it, nevertheless God, who has granted to the bishops the name even of his one and only [Son],[47] will not deny this to them as if they were saints and sitting in the seat of the apostles.

7. I would write more, my brother, were I not pressed by the

---

43. Lk 10.7; Mt 10.10; 1 Tim 5.18. Cf. Deut 24.14.
44. Mt 16.9, 18.18; Jn 20.23.
45. 1 Cor 3.10.
46. Phil 2.25.
47. *Unici sui nomen.* By this Pacian means that bishops bear the name of "Christ" since all those anointed with the consecrated oil are "christos." Cf. *Ep.* 3.7 where he is more explicit: *quia Christi appellatione signamur.* Also, see Augustine of Hippo, *De civitate Dei* 17.4ff.

early return of my son and were I not reserving a more complete account for you when you are either present or disclosing your entire case.

(2) Let no one look down on a bishop in consideration merely of the man. Let us remember that the apostle Peter designated our Lord as "bishop": "But you have returned," he says, "just now to the bishop and shepherd of your souls."[48] What shall be denied to the bishop in whom the name of God operates? He shall assuredly render account if he has done anything wrong, or if he has judged incorrectly or unrighteously. Nor is God's judgment prevented, so as to prevent his undoing of the works of a wicked builder. In the meantime, if his conduct is holy, he continues as a helper in the work of God. Behold what the Apostle writes to the lay people, "If you have forgiven anyone anything, I have also. For what I have forgiven, if I have forgiven anything, has been for your sakes in the person of Christ, so that we may not be overwhelmed by Satan; for we are not ignorant of his devices."[49] But if what the lay people forgive, the Apostle says he has forgiven, what a bishop has done, how can this be rejected? Therefore, neither charism, nor baptism, nor remission of sins, nor the renewal of the body were granted to his sacred authority, because nothing was entrusted to him through his own assumption of such; but rather, the whole has descended to him from apostolic authority. Know, my brother, that this very favor of penance is not granted indiscriminately to all; nor until there shall have been either an indication of the divine will or perhaps some visitation[50] may men be "loosed." Know also that with careful pondering and much weighing of circumstances, after many groans and much shedding of tears, after the prayers of the entire Church, pardon is not refused to true penitence, so that no one may thereby prejudge the future judgment of Christ.

(3) If, my brother, you would write to me what you believe in greater detail, you will be instructed more fully.

48. 1 Pet 2.25.
49. 2 Cor 2.10–11.
50. *Visitatio*. This word, often used in patristic writings, can mean "an apparition of God," "the benevolent presence of God," or "a visit of God [for punishment]," hence, "chastisement, punishment, affliction."

LETTER 2

PACIAN THE BISHOP TO SYMPRONIAN, his brother, greeting.

1. On this far-ranging question I will, as far as I am able, seek brevity. Nor will I, my brother, reply to you with any repayment of malice, although under the guise of fair questioning you cast and directed [at me] in your speech hidden arrows, which you yourself cunningly devised. We are bid "to pray for those who persecute" [us] and "to bless those who curse" [us].[1] For deceit belongs, so to speak, to the fox and violence to the lion. Either one is most hostile to man, but deceit is deservedly the more odious.[2] For although you believe that you are very well-informed, you question as if you are ignorant; when you think that you are teaching, you pretend to be taught. The Pharisees of times past used to call our Lord "rabbi" when they would set before him as obstacles ambiguous questions of the Law. They designated him as "master" when in fact they claimed all mastery for themselves.

(2) But do what you please, my brother. In return, you will hear everything from me without guile. I would rather be thought ignorant than malicious. I would rather be judged foolish than crafty. Therefore, before I explain the guiding principles of our faith, about which you are agitated, accept these few words concerning your letter, with which you prefaced your treatise.

2. You say that you were refreshed by my previous letter, and you immediately add that my answer was written with bitterness. If bitter things refresh, then I do not know what the effect of sweet things would be, unless it is that, as with potions of medicine,

---

1. Mt 5.44.
2. Cf. Cicero, *De officiis* 1.13.41.

what is bitter is apt to cure more readily than what is sweet. But I ask you, look at my letter again and see whether it is at all stained with venom, and what was disdainful, what was harsh in my answer. You say that I named many heresies, about which no one inquired. Come now, what did this matter to you unless you were a heretic? When you raised a question concerning our faith and said that you wished to be instructed, I wrote that the causes of ignorance were many, so that you might show which one had the greatest influence upon you, lest I become perturbed over many other issues I might unravel.

(2) Concerning the name "Catholic" I answered fully and in a conciliatory manner. For I said that it mattered to neither one of us what the other was called. But if you demanded to know the meaning of the name, whatever it might be, it is "wonderful"—whether it means "one in all" or "one above all"[3] or, an interpretation I have not mentioned previously, "the king's child"—that is, the Christian people.[4] Certainly this name, which has endured for so many centuries, was not bestowed upon us by ourselves, but by God. And truly I rejoice that, although you may have preferred other names, you agree that the name belongs to us. And what if you were to deny this? Then nature would cry out. Or if you still have doubts, let us say nothing about it. We will both be that which we are called, under the witness of the antiquity of the name. If, however, quite stubbornly you continue to ask, take care lest that "man of might" may exclaim to you, "Why do you ask my name? The name itself is wonderful."[5] I then sensibly added that we ought not to consider whence Catholics acquired this name, because neither was it traditionally considered to represent a charge against the Valentinians if they were named after Valentinus, nor against the Phrygians, if from Phrygia, nor against the Novatians, if after Novatian.

3. At this you are gravely upset, and rouse yourself as if pierced by a weapon's barb. For in your anger you exclaim, "Is it prejudicial to that holy man Cyprian that his people bear the name of

---

3. Cf. *Ep.* 1.4.   4. Cf. *De baptismo* 6.
5. Judg 13.18.

'apostate'[6] or 'Capitoline'[7] or 'Syndrene'[8]?" You jeer, but look here! I am not provoked. Have we Catholics been called by any of these names? Put the question to our century, my brother, and all of its years in succession, of whether this name has adhered to us and whether the people of Cyprian have been called by any other name than "Catholic." Never have I heard any one of these names. Now consider this: if someone could be called by a name which he knows was not given to him, what then? Such as these are mere insults, not names; and insults of those who are in rage, insults of those who are insolent. I, too, could call you by as many names, were I permitted to be angry. Do you call Cyprian holy, but his very own people "apostate"? How can you? "If the first-fruit is holy, the dough flour is also holy; and if the root is holy, so are the branches."[9] Am I the apostate, or is it Novatus? Novatus, I say who forsook his father, abandoned the Church, and caused his wife to miscarry?[10] Am I the apostate, or is it Novatian, whom a mere letter, even with him being absent, made a bishop,[11] whom the episcopal seat received without any consecration?[12] But concerning these points I will speak later. In the meantime, tell me yourselves what you are called. Do you

6. *Apostaticum.* This is a reference to the *lapsi* ("the fallen"), who had in varying degrees denied their Christian faith in the Decian persecution of 250–51. Cyprian argued that they were to be readmitted to the Church after penance and probation. Cf. Cyprian, *Ep.* 8.2.

7. *Capitolinum.* This term, applied to the *lapsi*, designates those who publicly took part in pagan sacrifices (cf. Capitolium, the hill in Rome on which was situated the great temple of Jupiter). Cf. Cyprian, *Ep.* 59.18; Tertullian, *Apologeticus* 6.

8. *Syndreum.* This term, which can be translated as "member of a council," perhaps refers mockingly to Cyprian's Council of Carthage (held in 251), which established procedures for readmitting the *lapsi* into communion with the Church.

9. Rom 11.16.

10. Here Pacian follows the account of Cyprian, *Ep.* 52.2.5: "Moreover, his father died of hunger in the streets, and after his death he did not even see to his burial. His wife's womb he kicked with his heel, causing a premature and abortive birth, and the murder of his child." Pacian returns to the subject in *Ep.* 3.6 and 3.19.

11. On this and other issues concerning the career of Novatian and his relationship with Cyprian, see the study by Henneke Güzlow, *Cyprian und Novatian* (Tübingen: Mohr, 1975).

12. Cf. *Ep.* 3.6; *Vita S. Cypriani* 16.

deny that the Novatianists are named after Novatian? No matter what name you impose on them, it will always adhere to them. Examine, if it seems right to you, all the historical records and believe so many centuries. You will respond, "Christian." But if I inquire into the origin of this sect, you will not deny that it is Novatian. And yet it is not the name of your Novatian which I censure and which, when so often asked about, you conceal in your letter by talking around the subject and with what might be called a closed heart. Admit this, my brother, admit this openly! There is no wickedness in a name. Why, when so often you have been questioned, do you hide yourself? Why do you feel ashamed at the origin of your name? When you first wrote I thought that you were a Cataphrygian. Do you not in fact acknowledge it in your second letter? Do you look spitefully at my name and shun your own? Consider what shame there is in a cause which shrinks from what it is called.

4. What do you busily attempt to correct, as though I had approached a rhetorician, or had to practice an art or offer debate on the verses of Virgil? What then had I said or on what verses of Virgil was I expounding? After I had named several heretics, I added, "And the ones now hidden by a dark fame."[13] And how do you think this has been drawn from a verse of Virgil if you had no knowledge at all of Virgil? Yet I did not set down the verse in its correct order, for I said, "The ones now hidden by a dark fame," just as, when speaking we are accustomed from the resources of human language to repeat anything which may have been said before. But you requoted the verse in its original order, in its correct context.[14] Did you have so much love for Virgil that you think it a sacrilege if you were to upset his verse? And yet I had learned this verse as a little child. How is it strange if I stumbled upon that which I used to know? Is there in you, my brother, such an industrious spirit that now at last you read those very things which you were ashamed that others had once read?[15] You might as well find fault with a person instructed in Latin for

---

13. *Ep.* 1.1. The words in Latin are: *Et quos fama recondit obscura.*
14. Virgil, *Aeneis* 5.302: *Quos fama obscura recondit.*
15. I have here followed Peyrot in making this sentence interrogative.

speaking Latin, as you might with a Greek for speaking Greek, with a Parthian for speaking Parthian, or a Phoenician[16] for speaking Punic. Medes, Egyptians, Hebrews each have their own language in accordance with the resources provided by the Lord, who has arranged language into one hundred and twenty tongues.[17]

(2) Has a bishop quoted a verse of poetry? What! Does the Apostle Paul feel ashamed when he quotes and accepts as true a particular Athenian verse? For in the Acts of the Apostles he puts it this way: "Just as even some of those among you have said, 'For we are his offspring.' Since therefore we are the offspring of God . . ."[18] And again, to Titus he said, "A certain one of them, a prophet of their own, said, 'Cretans are always liars, evil beasts, lazy gluttons'." And he added, "This testimony is true."[19] So we are making our mistake by this precedent. Nor are we rhetoricians; but whatever means of expression we use, we believe it to be of the resource given by God. Latium, Egypt, Athens, and Thracians, Arabians, Spaniards acknowledge God. The Holy Spirit understands all languages. Why do you say, "I will smear your letters all over with a long-lasting oil of cedar to protect them from the decay-causing enemies of the Muses"?[20] What Muses, I ask you? Those who invented letters and wrote the very pages which are preyed upon by the larvae of moths?[21] Tell me, I

---

16. Alternatively, "a Carthaginian."
17. Here I have followed the manuscripts' reading. Some editors, including Rubio Fernández, have conjectured that perhaps "seventy" was originally meant and that at some point in the tradition "*CXX*" was substituted for "*LXX*." Seventy was taken by some to represent a mystical number of perfection (e.g., Augustine, *Enarrationes in psalmos* 111.1; cf. Arnobius the Younger, *Commentarii in psalmos* 104 [105]). Still the correct reading could well be "one hundred and twenty," this perhaps referring to Acts 1.15: "At this time, Peter stood up and spoke before all the brethren; a company of about a hundred and twenty were gathered there" (Knox's translation).
18. Acts 17.28–29. The internal quotation is from the *Phaenomena* 5 of Aratus, a third century B.C. poet.
19. Titus 1.12–13. This ethnic insult was attributed by later writers to Epimenides of Crete (sixth century B.C.).
20. Cedar oil was used by the ancients to preserve books, as is attested by numerous classical authors.
21. These larvae were especially destructive of books. Cf. Cyprian, *De zelo et livore* 7.

beseech you, my brother, did the Muses invent letters? Do not all things come through the Lord and are not all things from God? Besides those one hundred and twenty tongues, was there yet another one of the Muses? Indeed, that idea was falsely alleged by Hesiod on Mt. Helicon,[22] but only for the fancy of the Athenians, "for whom," the Apostle says, "there was time for nothing but talk."[23] We, with the Apostle as our witness, continue to observe proper measures of all words and all kinds of languages as inspired by God. Yet I forgive you, my brother, if you rely upon your own founder and join together Novatian's philosophy, by which he shipwrecked religion, with the authority of Hesiod. But even so, you ought to have remembered the words of the Apostle, who says, "Take care lest any man mislead you through philosophy and empty deception."[24]

5. And now, what sort of thing is it which you think should be charged against Catholics, if at any time kings or governments have persecuted you?[25] Rather, on the contrary, it ought to be charged against you, that is, as often as Catholics have endured the wickedness and persecutions of kings, and pagan princes have persecuted us! Have you endured acts of hatred from Christians? But we have still more reason for complaint. Let him who did this consider with what intention and in what spirit he did it: to secure peace or effect discord. "But even if some of them have erred," he says, "do they destroy the faithfulness of God?"[26] And yet, do not suppose that there was any reason to complain about us—when through our faith princes had begun to be Christians, these very princes, favoring the Catholic, that is, their own side, were moved [to act] by their own sorrow—unless, perhaps, it is to be charged against Daniel that he was avenged by Darius;[27] or against that most holy woman Esther, when for her a chief minister of the king was put to death;[28] or against the three youths,

---

22. Cf. Hesiod, *Theogonia* 22–35.
23. Acts 17.21. Cf. Tertullian, *De anima* 3: *Athenis enim expertus linguatam civitatem cum omnes illic sapientiae atque facundiae caupones degustasset.*
24. Col 2.8. Cf. Cyprian, *Ep.* 55.16, *De bono patientiae* 1.
25. Like Peyrot, I have taken the sentence to be interrogative.
26. Rom 3.3.   27. Cf. Dan 6.23–24.
28. Cf. Esth 7.10.

when after their trial by flames the Babylonian king threatened the impious and the unbelieving because of them![29]

(2) Did not Peter put Simon [Magus] to confusion with the consent of the judge?[30] Did not Paul strike Elymas blind with the approval of Sergius?[31] And even at Jerusalem, he could have been freed from danger had he, when in bonds,[32] had any confidence [in them].[33] Do you not know that the authorities themselves serve the innocent and minister for the good on behalf of the righteous faction?[34] Just as the Apostle says, "Rulers are not a terror to good work, but to the evil. Do you wish, then, not to be afraid of power? Do what is good, and you will have praise from the same through the Lord. For he is a minister [of God] to you for the good."[35] And yet I, for my part, have offered protest about no one; I have taken my vengeance upon no one. Nor do I think that the Novatians, in whose sparse and dwindling membership I could well glory, if I wished, offer hindrance to me. Behold, no one levels charges against your people with the emperor, and yet you stand alone. Nevertheless it is inevitable that we "all will stand before the judgment seat of God,"[36] which is one thing I know the Novatians would complain, if their cause were acceptable to any princes.

6. It is more advantageous, you say, to prevail than to please. Yet those who are led by a burning desire to prevail make progress by contention. The Apostle, however, says, "But if anyone appears contentious, we have no such custom, nor does the church of God."[37] On the contrary, concerning the aim of pleasing he

---

29. Cf. Dan 3.29.
30. Cf. Acts 8.9–24; Ps.-Tertullian, *Adversus omnes haereses* 1: *Simon magus qui in actis apostolorum condignam meruit ab apostolo Petro iustamque sententiam*. Also, cf. Tertullian, *De praescriptione haereticorum* 33.1; Eusebius of Caesarea, *Historia ecclesiastica* 2.15.3; Ps.-Cyprian, *De rebaptismate* 16.
31. Cf. Acts 13.6–12. Sergius Paulus was a proconsul or governor.
32. Here I have accepted the manuscripts' reading (*ligatus*), accepted by all editors but Rubio Fernández, who conjectures *legatus*.
33. This presumably alludes to one or more of the events recorded in Acts 21–26. Cf. Acts 25.10–11, 26.31–32.
34. Here also I have adopted the reading of the manuscripts and Peyrot: *partibus* (cf. Rubio Fernández: *patribus*).
35. Rom 13.3–4.   36. Rom 14.10.
37. 1 Cor 11.16.

says, "I please all people in all things, not seeking that which may be advantageous to me, but to the many, so that they may be saved."[38] But you, while thinking of your own interests and not those of your brethren, would rather destroy by prevailing than restore by pleasing. To have overcome evil with good is indicative of reason; but to wish to gain the upper hand in whatever cause it may be is indicative of insane presumption. This idea does not come from the law of the apostles but from that of the Greeks, amongst whom it is thought, according to our records, that the whole character of the Lacedaemonians was inflamed with a desire for conquest. As does the filthy boar and the raging tiger! What else do they desire but to prevail rather than to please?

(2) You write that you have time to spare and for that reason such contentious matters amuse you. But to me, busy with Catholic concerns, your letters were delivered after about thirty days and returned after forty more.

7. You say that I am angry. God forbid! I believe that I am roused, like the bee which, when the situation arises, defends its honey with its sting. But in your mind go over the present correspondence on both sides. You will soon see whether it is with stings or with flowers that we contend on these pages. The Apostle indeed speaks of some similar individuals who must be muzzled.[39] But note this: we argue against you like doves, with the mouth rather than with the teeth.

(2) Would that it were true, as you say, that you wish to be instructed! Immediately I would with my own hands propose for you the ointments of the Holy Spirit. Do you love me? I have not harmed you, I know. But only then would you love, if you would not think otherwise, and you would approach my work with agreeable feelings.

(3) Do you marvel that the letters of Cyprian are pleasing to me? And why should they not be, these letters of a blessed martyr and Catholic priest? You thrust Novatian upon me! I hear that he was a "philosopher of the world."[40] I do not wonder greatly that

38. 1 Cor 10.33.
39. Cf. Titus 1.10–11.
40. *Philosophum saeculi.* Cf. Tertullian, *De praescriptione haereticorum* 7, where *philosophia saecularis* is discussed.

he fell short of the standard set by the Church of the living God.[41] I know that he abandoned the root of the ancient law, the source of the ancient people; envied Cornelius, after lending himself to the delusions of Novatus; was made bishop without the proper consecration, and therefore was not truly made bishop by the letter of those parties who pretended to be confessors, those who tore apart the limbs of their one mother.[42] These points, my brother, I will prove to you in my letters, by the admission of your own associates.[43] Thus, this "philosopher" of yours, "in seeking to establish his own wisdom," as the Apostle puts it, "did not subject himself to the wisdom of God";[44] "since through its own wisdom, the world did not acknowledge the wisdom of God."[45]

(4) For while you think that Novatian suffered first and add that Cyprian said, "My adversary has preceded me,"[46] see how clearly I can respond. Novatian never suffered martyrdom,[47] nor was such a thing heard or read from the words of the most blessed Cyprian. You have his letters in which he mentions Cornelius, the bishop of the City [i.e., Rome], a man of whom Novatian was at that time jealous, as offering resistance to the hostile princes, often standing as a confessor, often treated roughly; as having been appointed leader of many confessors and of many martyrs also; and as most gloriously having received the crown of

41. Cf. Cyprian, *Ep.* 55.16: "But quite different, dearly beloved brother, is the thinking of philosophers, in particular of the Stoics: they claim that all sins are equal and that it is quite wrong for a man of gravity to be easily moved to pity. But the fact is that a vast distance separates Christians and philosophers."
42. Cf. Cyprian, *Ep.* 45.1: "The body of the Church had been severed. They were to strive and labor to their utmost to join back together the limbs of that divided body, restoring the unity of the Catholic Church.... Instead, the opposing faction acted with perverse and self-willed obstinacy. They rejected the welcoming embrace of the mother, they cut themselves off from their source of life."
43. These points are treated in depth in Pacian's third letter and were, perhaps, also explored in his lost treatise, *Contra Novatianos*.
44. Cf. Rom 10.3.
45. Cf. 1 Cor 1.21.
46. The source of this quotation is unclear. Perhaps it is from a version of the so-called "Martyrdom of Novatian" (written in Greek) which in later times circulated among members of this group.
47. A number of later sources, including Socrates Scholasticus (*Historia ecclesiastica* 4.28), state that he did become a martyr.

martyrdom together with many others, while Novatian was still living and indeed even free from any danger. For [Novatian] had left the Church of Christ for this very reason: that the hardships of a confessor might not press in upon him. First, goaded on by jealousy, he could not put up with the episcopate of Cornelius; then, with the mockery of those letters of a few, he had attached himself to Novatus.[48] The letters of Cyprian will thoroughly teach you all of this information about Novatian.

(5) Furthermore, even though Novatian did endure some suffering, nevertheless he was not slain. And even though he was slain, yet he was not crowned [with martyrdom]. Why not? Because he was outside of the communion of the Church, he was outside the boundaries of concord, he was far away from that mother [i.e., the Church] of whom he who is a martyr must be a part. Pay heed to the Apostle! "And if I have all faith so that I could move mountains, but do not have charity, I am nothing. And if I divide up all of my possessions as provisions for the poor and if I hand over my body to be burned, but do not have charity, it is of no avail to me."[49]

(6) On the other hand, Cyprian suffered while in concord with all, in peace with all, in the company of the confessors; and, having often been a confessor in repeated persecutions and having been treated roughly with many a torment, at last he was given to drink of the saving cup![50] This is what it was to be crowned! Therefore, let Novatian have to himself his letters, his arrogance, his pride, by which while he is lifted up on high, he is dashed down to pieces. While he shows mercy to no one, he is himself cast out. Behold the man who, by an unyielding religious system, obstructs the way to salvation for his brethren! Behold the man who is confident that he bears the winnowing basket and that he is cleansing the threshing-floor of the Lord![51]

---

48. A follower of Felicissimus and priest of Carthage, he along with Fortunatus and Gordius opposed the election of Cyprian as bishop.

49. 1 Cor 13.2–3.

50. Cf. Cyprian, *Ep.* 28.1: "You have handed over to us here the crowns which your hands have wreathed, you have passed on to your brethren here the saving cup which your lips tasted first in pledge."

51. Cf. Mt 3.12; Lk 3.17. Also, cf. Cyprian *Epp.* 54.3, 55.25.

8. Take pity on yourself, brother Sympronian, lest Novatian deceive you by this guise, as though he were to be thought the more righteous because he has looked down on others in comparison to himself. Impudence often apes confidence; and the false appearance of a good conscience deludes those hopeless sinners. But, on the other hand, all humility is innocence, even that of the debtor, even that of the sinner, even that which softens its soul with the sinner. "Expunge me," Moses says, "from the book that you have written,"[52] so that sinners might not perish. "I had wished," the Apostle says, "that I myself were accursed and separated from Christ for the sake of my brethren, my kindred according to the flesh."[53] Both of these men certainly pray for sinners. And yet neither Moses nor Paul offends God because of this. Is Novatian better than they are? Is he the corrector of the prophets? Is he the teacher of the apostles? Is he now seen with Christ, as was Moses himself?[54] Is he now carried up into the third heaven on high, as was Paul?[55] Is he alone now to be heard, while all others have been neglected?

(2) It would have been sufficient to answer your letter in such a fashion. But, seeing that you have argued rather extensively concerning penance, that it ought not to be done or that it should take place before baptism, and you have filled the pages with innumerable citations of examples from his [Novatian's] treatise, I will respond to each point though this is more than is called for. I will not be silent about that which the truer faith holds. And since you have thought fit to command me to hear you out at great length, now in return, I ask you, kindly afford a like reception for our own treatise. The Lord will, perhaps, grant that we who have patiently offered our services to you may gain some profit from your patience also.

(3) May the Lord see fit to guard and protect you forever, and cause you to live as a Christian and as a Catholic, and come into agreement with us!

---

52. Ex 32.32.
53. Rom 9.3.
54. Cf. Mt 17.3.
55. Cf. 2 Cor 12.2.

LETTER 3

DACIAN THE BISHOP TO SYMPRONIAN, his brother, greeting.

1. The entire treatise of the Novatianists, which you have directed to me, crammed with propositions on all sides, simply amounts to this, brother Sympronian: that repentance should not be permitted after baptism; that the Church cannot forgive mortal sin; and that, beyond this, by receiving those who sin, the Church itself perishes.

(2) What an illustrious honor, what a singular power, what a great consistency it is to reject the guilty, to flee the touch of sinners, to have so little confidence in the Church's own innocence! Who lays claim to this, my brother? Is it Moses, or Paul, or Christ? But Moses wishes to be "expunged from the book"[1] for the sake of blasphemers, and Paul "to be accursed and separated for the sake of [his] brethren";[2] and the Lord himself prefers to suffer for the unrighteous! None of these, you will say. Who then? It was Novatian who taught these things. Can this be some spotless and pure man who did not follow Novatus; who never abandoned the Church; who was made bishop by other bishops; who was consecrated according to proper procedures; who succeeded to an episcopal see in the Church when it was [duly] vacant? "What does this matter to you?" you will say. And I answer, "Novatian taught these things." But, when did he teach them, my brother, or in what era? Immediately after the Passion of our Lord? No, it was after the reign of Decius,[3] that is, nearly three hundred years[4] after the Passion of our Lord. And what did he

---

1. Ex 32.32.
2. Rom 9.3.
3. Decius was emperor from 249 until 251.
4. I have followed the manuscripts' (and earlier editors') reading of *trecentos*

LETTER 3

do at that time? Did he follow such prophets as the Cataphrygians, or someone named Philumene, as Apelles did?[5] Or did he himself become the recipient of such great authority? Did he speak in tongues? Did he prophesy? Was he able to resurrect the dead? For he ought to have had at least one of these powers, since he introduced a gospel of a new Law! This, even though the Apostle declares against such, "Even if we or an angel from heaven proclaim a gospel other than that which we have proclaimed to you, let that one be accursed!"[6] "Novatian," you will say, "has understood this," but it was Christ who taught it. Has there been, accordingly, no discerning person from the time of Christ up to the reign of Decius?[7] Furthermore, after Decius, has every bishop been unable to bear his office, and all others [except Novatian] lax men, choosing rather to join themselves with the lost, to perish with the wretched, to be wounded through the wound of another one? Novatian claims the truth, and righteousness is set free; Novatian serves as the guide, and every error is put right!

2. "But come now," you will say, "let us dispute with specific examples and let us contend with reasoning." So far, I am confident. Content as I am with the very chain of tradition in the Church and with our communion with the ancient congregation [of Christians], I have learned no eagerness for discord; I have sought out no arguments for disputes. But you, having been excluded from the rest of the body [i.e., the Church][8] and separated from your mother [the Church][9] so that you may render account for your actions, as an unrelenting searcher into the innermost recesses of books you examine, you disturb everything

---

(or *CCC*). Rubio Fernández, perhaps in the interests of chronological accuracy, has supplied *CCL*.

5. Apelles was a disciple of Marcion. In his *Syllogismoi* he wrote extensively on the Old Testament, attempting to demonstrate that it was not trustworthy (cf. Ambrose, *De paradiso*, for surviving passages). His *Revelations*, which recorded the visions of his female disciple and prophetess, Philumene (or Philomena), unfortunately is lost.

6. Gal 1.8.

7. I have followed Peyrot and other editors in rendering this sentence and the next as interrogative.

8. Cf. *Ep.* 1.1.

9. Cf. *Ep.* 2.7.

which is concealed and rouse whatever is at rest. Our ancient predecessors, on the other hand, entered into no dispute. While the very freedom from anxiety among us is undisguised, everything that you have brought forth for your faction is defended! I myself do not know what Novatian did, what Novatus was guilty of, what caused the swelling pride of Evaristus,[10] or what message Nicostratus[11] conveyed. Since I despise your weapons, I have no experience with them. Yet, take care if you do battle with the unarmed truth! Still, let us await what you may put before us, what you have to say. Will truth be able to hold its ground though it is unarmed, or innocence though it is inexperienced?

(2) You, indeed, correctly state that the Church is a people born again of the water and the Holy Spirit, free from denial of the name of Christ; the temple and the house of God; "the pillar and the bulwark of the truth";[12] a holy virgin with the purest feelings; the spouse of Christ "from his bones and flesh";[13] "not having a spot or wrinkle";[14] observing the laws of the Gospels in their entirety. Who among us denies this? But we add moreover that the Church is "the queen in clothing embroidered with gold and adorned with diverse colors";[15] "a fruitful vine on the walls of the house of the Lord";[16] the mother of "young maidens without number";[17] "the one beautiful and perfect dove, the chosen of her mother";[18] the very mother of all, "built upon the foundations of the prophets and apostles, and with Jesus Christ himself as the corner stone";[19] and "a great house" made sumptuous with a diversity of every kind of vessel.[20]

10. Evaristus was an Italian bishop, perhaps among those who consecrated Novatian. In the view of Pope Cornelius he was one of the leading instigators of the Novatianist schism. Eventually deposed and succeeded by Zetus, he followed Novatus to Carthage and there continued his opposition to the Catholic hierarchy. Cf. Cyprian, *Epp.* 50.1, 52.1.

11. Nicostratus was a Roman deacon and confessor, and a follower of Novatian. He, like Evaristus, eventually went with Novatus to Carthage to support the schism. Pope Cornelius accused him of fraud against his patroness and of stealing church funds and channeling them to the Novatianists. Cf. Cyprian, *Epp.* 32.1, 50.1, 52.1.

12. 1 Tim 3.15.
13. Eph 5.30.
14. Eph 5.27.
15. Ps 45.12.
16. Ps 128.3.
17. Song 6.8.
18. Song 6.9.
19. Eph 2.20.
20. Cf. 2 Tim 2.20.

3. But these descriptions of ours will come later. For the present, let us consider those of yours. "The Church is a people born again of the water and the Holy Spirit." Well now, who has closed off the fountain of God to me? Who has snatched away the Spirit? In fact, with us is "the living water,"[21] the very water which gushes from Christ. But you, separated from the everlasting fountain, from where do you receive your birth? And likewise has the Holy Spirit not departed from the original mother; from where did it come to you? Of course, perhaps [the Spirit] has followed one who engages in strife and, having abandoned so many priests and not content with its consecrated dwelling-place, has truly loved the broken cistern of an impure fountain?[22] From where do your people possess the Spirit, those whom an anointed priest has not sealed? From where do they possess the water, those who have withdrawn from their mother's womb? From where do they possess spiritual renewal, those who have lost the cradle of nuptial peace?

(2) "The Church is a people free from denial of the name of Christ." Are there then no confessors among us, no martyrs, no pure and upright priests, who have been proven by prisons, by chains, by fire, and by the sword? "There were," you will say, "but by receiving those who had denied their faith, they perished." I do not say anything, nor do I produce testimony on this fact: that your Novatian, while he was still dwelling within the Church, wrote, recommended, and read aloud a short treatise on the subject of receiving those who had denied their faith or had lapsed.[23]

(3) In the meantime whom will you be able to persuade that, by receiving those who lapsed, the entire Church has fallen? That by the admission of penitents, the party of those who receive them back has become like someone who denies the faith?

---

21. Jer 2.13.
22. Cf. Jer 2.13.
23. It would appear that Pacian is here alluding to one of Novatian's "Roman" letters (*Ep.* 30, found in the correspondence of Cyprian) for which Novatian was the *scriptor* on behalf of the clergy at Rome. The stance taken in this letter is somewhat less rigorous on the matter of the reconciliation of the *lapsi* than that in Novatian's later pronouncements.

But even if a congregation somehow has been too lenient, have other congregations who did not approve of their actions but rather followed convention and kept communion, also lost the name "Christian"? Hear the voice of Jeremiah! "In those days they shall not say, 'The fathers have eaten sour grapes, and the children's teeth are set on edge.' But each one shall die for his own sin."[24] Nor is the Lord silent in the writings of Ezekiel, "As the soul of the father is mine, so also is the soul of the son; each one shall die for his own sin."[25] Likewise later he writes, "The son shall not receive the iniquity of the father, nor shall the father receive the iniquity of the son; the righteousness of the righteous shall be upon him."[26] You yourself bring forward the following example, "Even if these three, Noah, Job, and Daniel, were in their midst, they shall deliver neither sons nor daughters; they themselves only shall be delivered."[27] See, the very ones who have been placed in the midst of sinners and who cannot deliver others are saved. You, on the other hand, bind the whole world with the chains of a few; you condemn the entire Church because of the infirmity of a small part. What? Are all of those with you saints, those whom Novatus trained, whom Evaristus chose, whom Nicostratus taught, whom Novatian instructed? Have you escaped "the thorns and thistles"?[28] Do you have no weeds in your wheat? Is your grain already freed from impurities? Will he who purifies come to you without his winnowing-fan?[29] Shall you alone among all have no chaff?

4. But come now, proceed with the rest. "The Church is the body of Christ." Without doubt, the body, not merely a member; the body composed of many parts and members, made into one, just as the Apostle says, "For the body also is not one member, but many."[30] Therefore the Church is the full body, solid and spread over the entire world, like a state, I would say, whose parts are all united. Not like you, Novatians, are, some very small and insolent portion, and a mere tumor that has swelled up and separated from the rest of the body.

---

24. Jer 31.29–30.
25. Ezek 18.4.
26. Ezek 18.20.
27. Ezek 14.16, 14.18, 14.20.
28. Gen 3.18. Cf. Mt 7.16.
29. Cf. Mt 3.12; Lk 3.17.
30. 1 Cor 12.14.

LETTER 3

(2) "The Church is the temple of God." A truly magnificent temple, "a great house," having assuredly "vessels of gold and silver, but also of wood and earth, some esteemed,"[31] many, indeed, excellent ones destined for the manifold functions of various tasks.

(3) "The Church is a holy virgin with the purest feelings, the spouse of Christ." A virgin, it is true, but also a mother. A spouse, it is clear, but also a wife and a mate, "taken from her husband,"[32] and for that reason, "bone of his bones, and flesh of his flesh."[33] For about her, David says, "Your wife [shall be] like a fruitful vine on the walls of your house; your children like the young olive-branches around your table."[34] Abundant, therefore, is the progeny of this virgin, and without number are her offspring, by which the whole world is filled, by which the populous colony invariably swarms the encircled hives. Great is the care of that mother for her children, and tender is her affection. The good are honored, the haughty are chastised, the sick are cared for; no one perishes, no one is despised, the young are kept safe under the indulgent protection of the mother.

(4) "The Church is 'not having a spot or wrinkle.'[35]" That is, not having heresies: Valentinians, Cataphrygians, or Novatianists. For among these are certain spotted and wrinkled folds, envious of the decorations of the precious vestments [of the Church].[36] But the sinner and the penitent are not a spot on the Church, because as long as such a person sins and does not repent, he is placed outside of the Church; when he ceases to sin, he is already cured. On the other hand, the heretic tears, divides, spots, and wrinkles the garment of the Lord, which is the Church of Christ. "For while there are schisms and quarrels among you," says [the Apostle], "are you not of the flesh and do you not walk as men?"[37] And moreover, "Their words will gradually spread like a cancer."[38] This is the spot upon [the Church's] unity, this is the wrinkle. Lastly, when the Apostle speaks of these things, he is bringing to our attention the love and affection of Christ. "Just as

---

31. 2 Tim 2.20.
32. Gen 2.23.
33. Gen 2.23. Cf. Eph 5.30.
34. Ps 128.3.
35. Eph 5.27.
36. Cf. Ps 45.12.
37. 1 Cor 3.3.
38. 2 Tim 2.17.

Christ," he says, "loved the Church and gave himself up for it,"[39] so that he might rebuke the heretics because they do not know how to love. But why is this to be denied to the wretched penitent, who wishes both to love and to be loved?

5. "The Church is that which keeps the laws of the Gospels in their entirety." Truly "in their entirety" because it denotes them all, because it denotes them completely. Where a reward is given to the faithful, where tears are not denied to the wretched, where the weeping of those who beseech [God] is heard, where the wounded are bandaged, where the sick are healed, where neither arrogant "health" nor disdainful "righteousness" claims anything for itself, where charity long endures, attentive to all, "believing all things, hoping all things, enduring all things"[40]—whence is the statement of the Apostle, "Who is weak, and I am not weakened? Who is made to stumble, and I am not distressed?"[41]—where the entire brotherhood, mourning together, bears its own burdens, secure in mutual affection, with everyone "sustaining each other in love, making every effort to preserve the unity of the Spirit in the bond of peace":[42] this will be the Church, brother Sympronian. This will be the people born again in Christ from the water and the Holy Spirit.

(2) "I do not know," you say, "whether sin can be remitted by bishops since the Lord has said, 'He who denies me before men, him I will deny before my Father who is in heaven.'"[43] Why then did your Novatian teach this very thing as a priest, before he had illegitimately assumed the episcopate, long before Cornelius was made bishop of Rome, and before Novatian was envious of his priesthood? You have the testimony of Cyprian; Cyprian, whose reputation not even you have been able to blacken. For in a certain passage he wrote to Antonianus[44] as follows, "It was added also—when Novatian was then writing and reciting with his own voice what he had written, and when Moses,[45] then a confessor

---

39. Eph 5.25.
40. 1 Cor 13.7.
41. 2 Cor 11.29.
42. Eph 4.2–3.
43. Mt 10.33.
44. Antonianus was a North African (perhaps Numidian) bishop who wrote to Cyprian to pledge his support of both Pope Cornelius and Cyprian in the face of the threat by Novatian and his schismatics.
45. Moses was a prominent member of a group of confessors at the outset of

and now a martyr, was subscribing—that reconciliation should be granted to the lapsed who were sick and near death. This letter was sent throughout the world and brought to the notice of all the churches."[46]

(3) What do you say, brother Sympronian? Novatian wrote such a thing and, so that he might add the assent of his immoderate will, recited it also when it was written. A witness is his very pledge; a witness is the hand which wrote it; a witness is the tongue which read it. And to this point in time Cornelius, on whose account all of this jealousy of yours bursts forth, was not yet bishop. It was long after this that Cornelius, in the company of numerous fellow bishops, numerous confessors and soon-to-be martyrs—just as the same Cyprian writes—gave his assent.[47] If it is never permitted to grant reconciliation to the lapsed, if access to penance is to be denied, then Novatian, who after all wrote, recommended, and recited this, is involved in the offense. Where in those days was his impatient rigor? Where then was that fierce judgment? If no one had preferred Cornelius to your man, the authority of Novatian, with his writings, would have remained.

(4) And now this entire opinion causes displeasure. Now arrows are shot at us, with those men supplying them by whose authority the cause, against which they direct the arrows, gained its strength!

6. But when did the Novatianists begin this heresy of theirs? Listen, I beg you, and consider carefully the entire course of your error. Cornelius, who at this point was made bishop of Rome by sixteen bishops, had succeeded to the position of the vacant see, and in that virginal chastity which he possessed, endured repeated persecutions at the hands of the enraged prince.[48] As it so happened, at that time a certain presbyter, Novatus, having

---

the Novatianist schism and was among the first confessors imprisoned when Pope Fabian was martyred in the Decian persecution. After almost a year in prison he died. According to Cyprian (and Pacian) in this passage, even that honored confessor and martyr, who was well known for his strict stance on penance, approved of this position.

46. Cyprian, *Ep.* 55.5.   47. Cf. Cyprian, *Ep.* 55.6.
48. Cf. Cyprian, *Ep.* 55.8.

defrauded the widows of the church at Carthage, robbed orphans, embezzled the money of the Church, cast his father out of his house and allowed him to die of hunger and without burial, and having kicked the womb of his pregnant wife and caused her to abort her child, came from Africa to Rome.[49] And at Carthage, when the brethren in the Church pressed hard upon him in pursuit and the day of the investigation of his activities was imminent, he went into hiding.[50]

(2) Not long after, when this Novatian was disturbed about the episcopate of Cornelius—for he had hoped to have it for himself—Novatus together with some partisans of his side, as is usual in such cases, urged him on when he was wavering, encouraged him when he was uncertain, and exhorted him to hope for something great. He came across some people, out of the number of those who had escaped the storm of that persecution, among whom he aroused against Cornelius this very hatred on the subject of receiving the lapsed. He gave to Novatian their letters. And Novatian, by the authority of these letters, although there was already a bishop sitting at Rome, assumed for himself the title of the "other" bishop in opposition to the proper tradition decreeing a singularity of the priesthood;[51] he accused Cornelius of having been in communion with the lapsed; and he asserted his own blamelessness. Against such a man am I to render account? Against such a man am I to defend the cause of modesty? Against such a man is purity of life to be vindicated?

7. "But," you will say, "why do also you, bishops, approve of such things?" Let another person raise this issue, but you, a disciple of Novatian, defend it! Let this cause seem to others inexcusable; to you it should be welcome.[52] Whoever is guilty in your

---

49. Cf. Cyprian, *Ep.* 52.2.

50. Cyprian, in *Ep.* 52.3, notes that it was the onset of the Decian persecution which allowed Novatus to escape judgment.

51. Cf. Cyprian, *Ep.* 45.1: "As the discord spread, breaking out afresh and even more violently, they appointed their own bishop: they set up outside the church and in opposition to it an illicit head, in defiance of the sacred ordinance firmly laid down and instituted by God concerning Catholic unity."

52. Pacian here seems to be arguing that Sympronian should let others condemn the alleged laxity of the Catholics, since for him and his fellow partisans such laxity could only mean a gain in strength.

own behalf, he is innocent in your sight. Do not accuse another of a crime from which you cannot clear yourself. Come now, should we bishops in every way owe a debt of shame because we have received the name of "apostles," because we are sealed with the appellation of "Christ"?

(2) "The Lord," you say, "denies the man who denies him; I do not wish that you should acknowledge a man who denies [the Lord]."[53] Who acknowledges the man who denies [the Lord]? Is it the person who compels him to penance, rebukes him, shows him his crime, lays bare his wounds, reminds him of eternal punishments, and reforms him by "the destruction of the flesh"?[54] This is what it is to chasten, not to acknowledge. The Lord says unto us, "You are the salt of the earth."[55] We therefore salt rightly when we declare such things, nor will its authority be slight, whoever shall hear us. You see that the decree of the Lord is not trampled upon, but enforced by us; severity is not discarded, but his will is thrown open.

(3) "But," you will say, "you forgive sins to the penitent, whereas it is allowed to you to remit such sin only in baptism." Not to me at all is it allowed, but to God alone, who in baptism both forgives the offense and does not reject the tears of the penitents. But what I myself do, I do not do by my own right, but by the Lord's. "We are God's helpers," he says, "you are[56] God's building."[57] And again, "I planted, Apollos watered; but God gave the growth. Therefore, neither is he who plants anything, nor is he who waters; only God, who gives the growth."[58] Therefore, whether we baptize, or compel to penance, or grant pardon to the penitents, we do this on the authority of Christ. This you must see—whether Christ has this power, whether Christ has done this.

8. "If the remission of sins," you say, "could be given to the penitents, baptism would not be necessary." A most ridiculous analogy! For baptism is the sacrament of the Lord's passion; the

---

53. Cf. Mt 10.33. 54. 1 Cor 5.5.
55. Mt 5.13.
56. I have here followed the manuscript reading preferred by Peyrot: *estis* (cf. Rubio Fernández's *est*).
57. 1 Cor 3.9. 58. 1 Cor 3.6–7.

pardon granted to penitents is the due reward of the one confessing. The former all people can obtain, because it is the gift of the grace of God, that is, a gratuitous gift. But penitence is the task of a few, who arise after their fall; who recover after being wounded; who are aided by tearful prayers; who are restored to life through "the destruction of the flesh."[59]

(2) You assert that to no avail did I cite that instance when God said, "I prefer the repentance of a sinner rather than his death."[60] What if I had added that precept of Isaiah, "When you have returned and shall lament, then shall you be saved and you will know where you have been"?[61] What if I had added the word of the Apocalypse, "Remember from where you have fallen, and repent and do the works you did at first"?[62] "These things," you will say, "were spoken to the gentiles before baptism." But hear the Apostle! "Now we know that whatever the law says, it says and speaks to those who are under the law."[63] Therefore, the condition of repentance will not constrain those who lived without the law. And even if they had repented, they had done it out of an unconstrained faith, not by any bond of repentance imposed by the law.

(3) "Therefore," you will say, "the Jews at least, who repented before baptism, cannot repent after baptism." Who taught you this, brother Sympronian? Who convinced you that he who may have repented before ought not to repent afterwards? But we will consider this matter at a later time. In the meantime, if the Jews were precluded from repentance after baptism because they had fulfilled this before, grant that the gentiles at least, who did not know the law of repentance before, ought to repent afterwards. But I do not wish that you should be deceived even concerning the Jews. For it was on this very account that they repented before, because they had corrupted their long-established baptism, and they used to repent, as it were, after possessing faith, for having betrayed their faith. Hear the Apostle! "For I do not wish you to be unaware, brethren, that all of our fathers were under the cloud, and all passed through the sea; and all were baptized in

---

59. 1 Cor 5.5.
61. Isa 30.15 [LXX version].
63. Rom 3.19.

60. Ezek 33.11. Cf. Ezek 18.23, 18.32.
62. Rev 2.5.

Moses in the cloud and in the sea; and all ate the same spiritual food; and all drank the same spiritual drink. Indeed, they drank of that spiritual rock that followed; and in fact the rock was Christ."[64] Therefore it was this baptism they had violated, and for that reason they used to repent.

9. Let us next see what you say. "If God orders man to repent more often," you declare, "he allows them to sin more often." What are you saying here? Is it the case that he who more often reveals the remedy for a misdeed points to the misdeed? And when a physician effects a cure, does he teach one to be constantly wounded? God does not wish man to sin even a single time, and nevertheless he delivers him from sin. Nor yet when he delivers does he teach sin; just as he who rescues someone from a fire, does not teach how to start it; and he who rescues the shipwrecked from the cliffs does not drive him upon the rocks. It is one thing to be delivered from danger, another to be forced into danger. And perhaps I might be able to believe your assertion, if penance were considered a pleasure, penance which necessitates burdensome toil, which calls for "the destruction of the flesh,"[65] and which involves incessant tears and unending groans of sorrow. Will the one who is cured, in that case, desire again to go under the surgeon's knife, again to be cauterized? Will he desire to sin again, and do penance again, when it is written, "Do not turn to sin anymore, lest something worse happen to you,"[66] and further, "On him who sins constantly I have no mercy"?[67]

(2) But if, as you say, he is forced into sin, he to whom the medicine of penance is shown, I ask you: what then will that one do, who is shut out even from penance? He who has his whole wound laid open, and yet despairs of any remedy? He who is altogether and continually denied any access to life?

(3) "In baptism," you will say, "we die once and no more according to the Apostle, 'Do you not know that whoever of you have been baptized in Jesus Christ have been baptized in his death? Therefore you have been buried with him by baptism into death so that just as Christ arose again from the dead, so

---

64. 1 Cor 10.1–4.
66. Jn 5.14.
65. 1 Cor 5.5.
67. Cf. Sir 12.3.

you, too, may walk in the newness of life.'"⁶⁸ What is so extraordinary here? The Apostle was teaching that we were renewed so that no one might sin. And yet it followed that he who had sinned should repent. The one is to live unimpaired, the other one, cured. The innocent should bear a crown; the penitent, a pardon. The one should receive a reward; the other, a remedy. And lastly, the same Apostle says, "For when we were still sinners, Christ died for us. Much more then, now that we have been justified by his blood, shall we be saved from the wrath through him."⁶⁹ From the wrath, it is clear, which was due sinners. But if he did not allow the gentile people to die, much more will he not permit those who have been redeemed to perish. Nor will he cast away those whom he has bought at a great price. Nor is the loss of his servants of little consequence to him. "Assuredly, he who has risen again will die no more,"⁷⁰ as it is written. Yes, and what's more, he himself is our "advocate with the Father."⁷¹ This very one "intercedes for our sins."⁷² He is no powerless patron of the wretched, no inadequate intercessor!

10. Answer, my brother. Can it really be that the devil is able to overwhelm the servants of God and Christ is not able to set them free?

(2) You say that the repentance of Peter took place before the passion of our Lord. No one brought this to your attention. And yet Peter had already been baptized. For to him the Lord had said, "He who has been washed once does not need to be washed again."⁷³ Later, however, he received the remedy of Christ, but he repented before that and possessed holiness before he attained this remedy. Nor would his repentance have been recorded as a memorial, unless in some way it had profited the penitent. "He wept," it is said, "most bitterly."⁷⁴ Do you not wish that the believer should do what Peter did? Do you not wish that what profited Peter should profit us? Come now, did not my Thomas, after the resurrection of the Lord, still have doubts about the resurrection? Was he not singled out by the Lord as one guilty of

---

68. Rom 6.3–4.
69. Rom 5.8–9.
70. Rom 6.9.
71. 1 Jn 2.1.
72. Cf. Rom 8.34.
73. Jn 13.10.
74. Mt 26.75.

faithlessness, when he was shown the marks of the nails, the pierced hands, and the wound in the side, when the Lord said to him the following, "Do not be doubting, but believing"?[75] What then? Was he ashamed to repent? Was he not humbled? Did he not immediately acknowledge his God and his Lord? Does not his very confession recommend him?

11. In the same way, you now cleverly dispose of the fundamental argument which I have set down: that power was given to the bishops, and that "whatever they bound on earth should be bound also in heaven; and whatever they loosed on earth should be loosed also in heaven."[76] You say that this refers not to the faithful but to the catechumens; so that, in the case of people yet to be baptized sins were allowed either to be "loosed" or retained. Finally, you join together portions of Scripture from two of the evangelists, so that they would seem to be one; and you add that what Matthew detailed less fully, John completed. You did this so that, whereas the Lord had said, according to Matthew, "Go and teach all nations, baptizing them in the name of the Father, and of the Son, and of the Holy Spirit,"[77] he made his words complete in John, saying, "Whosesoever sins you pardon, they will be pardoned him; and whosesoever sins you retain, they will be retained."[78] This you did so that the "loosing" and "binding" may seem to have referred to the gentiles who were yet to be baptized because the former evangelist spoke first of the gentiles, but the latter "completed" the teaching on "loosing" and "binding." What are you saying here? Did the two evangelists record meanings divided in half between them and only half complete? Were they both deficient either in language or in reason? Or did not, in all things, the Holy Spirit fill every part of each man, carrying out entirely the sense proposed and defining the words to their fullest? "No one adds further provisions to a man's testament when it has been confirmed."[79] Shall a different covenant change the covenant of God?[80] What is this desire to prevail

---

75. Jn 20.27.
77. Mt 28.19.
79. Gal 3.15.
76. Cf. Mt 16.19, 18.18; Jn 20.23.
78. Jn 20.23.
80. Pacian's comment here captures something of Paul's original intended meaning for the passage cited above.

within you, that you would dare such a thing? What is this which, according to Matthew himself, the Lord had said before his own passion? "Whatever you shall bind on earth shall be bound also in heaven; and whatever you shall loose on earth shall be loosed also in heaven."[81] The Lord had foretold this in the Gospel of Matthew, and there had made no mention of the gentiles. Why then do you join to this the passage from John, where he has set down what is referring to himself, and so set it down to keep it distinct from the gentiles? Had he wished to refer to the gentiles, he could surely join together that which he himself set down elsewhere.

(2) All you seek, therefore, you have in Matthew. Why did you, who teaches a bishop, not read the book in its entirety? Look back to the beginning of that injunction. According to the record of Matthew himself, the Lord spoke in the previous passage to Peter—he spoke to a single individual, so that from one he might lay the foundation of unity—not long after delivering the very same injunction to all. How, nonetheless, does he begin his words to Peter? "And I say to you," he says, "that you are Peter, and upon this rock I will build my church; and the gates of hell shall not gain in strength against it. And I will give you the keys of the kingdom of heaven; and whatever you shall bind on earth shall be bound also in heaven; and whatever you shall loose on earth shall be loosed also in heaven."[82] Tell me, my brother, did he say this concerning gentiles only? "Upon this rock," he says, "I will build my church." Does he call nations which have not yet been baptized his Church? Is a man who is not yet reborn the body of Christ? What do I loose to the gentiles? That which is not bound? For if it is not taken into account, it is not bound. Why do I bind that which I have no right to bind? The gentile is free from the law. See now, on the other hand, whether both words [i.e., "loose" and "bind"] are suited to the baptized. He is loosed by pardon because he was held by sin. He is bound by an expiatory offering because he had been loosed by faith and set free through grace. But if I concede that this privilege of loosing and

81. Mt 16.19, 18.18. Cf. Jn 20.23.
82. Mt 16.18–19.

LETTER 3

binding was directed to the gentiles also, even more do I prove that it pertained to the baptized. For if the person who had no chain could be loosed or bound, how much more he who was held by the laws of faith?

12. You say that Matthew stated, "If your brother sins against you, go and rebuke him between you and him alone."[83] And then, immediately after, the Lord added, "Whatever you shall loose on earth shall be loosed also in heaven,"[84] so that it would seem to have pertinence to an offense committed against a brother. But look, do you not see what he says above? "If your brother sins against you." But here he adds, "Truly I say to you, whatever you shall loose on earth . . ."[85] The former statement was a command to one, the latter a privilege of loosing granted to many;[86] the former that same one looses, against whom it is committed; the other, the Church. The former is obtained without a priest, without the brethren; the latter, from all. "Whatever you shall loose," he says. He has made no exceptions at all. "Whatever," he says, whether it is great or small. Listen to what he says to Peter further on: that he who sins against man is to be forgiven "seventy and seven times"[87] in order to show that in other cases it can be forgiven at least once. Yet he who sins against Peter offends the Lord, just as he himself points out to Samuel, "They have not regarded you of no importance, but rather, me."[88] Therefore, what is commanded to us so often is allowed to the Church just once.

13. Now let us return to the "lost sheep," the "piece of silver" and the "younger son,"[89] examples upon which I touched briefly in my previous letter. You returned to them again in full, teaching and demonstrating indeed that the "piece of silver" and the "sheep" and the "younger son" refer to publicans and sinners, that is, ignoble people, and not to the image of the Christian people, nor to the likeness of the faithful. I congratulate myself

---

83. Mt 18.15.
84. Mt 16.19, 18.18. Cf. Jn 20.23.
85. Mt 18.18. Cf. Mt 16.19; Jn 20.23.
86. The singular is employed in the first biblical passage quoted (*in te*), while the plural is used in the second (*vobis, solveritis*).
87. Mt 18.22.
88. 1 Sam 8.7.
89. Cf. Lk 15.

on being so taught, but I am annoyed that I have not understood. For what shall I say? "Whatever the law says, it says to those who are under the law."[90] And I agree that certainly this was spoken principally to the former group, but as a likeness of the faithful, as an image of those who should come in the future, just as the Apostle says, "But these things were happening to them as an example; and they have been written for our correction, on whom the ends of the ages have fallen."[91] And again, "All of these were shadows of good things to come for them."[92] Certainly you yourself concede that these things were spoken to publicans and sinners, that is, to a lowly people and therefore the younger one. Say then, is not the Christian people itself that younger one? Has it not grown together into the root? Has he not bound together these members into one? "Built," as it is written, "upon the foundation of the apostles and the prophets, with Jesus Christ himself being the cornerstone."[93] "Is he the God of the Jews only? Is he not that of the gentiles also? Yes, of the gentiles also. For there is one God, who justifies the ungodly[94] by faith and the uncircumcised[95] through faith."[96] Certainly that lowly people whom the Lord was comparing to the "younger son," the "piece of silver," and the "little sheep" was the Church, from which came the apostles, the whole assembly of believers, and the Christian people. To this body, then, are joined our members also, and all portions of believers, so that out of the wild olive tree of the gentiles they might grow together into a good olive tree,[97] as the Apostle says, "sharing in the richness of its produce";[98] and so "we all might be one in Christ, Jew and Greek, slave and free."[99] If, therefore, we are one body with those lowly ones, those things which the lowly among the ancients heard were also spoken to us; and thus, whatever was declared to a part of the body was announced to the whole body.

14. I will speak still more plainly. This later, this poor, this

90. Rom 3.19.
91. 1 Cor 10.11.
92. Heb 10.1.
93. Eph 2.20.
94. Here I have followed the manuscripts' reading, *impium*, preferred by Peyrot. Rubio Fernández supplies the Greek word *peritomen*.
95. *Acrobystiam*. Rubio Fernández again supplies the original Greek word, *akrobystian*.
96. Rom 3.29–30.
97. Cf. Rom 11.17, 11.24.
98. Rom 11.17.
99. Cf. Gal 3.28.

undistinguished people was an image of the Church, the humble and modest soul, the soul delivered through Christ. It was this people the Lord came to save, this people which he "did not abandon in hell."[100] This people represents that sheep which is carried back on his shoulders, that is, with the effort and might of patience. This is the piece of silver which is sought and, when found, shown to the neighbors. Do you see that its likeness bears a resemblance to penitents? Do you see that mercy is extended even to our own era? Do you see that whatever was spoken to the Church at its birth relates also to the Church in its fullness? Consequently, the Lord at that time added, "Thus, there will be more joy in heaven over one sinner who repents than over ninety-nine righteous persons who need no repentance."[101] For if all these things were written as our reminder, to whom then shall that sinful, humble people be compared, unless to the penitent people? And if, with the figures recurring in such a regular order, the ninety-nine sheep that were safe represent the whole Church, but the one that strayed is that small portion of offenders and the piece of silver which was lost is that wretched sinner, let the son who returns after his evil ways be judged on the pattern of him who is redeemed. You now see that I rightly set down, when I consider the matter of the cure of penitents, that the Lord said, "Those who are well do not need a physician, but rather, those who are sick."[102] Rightly also this, "Blessed are those who mourn, for they shall be comforted."[103] Whatever was said about publicans and sinners will apply to all who are sick and to all who are wretched.

15. You say, "It was only about martyrs that it was written, 'Blessed are those who mourn.'" Does no one then lament his own sins besides those? Does David not cry out, "Every single night I will wash my bed [with tears]"?[104] And also, "For I have eaten ashes as if they were bread, and was mingling my drink with tears"?[105] Does Jacob not say, "Very hard to bear are the years of my life"?[106] Does the Apostle not write to Timothy, "longing to see you, being mindful of your tears"?[107] And yet he was not saying

---

100. Ps 16.10.
102. Mt 9.12; Mk 2.17.
104. Ps 6.6.
106. Gen 47.9.
101. Lk 15.7.
103. Mt 5.4.
105. Ps 102.9.
107. 2 Tim 1.4.

this about a martyr. What now? Do the wretched penitents have dry eyes? And do those who grieve that they have sinned not know how to weep? And do we ourselves, the communicants, we the faithful, not have tears? Does any one of us find pleasure in rejoicing when the world rejoices? But as for you, Novatians, "Even now you have been satisfied, you have become rich, you have begun to reign without us."[108] It is not therefore only the one in misery who ought to be commiserated with.

(2) After this you present and quote that which is written by the Lord, "Every sin and blasphemy shall be forgiven people. But whoever sins against the Holy Spirit, it shall not be forgiven him, neither here nor in the future."[109] Either I am mistaken or this particular example makes a case against you. For if every sin and blasphemy shall be forgiven, you see that pardon is not denied to penitents; thus every sin, thus even blasphemy itself. According to Luke, you have this addition, "And whoever sins against the Son of Man, it shall be forgiven him."[110] What more can be said than this as to the mercy of God, the clemency of the Judge? Or "does your eye look on with envy because the head of the household is good? Is he not allowed to do what he wishes?"[111] Rather, "Who are you to judge a servant [of another]? It is before his own lord that he may stand or fall. Indeed, God has the power to make him stand."[112]

(3) But "whoever has blasphemed against the Holy Spirit," you say, "it shall not be forgiven him."[113] It is your usual practice to review the texts in their entirety. Why did you not read here what "against the Spirit" means? You have it written earlier on the page that, when the Lord was casting out demons by his word and was performing many miraculous deeds by the power of the Spirit, the Pharisees said, "This man does not cast out demons except through Beelzebub, the prince of the demons."[114] This is what it is to have sinned against the Holy Spirit, to have blasphemed against those things which were brought about by the Holy Spirit. For in other sins we either fall through error, or are

108. 1 Cor 4.8.
109. Mt 12.31–32.
110. Lk 12.10.
111. Cf. Mt 20.15.
112. Rom 14.4.
113. Mt 12.32.
114. Mt 12.24.

conquered by fear, or are overcome by the weakness of the flesh. This is the blindness of not seeing what you see, ascribing to the devil the works of the Holy Spirit, and calling that very glory of the Lord, by which the devil himself is conquered, the power of the devil. It is this then that shall not be forgiven. The other things, brother Sympronian, are forgiven to good penitents.

16. After this, in such a manner you put forth arguments regarding the "branches" and the "vine." In the Gospel of John, the Lord says, "I am the true vine, and my father is the cultivator. Every branch in me which does not bear fruit, he will remove, and every one that bears fruit, he will prune."[115] You see therefore that on the branches fruit is required; that is to say, the good works of repentance, just as John [the Baptist] says, "Bring forth fruit accordingly, worthy of repentance."[116] You see that the branches are pruned, which represent the "destruction of the flesh,"[117] the loss of joy, the forfeiture of one's possessions, and the toils of life. These, strictly speaking, are the acts of penitents. You see also that the cultivator is God, who does not destroy even the branches themselves, but rather prunes and gathers them, some certainly for the fire, others for renewing and preparing once again his vineyards.

(2) "Eli the priest," you say, "speaks, stating, 'If a man sins against another man, they shall offer entreaties on his behalf; but if he sins against God, who shall offer entreaties on his behalf?'"[118] In the same way John writes, "If anyone knows that his brother commits a sin which does not lead to death, he shall implore [God] on his behalf, and God shall give him life. Indeed, there is a sin that leads to death; I do not say that you should pray about that."[119] You see that all of this refers to sins still remaining, not to those persons who have at any time sinned and have begun to repent before anyone asks on their behalf. It is too long a task for us to go over such instances. Observe every one of the sins for which the Lord makes threats; you will at once see that they are current ones. But if someone's past righteousness shall

---

115. Jn 15.1–2.
116. Mt 3.8.
117. 1 Cor 5.5.
118. 1 Sam 2.25.
119. 1 Jn 5.16.

not be beneficial to the righteous individual in the time of his iniquity, then neither shall his iniquity which has been forsaken harm the wicked individual in the time of his righteousness.[120] For it is written, "Let the unrighteous person forsake his ways and the wicked his thoughts; and let him return to God and he shall obtain mercy."[121] But if God has punished even past sins and has decreed punishment and suffering for things past and overlooked, well then, is it not within his power to change his sentence? Did he not deliver Rahab,[122] Nebuchadnezzar the king,[123] the Gibeonites,[124] the Ninevites,[125] and Segor[126] from the destruction which had been foretold for them? Did Joel the prophet not bring forth such an idea in his name? "Return to the Lord your God, together with fasting, with weeping, and with mourning, for he is merciful, patient, generous, full of compassion, and causes repentance of evils. And who knows if he, having returned, will repent, and leave a blessing behind him?"[127] Therefore, if you have proved in any way that punishment is decreed for sinners, you must allow this: either such is decreed for persisting sins, or to God is left the freedom of changing his sentence, upon your repentance, for a more favorable one.

17. You say that it is further written, "Now, if your hand or your foot causes you to sin, cast it from you."[128] What this means Moses foretold, as the book of Deuteronomy testifies, "But if your brother, or your daughter, or your wife who is in your embrace, or a friend who is like your own soul—for these are our eyes and our hands—entices you, saying, 'Let us go and serve other gods which you have not known,' you shall denounce him," he added later in the text, "and your own hand shall be upon him to put him to death."[129] Do you see then that this was not said about penitents, but about those who not only themselves persevere in wickedness, but also do not cease to put obstacles in our way? It

---

120. Cf. Ezek 18.24.
121. Isa 55.7.
122. Cf. Josh 6.25.
123. Cf. Dan 4.34.
124. Cf. Josh 9.26.
125. Cf. Jon 3.10.
126. I.e., ancient Zoar. Cf. Gen 19.22–30 [LXX version].
127. Cf. Joel 2.12–14.
128. Cf. Mt 5.29–30.
129. Deut 13.6; Deut 13.8–9 [LXX version].

is these very ones, however dear they may be, that must be relinquished; however useful they seem, they must be abandoned.

(2) Further, you argue that the Apostle Paul said, "Banish evil from among you."[130] Certainly the evil which persists. But repentance is not an evil, since David declares, "It is a good thing to make confession before God."[131] But, nevertheless, the person not performing penance is not with me, nor is he joined together to the party of the saints, nor is he in communion with the Church. But the Apostle states, "If any man who is called a brother is also either a fornicator, or serves the idols, or is greedy, or is a reviler, or a drunkard, or a predator, with such a one, do not even eat."[132] Do you see that not without reason does it specify, "if any man is . . ."? This is to say, one who does not yet repent, one who has not yet ceased to be shameless. And certainly the same has been said about the greedy, about drunkards, and about revilers. Answer me, my brother, is no one of this sort included in your communion? Thus it is that God proclaims through Isaiah, "The impious and the sinners shall perish together."[133] Not the penitent, nor those who are attending to works of mercy. These are the ones to whom God speaks again through the very same Isaiah, "Even if your sins are like crimson, I shall whiten them like snow; even if they are like scarlet, I shall make them as white as wool."[134]

18. "Nevertheless," you say, "the Apostle has condemned him who goes astray, for in the first letter to the Corinthians he says the following, 'Indeed I, who am absent in body but present in spirit, have already passed judgment upon him who has allowed such a crime. In the name of our Lord Jesus Christ, when you are all gathered together, with the power of God, deliver such a one to Satan for the destruction of the flesh, so that his spirit may be saved in the day of the Lord.'[135]" Note, my brother, first that he does not condemn those with whom this person is in communion. He alone who had allowed such a crime is delivered to Satan; he alone is separated out, the communion of the saints is

130. 1 Cor 5.13.
132. 1 Cor 5.11.
134. Isa 1.18.
131. Ps 92.1.
133. Isa 1.28.
135. 1 Cor 5.3–5.

kept intact. You Novatianists condemn all churches because of one sinner. Next, you can see that this same unclean sinner is not delivered unto death, but to Satan, to be punished, to be treated roughly, to repent. Lastly, he says, "for the destruction of the flesh." Not however, of the soul, not even of the spirit, but "for the destruction of the flesh" only; temptation of the flesh, certainly, tribulations, harm to the members, just as in another passage he says of those who lack self-control, "But such people shall suffer tribulation of the flesh."[136] Do you want to know [more]? In the second letter to the Corinthians, Paul himself absolves the very same unrighteous man, for concerning him he remarks, "Sufficient for such a man is this punishment which was inflicted by many. So that now, instead, you ought rather to forgive and console him, lest perhaps such a person should be overwhelmed with too great a sorrow. Therefore, I beseech you to affirm your love for him."[137] And likewise in the text below this, "If there is anyone whom you have forgiven anything, I also forgive. For that which I have forgiven, I have forgiven it for your sakes in the person of Christ, so that we may not be overwhelmed by Satan."[138] Do you see the indulgence of the Apostle, which moderates even his own sentences? Do you see his most merciful leniency, which is so far removed from your own severity? Which differs so much from the countenance which Novatian presents? Which, instead, looks to the common life and salvation of all people?

19. But you also attack us with the severity of a grim judge. You state that, "According to the law of heaven, it is not permissible to break one of the commandments"; and that "lambs ought not to associate with wolves"; and that "everyone who consents to such dealings is rightly an object of reproach"; that "'he who touches pitch is defiled'[139]"; that "'there is no fellowship between light and darkness, or of the temple of God with idols, nor agreement of Christ with Belial'[140]"; and, for that reason, David says, "You were observing a thief and used to associate with him, and with adulterers you used to throw in your lot."[141] And what do

136. 1 Cor 7.28.
137. 2 Cor 2.6–8.
138. 2 Cor 2.10–11.
139. Sir 13.1.
140. 2 Cor 6.14–15.
141. Ps 50.18.

you say lastly? That we abolish the commandments of God. But do we alter even a detail of the law, or is it the Novatianists rather who have violated all the laws of the Church, all the laws of amity, who after so many years of peace, so many accords of religious observance, have produced new ordinances for you, novel customs, all the while feigning under an unrelenting countenance a private type of righteousness? Do we receive wolves into the Church, we who shun the very countenances of heretics? Or is it, rather, the Novatianists, who, although they themselves are rapacious wolves, shrink from the poor sheep who are little more wretched than they themselves? Do we give assent to the wicked? Do we "touch pitch"? Do we embrace the darkness? Do we join ourselves to the idol and to Belial? Or is it those who have received Evaristus, Nicostratus, and the rest who separated from the Church, defiled in word, in deed, and in life? Do we have dealings with adulterers and thieves? Or is it those who have preferred Novatus to their own life and head, after he had embezzled the money of orphans and widows; those who have preferred the murderer of his own wretched parent and of his wife's offspring; those who have preferred a man who was not only unrepentant [of his crimes], but even glorying in them?

(2) Yes, the Apostle Paul did say, "Lay hands hastily upon no man."[142] Yet, this same one teaches that either slowly or after repentance it must not be refused.

20. "But," you say, "after the destruction of Jericho, Achan, the son of Carmi, was put to death for stealing a garment."[143] Come then, slay all who have stolen our money and our books,[144] and invoke your fury against the bones of Novatus. Accept once more that yoke "which neither we nor our fathers have been able to bear."[145] Why are you, Novatianists, slow to demand "an eye for an eye, a tooth for a tooth,"[146] to require "a life [for a life],"[147] to revive once again the commerce in circumcision and the Sabbath?

---

142. 1 Tim 5.22.
143. Cf. Josh 7.
144. Here I have followed the manuscript reading of *librorum*. Rubio Fernández conjectures *liberorum*.
145. Acts 15.10.   146. Deut 19.21.
147. Deut 19.21.

Put to death thieves. Stone insolent people.[148] Choose not to read in the Gospel that the Lord spared even the adulteress who confessed when no one had condemned her;[149] that he absolved the sinner who washed his feet with her tears;[150] that he saved Rahab at Jericho, itself a city of the Phoenicians;[151] that he set Tamar free from the sentence of the patriarch;[152] that also when the Sodomites perished, he did not destroy the daughters of Lot, and would have likewise delivered his sons-in-law had they believed in the destruction that was imminent.[153]

(2) Come then, do you not remember that the Lord says in the writings of David, "With those who hated peace, I was peaceful"?[154] And also that he is not silent about the sentence of Solomon, "A brother helping a brother will be exalted"?[155] What does the Apostle say? "Brethren, even if a person is caught in some misdeed, you who are spiritual, instruct such a one in the spirit of gentleness, taking care that you yourselves are not tempted. Bear each of you the other's burdens, and in this way you will fulfill the law of Christ."[156] And, something which I have already quoted previously, "For I wish to be accursed and separated from Christ for the sake of my brethren, my kindred, according to the flesh."[157] And again, "I have become all things to all men, so that I might gain all."[158] This is: to share in the groans of the wounded, the suffering of the sick, and the death of the dying; to be able to bring together the fall of his brethren with his own upright standing; to detach something from his own healthy condition and apply it as a cure to those losing strength.

21. What advantage is it to you to harden yourselves with a disdainful and severe countenance, to be unbending, holding your necks high, to turn away your faces from the wretched, to close your ears and eyes to them? Have you, I pray, never fallen? Is there no blemish upon your own characters? No mote, I pray, in your eyes?[159] "Who will boast that he has a pure heart, or that he

---

148. Cf. Deut 21.18–21.
149. Cf. Jn 8.1–11.
150. Cf. Lk 7.36–50.
151. Cf. Josh 6.17–27.
152. Cf. Gen 38.6–30.
153. Cf. Gen 19.1–29.
154. Ps 120.7.
155. Cf. Prov 18.19.
156. Gal 6.1–2.
157. Rom 9.3. Cf. Pacian, *Epp.* 2.8, 3.1.
158. 1 Cor 9.22.
159. Cf. Mt 7.3–5; Lk 6.41–42.

is free from sins?"¹⁶⁰ All of you, I suppose, are just, benevolent, and temperate; your members are all sound, your entire body is intact; you have no need of a physician nor of medicine for weaknesses! Enter then heaven immediately, make your way into the approaches to paradise even as the [fiery] sword yields before you;¹⁶¹ exclude from your gifts so many people of ours who confess the one and only God! But even if such as these are in a far different state from that which the unbending rigor of your nature and cruelty pretend, you must see now, O Novatians, that God can have mercy; that a remedy, however late it may be, is available to wretched brethren who confess what is past; that the wounded man, whom the Levite and the priest passed by, can be healed by Christ;¹⁶² that the prayers of the Church are not to be refused to the humbled; and that the hands of priests are to be offered in support to those brethren who deserve pity.

(2) But we understand, just as you reproach [us], that the Church of God is a dove, not bitter with gall, not violent nor apt to rend with talons, but white, with small and tender plumage. We know, too, that since it is "the well of living water"¹⁶³ and "a fountain enclosed,"¹⁶⁴ it is defiled with no filth from a heretical abyss; that it is also a garden enclosed and filled with herbs great and small alike, some of little value, some precious; and that it is also the eight souls from the Ark,¹⁶⁵ among whom, however, was Ham¹⁶⁶ and those thousands of birds and beasts, in pairs and in sevens, clean and unclean alike.¹⁶⁷ But we consider the "dry cisterns"¹⁶⁸ and the "clouds carried about by winds"¹⁶⁹ to represent the spiritual barrenness of the heretics and the assaults of demented voices.

(3) Nor do we promise freedom, since we ourselves are the servants of punishment; but we confess our misdeeds and call upon others likewise to confess theirs and to believe in him "who justifies the wicked person by faith" and "who revokes the sentence

---

160. Prov 20.9 [LXX version].
161. Cf. Jerome, *Ep.* 60.3: *flammea illa rhomphaea custos, paradisi*.
162. Cf. Lk 10.30–37.
163. Cf. Jn 4.10–15, 7.37–39.
164. Song 4.12.
165. Cf. Gen 6.18, 7.7, 7.13; 1 Pet 3.20.
166. Cf. Gen 9.22–27.
167. Cf. Gen 7.2–3.
168. Cf. Jer 2.13; 2 Pet 2.17.
169. Cf. 2 Pet 2.17; Jude 12.

pronounced against wickedness."¹⁷⁰ When we are on guard against you, we also mark warily false prophets and ravenous wolves.¹⁷¹ And we think that just as Jannes and Jambres resisted Moses,¹⁷² so you keep resisting the Catholics. In consequence, the Apostle sets forth the following, "Now just as Jannes and Jambres resisted Moses, so do these also resist the truth: corrupted people, people rejected by God; but they shall proceed no further. For their folly shall be obvious to all, just as that of the former two also was."¹⁷³ That this was spoken against you is clear; for you could neither proceed any further, nor conceal your folly.

22. "He who is washed from [touching] a dead man gains nothing."¹⁷⁴ That is to say: he who is washed in a heretical fountain, and in like fashion, he who is anointed with the oil of the sinner¹⁷⁵—that is, he who is filled with an unclean spirit. Therefore you shall also be children of blood. For you do not desire communion with your brethren, but rather, their blood. Your profession of faith is a false faith. A heretical congregation is an adulterous woman; for the Catholic congregation never, from the very beginning, left the marriage couch and nuptial chamber of her Spouse, nor ardently desired unsuitable and strange lovers.¹⁷⁶ You have painted a banished form with new colors; you have withdrawn your marriage couch from a long-standing marriage; you have left the body of a mother, the wife of the one husband, adorning yourselves with new techniques of pleasing, new allurements of seduction.

(2) For although you bring forward as a witness against me the most blessed Cyprian—because in his letter on the subject of the "lapsed" Christians he says that Noah, Daniel, and Job prayed for sinners but did not succeed in their request,¹⁷⁷ since our Lord

---

170. Cf. Rom 3.26, 3.30.
171. Cf. Mt 7.15.
172. According to post-biblical Jewish tradition, Jannes and Jambres were the magicians at Pharaoh's court who attempted to reproduce the miracles of Moses and Aaron. Cf. Ex 7.11, 7.22. The manuscripts read *Mambrem* here; I have furnished the modern, commonly-accepted form of the name for this passage and for the biblical quotation which follows it.
173. 2 Tim 3.8–9. 174. Sir 34.30.
175. Cf. Ps 141.5. 176. Cf. Ezek 16.32.
177. Cyprian, *De lapsis* 19.

LETTER 3

says, "Even if the three, Noah, Job, and Daniel, were in the midst of them, they shall deliver neither sons nor daughters; but they themselves alone shall be saved"[178]—if only you truly put your faith in the testimony of Cyprian! If only you gave your assent to judgments so salutary! For when Cyprian was urging to penance the lapsed, who were unwilling to do penance because they said that they had been taken back into communion by confessors or martyrs, he taught and demonstrated that not even those patriarchs mentioned above succeeded in gaining anything for the unrepentant. For who can deliver a person who does not wish it? Who can humble himself for those who are proud? Who can obtain anything for those who are unrepentant? So when he said such a thing he was compelling them to the remedies of penance. Nor did a man of such authority and merit in any way contradict himself, but rather taught that prayers must flow forth from the sinners and confession of sin must be held dear. Yet, it is these very examples of Cyprian, in which he relates that both Moses and the other holy ones who beseeched God on behalf of sinners did not obtain their request, which upset you.

23. What is that? Do you not see for whom Moses was unsuccessful in his request? When he had returned to his people, what did he hear in the camp? The voices of drunkards and the music of idolatrous worship were resounding throughout it.[179] The people up until that time were still persevering in their iniquity, still remaining in the very crime, but repentance they did not practice. And yet, who of us told you that Moses did not obtain his request? God, indeed, had said to him, "If anyone has sinned before me, I will delete him from [my] book."[180] He had spoken, however, with the authority of a judge and with the power of a lord. But see how quickly he reversed the sentence imposed against the wickedness of the people.[181] Listen now. Immediately, in the same passage the prophet relates, "And Moses prayed in the presence of the Lord God, 'Why, O Lord, do you rage in anger against your people?'"[182] And so on. Again, later in the

178. Ezek 14.20.
180. Ex 32.33.
182. Ex 32.11
179. Cf. Ex 32.
181. Cf. Joel 2.13.

text, "And the Lord became merciful regarding the evil he had said he would do to his people."[183] Do you see that the anger of God was calmed? Do you see that the offense was reconciled? And this for a people not praying, nor even repenting of what they had done!

24. "But Noah," you say, "and Daniel and Job were not able to deliver their sons or daughters." And the meaning of this is that they could not do this if they should petition on behalf of those who did not request it themselves, or if they should pray for a person who persevered in wrong-doing, or if they should plead not for individuals, not for a few people, but for many thousands. Yet Noah delivered his own household from the general ruin;[184] and Job received all which he had lost;[185] and Daniel by prayer removed that sword which was hanging over the wise men of Babylon.[186] Lot certainly prayed for the safety of a city,[187] and Paul for the passengers of a ship.[188] Thus it is that they who know how to repent are absolved by the righteous ones.

(2) Lastly, look at the very words which you say are written, "They alone shall be saved."[189] Who are they? The very ones who pray for sinners shall pray for such without punishment. And why do you condemn the Church? Why do you forbid the penitents to be prayed for, if we are allowed to pray even for those on whose behalf our petition may not be granted? Therefore, read my Cyprian with more care. Read the whole of his letter concerning the "lapsed"; read another one which he wrote to Antonianus, in which Novatian is hard pressed by examples of all kinds.[190] Then you will know what Cyprian pronounced as to the healing of penitents. I say that Cyprian is opposed to you and that he adhered to Catholic traditions. And you may hear Tertullian himself—not after he had fallen into heresy, for you have taken much from this source!—in a letter, the same which he published while a Catholic, confess that the Church can forgive sins.

25. You see then that the Church is "the queen in clothing embroidered with gold and adorned with diverse colors";[191] con-

183. Ex 32.14.
185. Cf. Job 42.10.
187. Cf. Gen 19.20–22.
189. Ezek 14.20.
191. Ps 45.12.

184. Cf. Gen 8.
186. Cf. Dan 2.
188. Cf. Acts 27.21–25.
190. Cyprian, *Ep.* 55.

LETTER 3

sisting, that is, of a variety of many bodies and many people. This embroidery is not of one color, nor does so great a diversity all glisten in a single garment. One part of her garment covers, another decorates. A certain portion is fitted to her bosom, another is drawn along behind in the lowest fold and becomes soiled in the very act of walking. A part is likened to the purple of the martyrs; another part to virgin silk. A part is sewed on beneath in the folds or repaired by the stitches of a needle. "For one in this way, and another in that way."[192] And yet, in all these she is made one queen.

(2) Therefore, she is also "a fruitful and rich vine,"[193] having many branches and the varied tresses of many a tendril. Look then! Is it really possible that there are everywhere huge clusters of grapes, and that every grape is bursting with ripeness? Have none of these suffered distress from the winter cold? Have none endured the rough hail? Have none reason to accuse the scorching heat of summer? One bud bristles with more shoots; another is stronger, another more pristine. One bursts forth into fruit, while another abounds in leaves alone. Yet she is a vine, beautiful in every part.

(3) She also is the mother of "young maidens without number."[194] Calculate now, if you can, the Catholic flocks and count on your fingers the multitudes of our people. Not only those who are scattered throughout the whole world and fill entire regions, but those, brother Sympronian, who reside with you in the closest vicinity and in the neighboring city. Consider how many of us you, as a single individual, see, how many of my people you alone encounter. Is it not the case that you are absorbed like a drip of rain in great fountains, like a drop of liquid by the ocean? Tell me, please tell me, are these same "young maidens" the offspring of your people? Have you alone borne them? This queen, I declare, is ours, "the chosen one of her mother and perfect."[195] Nothing, indeed, is chosen unless it is better and greater than another; nothing can be perfect unless it is full.

26. And now consider this: whether she is not specially "built upon the foundations of the prophets and the apostles, with

---

192. 1 Cor 7.7.
193. Ps 128.3.
194. Song 6.8.
195. Song 6.9.

Jesus Christ himself as the cornerstone,"[196] if her beginning came before yours, if her beliefs arose before yours, if she has not left her former foundations, if she has not moved them, if she has not been separated from the rest of the body, and if she has appointed her own rulers for herself and also particular guiding documents. But if she has made any interpretations contrary to tradition, if she has invented any new injunction, if she has inflicted on her own body a repudiation of ecclesial harmony, then clearly she appears to have departed from Christ, then clearly she appears to stand outside of the prophets and the apostles.

(2) She, therefore, will be "a great house," made sumptuous with a diversity of every kind of vessel, a house in which glistens pure gold, in which gleams malleable silver, but which also is considered worthy, as it is written, of "vessels of wood and earth."[197] For a great house employs many services and is concerned with various works. It does not seek silver only, nor is it delighted with golden ornamentation alone. Now and then, what is of little account adds grace to things great; and among noble circles, small things are sometimes no less pleasing. No artisan despises his own works, nor does he consider that which he has made to be worthless. And from what cause was it, do you think, that Christ suffered for sinners, except that he was unwilling to lose anything which he himself had fashioned? From what cause was it, do you think, that even now he intercedes with the Father on behalf of the wretched, except that he does not reject the person of little worth, even though that one may be most insignificant. He intends to lose not one of those whom he has accepted, although they may certainly be compared to vessels of wood and earth; and so he places all vessels together in his house.

27. Finally, brother Sympronian, do not feel annoyed to be included with the many. Be willing at last to scorn the festering hangnail sores of the Novatianists and those nail clippings of yours. Be willing at last to look with respect to the flocks of the Catholics and the people of the Church, whose presence extends

---

196. Eph 2.20.
197. Cf. 2 Tim 2.20.

LETTER 3

so far and so wide. "Where there is one," you will say, "there I am also; and where there are two, there is the Church."[198] "Where there is one"— yes, but only in harmony; "where there are two"—yes, but only those making peace. "Where one is, there is the Church also," but how much more where there are many? "Two," the Scriptures say, "are better than one, and a threefold cord is not broken."[199] Listen to David, "I will sing to your name in a great congregation."[200] And again, "Amidst a mighty throng I will praise you."[201] And, "The God of gods has spoken; and he has summoned the earth, from the rising of the sun to its setting."[202] What seed of Abraham, which is "as numerous as the stars and the sand,"[203] shall be content with your scanty means? "In you," God says, "shall all the peoples of the earth be blessed."[204] Tell me, is it really possible that Novatian can accomplish this? It is not such an insignificant thing which the Lord has redeemed with his own blood, nor is Christ so poor.

(2) Acknowledge now, my brother, the Church of God which is spreading widely her pavilions and fixing the wooden stakes of her curtains on the right and on the left. Understand that "from the rising of the sun to its setting, the name of the Lord is worthy of praise."[205] Please see, see, I implore you, that while the Novatianists are struggling over words, the spiritual riches of the Catholics are being dispersed throughout the world.

(3) I have now instructed you on all the points about which I have been consulted by you. I have passed over no major argument of your propositions. I have responded even to small points and individual terms. If you inquired in the spirit of one asking for information, I have revealed such to you with affection. If you inquired in the spirit of one attacking, I have argued my case no less spiritedly. I will add, when I shall have the time, another letter also in which I will not refute your views, but rather, set forth ours. And if you read it in a spirit of friendship

---

198. Cf. Tertullian, *De baptismo* 6.1: *Ubi tres, id est pater et filius et spiritus sanctus, ibi ecclesia, quae trium corpus est.*
199. Cf. Eccl 4.9, 4.12.
200. Ps 35.18.
201. Ps 35.18.
202. Ps 50.1.
203. Gen 22.17.
204. Gen 22.18.
205. Ps 113.3.

and without disdain, perhaps it will not offend you. Meanwhile, in the present letter, I ask you to examine each and every part of it thoroughly. For all that is read in haste passes by unnoticed. If you desire the nobler spiritual gifts and possess a spirit which is open to good instruction, you will not easily disregard things so true. May the Lord see fit to guard and protect you forever, and cause you to live as a Christian in accordance with spiritual harmony.

ON PENITENTS

ALTHOUGH I HAVE SPOKEN several times, albeit with no particular scheme in mind, concerning the treatment of penitents, still, being mindful of the concern of the Lord, who for the loss of one little sheep did not spare his own neck and shoulders, carrying the fragile sinner back to the flock made whole again, I shall try so far as I am able also to describe with my pen the example of such great goodness, and, as a servant, I shall imitate with the humility which is here seemly the purposefulness of the Lord's work.

(2) I fear but one thing, dearly beloved: that through resistance to my intended solicitude, I should, by impressing upon you what is now occurring, rather prompt than repress sins. Perhaps, after the example of the Athenian Solon, it would be better to be silent concerning great acts of wickedness than to warn against them,[1] the morals of our age having gone so far that people believe themselves urged when in fact they are forbidden. For this, I think, has most recently been the effect of my treatise, *The Fawn*,[2] to such a degree that the more earnestly this festival was branded with disgrace the more diligently it was practiced. And all that censuring of abominable behavior, so clearly stated and often repeated as it was, seems not to have repressed, but rather to have taught licentiousness. Alas, woe is me! What kind of crime have I committed? I suppose that they would not have known how to hold the festival of the Fawn unless I, by censuring it, had indicated such to them!

(3) But be that as it may. Rebels from God, those placed outside the Church, are also irritated by the effrontery of chastise-

---

1. Cf. Cicero, *Pro Quinto Roscio* 25.70.
2. Unfortunately, as was noted in the introduction, this treatise (Latin title, *Cervulus*) is not extant.

ment, undoubtedly indignant that their own morals can be criticized by anyone. And just as filth is apt to stink most when you stir it, and a destructive fire to burn more strongly if you turn it, and mad frenzy to appear more fierce if you provoke it, so such people, by turning their heel, have broken the pricks[3] of the unavoidable reprimand, but not without being hurt and wounded by their own resistance.

2. Do you, however, dearly beloved, remember that it is stated by the Lord, "Rebuke a wise man and he will love you; rebuke a fool and he will hate you"?[4] And furthermore, "Those whom I love, I reprimand and chastize"?[5] And therefore in lovingly following and not obstinately opposing, believe that the gentle and careful attention of this work of mine, undertaken according to the will of the Lord by me, your brother and priest, comes from love rather than stern severity.

(2) Furthermore, let no one imagine that this very sermon on the institution of penance is drawn up for penitents alone, lest for this reason whoever is not placed in that position scorn what will be said here as intended for others. Rather, the discipline of the entire Church is tied, as it were, into this clasp, since catechumens have to take care that they do not pass into such a state, and the faithful that they do not return to it; but the penitents themselves have to work hard that they arrive swiftly at the fruit of this labor.

(3) In my topics of discussion, nevertheless, the following order will be maintained. First, I expound upon the degrees of sins, lest anyone think that the most extreme peril is imposed upon all sins no matter what they are. Then I shall speak concerning those among the faithful who, ashamed of the remedy offered them, exhibit an ill-timed sense of modesty and engage in Church fellowship with an impure body and a corrupted mind. Being most timid in the sight of men but totally shameless

---

3. This phrase derives from a well-known, traditional Latin expression, *advorsus stimulum calces*, meaning "kicking against the pricks" and originally pertaining to the action of a horse using the back of its hoof to kick against thorns. Cf., for example, Terence, *Phormio* 78.
4. Prov 9.8.
5. Rev 3.19.

before the Lord, they contaminate with their profaned hands and polluted mouth the altar which is to be regarded with an awe-filled reverence even by the saints and the angels. Thirdly, my sermon will treat those who, having duly confessed and laid bare their misdeeds, either do not know or refuse the remedies of penance and the very acts belonging to the ministry of confession. Lastly, we shall strive to show most clearly what will be the punishment of those who either perform no penance or even neglect it, and who therefore perish in their wound and arrogance; and what, on the other hand, will be the crown, what will be the reward of those who purge the stains of their consciences by right and regular confession.[6]

3. First, therefore, as we have proposed, let us consider the ways of those who sin, diligently seeking out what are sins, what are misdeeds, so that no one may think that, because of the innumerable faults arising from the deceitfulness of which no man is free, I bind the whole human race under a single indiscriminate law of penance. Among Moses and the ancients, those guilty of even the least sin, and, so to speak, of a mere token's worth,[7] were immersed in the same shifting tide of misery as those who had broken the Sabbath,[8] those who had touched what was unclean,[9] those who had consumed forbidden food,[10] those who had been murmuring,[11] or those who had entered the temple of the Most High King when their own abode was infected [with leprosy] or their own garment defiled[12] or when under these defilements they had touched the altar with their hand or come into contact with it by their garment.[13] So much so that it would be easier to ascend to heaven or better to die than to have to keep every one of these injunctions!

(2) Therefore, from all of these sins and from many carnal offenses besides, so that each person might more easily attain his

---

6. *Ordinaria confessione.* That is, confession which conforms to the ecclesiastical *ordo* or *disciplina.*

7. The key term used here, *quadrantis,* denotes a Roman coin having the value of one quarter of an *as,* itself a copper coin of small value.

8. Cf. Ex 35.2. 9. Cf. Lev 11.24–40.
10. Cf. Lev 11.1–23. 11. Cf. Ex 16.7–8.
12. Cf. Lev 14.34–53. 13. Cf. Lev 13.47–59.

desired end, the blood of the Lord has delivered us, redeemed as we are from the servitude of the Law and liberated in the freedom of the faith. And thus the Apostle Paul says, "And indeed, you have been called to freedom."[14] This is that freedom: that we are not bound by all those things whereby the ancients were constrained. But, if I may say it this way, with the thicket of our faults [being forgiven] and the indulgence of remedies marked out, we are constrained to a few, necessary rules. These, whether to keep or avoid, were very easy for believers, so that he who was ungrateful for so great a forgiveness and did not keep even these few, could not deny that he most truly deserved hell. But what these are, let us now see.

4. After the passion of the Lord the apostles, having discussed and considered all things, delivered a letter to be sent to those of the gentiles who had believed. And of this letter, the main point was as follows: "Apostles and elders, the brethren, to those brethren who are of the gentiles in Antioch and in Syria and Cilicia: greeting. Since we have heard that certain persons who have gone out from us and have troubled you with words . . ."[15] Likewise further on, "For it has seemed proper to the Holy Spirit and to us to impose upon you no greater burden than these things: it is necessary for you to abstain from that which has been sacrificed to idols,[16] and from blood, and from fornication.[17] You shall do well if you keep yourselves from such. Farewell."[18] This is the whole conclusion of the New Testament.

(2) The Holy Spirit, disdained in those many ordinances, has bequeathed these injunctions to us under the terms of mortal danger. Other sins are remedied by the compensation of better works.[19] But these three crimes are to be dreaded like the breath of some kind of basilisk,[20] like a cup of poison, like a deadly

---

14. Gal 5.13.   15. Acts 15.23–24.
16. *Idolothytis*. This Latin term, derived from the Greek *eidolothyta*, occurs often in the New Testament and Latin patristic literature.

17. Cf. the Vulgate's reading here: *ut abstineatis vos ab immolatis simulacrorum, et sanguine, et suffocato, et fornicatione*. Acts 15.29.

18. Acts 15.28–29.

19. Cf. Tertullian, *De paenitentia* 6: *hac paenitentiae compensatione redimendam proponit impunitatem.*

20. A type of snake—sometimes identified in antiquity with the Egyptian co-

arrow. For they do not know how merely to injure the soul, but also to snatch it away. Stinginess will therefore be redeemed by generosity, insult will be compensated for by apology, grief by delight, harshness by gentleness, fickleness by seriousness, perversity by honesty. And so in all cases amends are made by the practice of the opposite. But what shall he who is contemptuous of God do? What shall the blood-stained individual do? What remedy shall the fornicator have? Shall he who has abandoned the Lord be able to appease him? Or he who has shed another's blood be able to preserve his own?[21] Or he who has violated God's temple by fornication be able to restore it? These, my brethren, are capital sins; these are mortal sins.

(3) Now hear John and be confident, if you can. "If anyone knows," he says, "that his brother commits a sin which does not lead to death, let him entreat about this and the Lord shall give him life, if he has not committed a sin which leads to death. Indeed, there is a sin that leads to death; I do not say that you should pray about that."[22]

5. But if it pleases you, listen also to what I say about each of these sins separately. God addresses Moses in the following manner when that man is praying for the people who had blasphemed. "Whoever has sinned against me," he says, "I will delete him from my book."[23] And concerning the murderer, the Lord judges thus: "Whoever kills with the sword," he says, "shall die by the sword."[24] And about the fornicator, the Apostle says, "Do not defile the temple of God, which temple you are; but he who defiles the temple of God, God shall destroy him."[25]

(2) These things are written, dearly beloved brethren, and carved on everlasting monuments, written and inscribed, I say,

---

bra—which was said to kill merely by looking at or breathing on its victim. Cf. Ps 91.13 [LXX version].

21. It is clear here and throughout his sermon that Pacian interprets the *abstineatis vos ab . . . sanguine* of Acts 15.29 as a prohibition of murder. See note 17 above.

22. 1 Jn 5.16.
23. Ex 32.33.
24. Mt 26.52. Cf. Gen 9.6; Ex 21.12; Rev 13.10.
25. 1 Cor 3.17.

not on wax and paper and brass or with the pen, but in the book of the living God. "Heaven and earth shall pass away," he says, "one iota or one stroke of a letter cannot pass away before all is fulfilled."[26] What then? Must we die? Many also have in their minds fallen into these sins. Many are guilty of blood; many, surrendered unto idols; many, adulterers. I say, moreover, that it is not hands alone that are involved in murder, but every design, too, which has driven the soul of another to death; and that not only those who have made burnt offerings of incense on profane altars but all who have desolated the Church.[27] And each and every sexual desire that strays beyond the marriage couch and lawful embrace is bound by the sentence of death. Whoever shall have done these things after coming to the faith shall not see the face of God. Those who are guilty of such great offenses are in despair. But what have I done to you? Was it not in your power that it should not occur? Did no one warn you? Did no one foretell it? Was the Church silent? Did the Gospels say nothing? Did the apostles threaten nothing? Did the priest ask nothing? Why do you seek consolations too late? You should then have done such things when you could have. This is a hard saying:[28] "But they who call you happy lead you into error and disturb the path of your feet."[29] He shows the way of wickedness to the innocent, who, after their crimes, flatters the guilty.

6. "Are we then to perish?" someone will say. "And where is the merciful God, 'who did not devise death nor rejoices in the destruction of the living'?[30] Shall we die in our sins? And what will you, priest, do? By what gains will you offset so many losses to the Church?" Accept the remedy if you begin to despair, if you acknowledge yourselves as wretched, if you fear. He who is too confident is unworthy. "Upon this man I will look," says the Lord, "only upon him who is humble and peaceful, and trembles at my words."[31]

(2) I appeal therefore first to you, my brethren, who, having

---

26. Mt 5.18.
27. Peyrot conjectures a gap in the text here, based on the asymmetrical nature of the phrasing.
28. Cf. Jn 6.60.   29. Isa 3.12.
30. Wis 1.13. Cf. Ezek 18.32, 33.11.   31. Isa 66.2.

committed crimes, refuse penance! You, I say, who are timid after being shameless, who are bashful after sinning! You who are not ashamed to sin, but are ashamed to confess! You who with an evil conscience touch the holy things of God and do not fear the altar of the Lord! You who approach the hands of the priest and who come within the sight of the angels[32] with the boldness of innocence! You who insult the divine patience! You who bring to God a polluted soul and a profane body, as if, because God is silent, he does not know! Hear what the Lord has done, and then what he has said.

(3) When the people of the Hebrews were bringing back the Ark of the Lord to Jerusalem, Uzzah,[33] from the house of Abinadab[34] the Israelite, who had touched the side of the Ark without having examined his conscience, was slain.[35] And yet he had drawn near not to take anything from it, but to hold it up when it was leaning because of the stumbling of a young ox. So great a concern was there of reverence toward God that God did not accept bold hands even out of help. The Lord also proclaims the same thing, saying, "Everyone who is clean shall eat of the flesh, and whichever soul touches the flesh of the sacrifice of well-being and has his uncleanness upon him, that soul shall be cut off from his people."[36] Are these things which existed long ago, and now they do not happen in this way? What then? Has God ceased to care for what concerns us? Has he withdrawn beyond the view of the world, and does he look down from heaven upon no one? Is his forbearance really ignorance? God forbid, you will say. Therefore he sees what we do but he waits, indeed, and endures patiently, and he grants an opportunity for repentance and holds out his own Christ to postpone [the end], so that they whom he has redeemed may not readily perish. Understand this well, you sinner: you are observed by God; you can appease him if you want to.

7. But allow that it is a thing of the past that the unclean were

---

32. Angels were thought to be specially present during the sacrament of the Eucharist. Cf. John Chrysostom, *De sacerdotio* 6.4; Ambrose, *Expositio evangelii secundum Lucam* 1.28; and Pope Gregory I, *Dialogi* 4.58.
33. The Latin reads *Otias* or *Ozas*. 34. The Latin reads *Aminadab*.
35. Cf. 2 Sam 6.6–7.   36. Lev 7.19–20.

not permitted to approach the table of God. Open the writings of the apostles and learn what belongs to recent times.

(2) In the first letter to the Corinthians, Paul has put forth these words: "Whosoever," he says, "shall eat or drink of the cup of the Lord in an unworthy manner shall be guilty of the body and of the blood of the Lord."[37] And likewise further on, "For he who eats and drinks in an unworthy manner eats and drinks judgment against himself, not discerning the Lord's body. For this reason," he says, "many among you are weak and sick, and many sleep. But if we would judge ourselves, we should surely not be judged. However, when we are judged, we are rebuked by the Lord, so that we may not be condemned with this world."[38]

(3) Do you tremble or not? "He shall be guilty," he says, "of the body and of the blood of the Lord." One who is guilty of taking human life could not be absolved. Shall the violator of the body of the Lord escape? "He who eats and drinks in an unworthy manner," he says, "eats and drinks judgment against himself." Awake, O sinner! Fear the judgment which is present deep within you, if you have done any such thing! "For this reason," he says, "many among you are weak and sick, and many sleep." If, then, anyone does not fear the future, let him at least dread his present sickness and his present death. "When we are judged," he says, "we are rebuked by the Lord, so that we may not be condemned with this world." Rejoice, O sinner, if in this life you are either cut off by death or wasted by illness, so that you may not be punished in the age to come. See what great evil he commits, who comes unworthily to the altar, he to whom it is reckoned a remedy when he either labors under infirmity or is destroyed by death!

8. But if your own soul is of little value to you, then spare the people, spare the priests.[39] The Apostle declares, "A small amount of yeast leavens the whole lump."[40] What will you do, you because of whom the whole lump is corrupted? You because of whom the whole brotherhood [of Christians] shall suffer? Shall

---

37. 1 Cor 11.27.
38. 1 Cor 11.29–32.
39. A typical use of alliteration by Pacian: *quod si vestra vobis vilis est anima, parcite populo, parcite sacerdotibus.*
40. 1 Cor 5.6; Gal 5.9.

you who has the guilt of so many souls live? Shall you be excused when the innocent have charged you with their [uncleanliness caused by] communion [with you]? When the Church has named you as the originator of her ruin? Behold again, the Apostle says to the priest, "Lay hands hastily upon no man, nor participate in other men's sins."[41] What will you do, you who deceive the priest? You who either mislead him if he is ignorant [of your deeds], or, if he does not possess full knowledge of them, perplex him through the difficulty of proving it? I ask you, therefore, my brethren, by that Lord from whom no secrets are hidden, to stop concealing the wounds of your consciences, even in consideration of my own danger. Wise people, when they are sick, do not fear the physicians, not even when they are about to cut, not even when they are about to burn them in the secret parts of their bodies. We have heard of some individuals who, not being ashamed even about parts of the body withdrawn by modesty from sight, have endured the most serious pains of the knife and of cautery and even of stinging powders. And how great is this which people have taken upon themselves? Shall the sinner be afraid? Shall the sinner be embarrassed to purchase eternal life by his present shame? And shall he withdraw his ill-concealed wounds from the Lord when the Lord stretches forth his hands? And has he who has injured the Lord anything to be embarrassed about? Or is it better that he should perish in such a manner that you, afraid of shame, shall die without shame? Although you are not making a place for shame, you would gain more through its loss, you for whom it were better to perish for your own sake! But if you are embarrassed before the looks of your brethren, have no fear of them since they are partners in your plight. There is no body that rejoices in the afflictions of its own members. Rather, the body grieves together with them and strives with them for a remedy. The Church is in the body and in the member; the Church, truly, is Christ. And so it happens that the person who is not silent about his sins before his brethren, when he is assisted by the tears of the Church, is absolved through the supplications of Christ.

9. Now let the topic of discussion be those individuals who,

---

41. 1 Tim 5.22.

while well and wisely confessing their wounds [i.e., sins] for the purpose of penance, know neither what penance represents nor what the cure is for their wounds. In this they are like those people who bare indeed their wounds and bodily swellings, and acknowledge them also to the physicians who take care of them. But when warned what is to be applied [to such wounds], they disregard it and refuse what they ought to drink. This is just as if someone should say, "Look! I am sick. Look! I am wounded. But I do not wish for my stomach to be cured."[42] Such was the case. But now see something still more foolish.

(2) Another disease is added to the original cause and a new wound inflicted, and all that is just contrary is applied, all that is dangerous is drunk. Under this evil especially does this brotherhood [of Christians] toil, adding new sins on top of old faults. Therefore it has burst forth into vice, and more grievously still, is now racked by a most destructive wasting disease. What then shall I, who as priest am compelled to cure, now do? It is very late in such cases. But even so, if there is any one of you who can bear to be cut and cauterized, I can still do it. Behold the scalpel of the prophet: "Return," he says, "to the Lord your God, and together with fasting and weeping and mourning rend your hearts."[43] Do not fear this incision, dearly beloved. David bore it.[44] He lay in filthy ashes and had his appearance disfigured by a covering of rough sackcloth.[45] He who had once been accustomed to precious stones and to the purple, clothed his soul in fasting. He whom the seas, the forests, the rivers used to serve, and to whom the bountiful land promised wealth, now consumed in floods of tears those eyes with which he had beheld the glory of God. This ancestor of Mary, the ruler of the Jewish kingdom, confessed that he was unhappy and wretched.

---

42. For various editors' conjectures on this passage, see the notes to lines 222–223 (p. 65) in the Anglada Anfruns edition.

43. Joel 2.12–13.

44. Cf. 2 Sam 12.15–16.

45. Cf. Tertullian, *De paenitentia* 9. The performance of penance in sackcloth and ashes is often mentioned in the Bible. Many early Christian ascetics requested that they be placed on the earth to die (eventually) in ashes and sackcloth. Cf., for example, Sulpicius Severus, *Ep.* 3 (death of St. Martin of Tours); Jerome, *Ep.* 108 (death of Paula). Also, see Isidore of Seville, *Etymologiae* 6.19.79.

(3) That king of Babylon, too, forsaken by all, performed penance and was worn out by seven years of squalor. His unkempt long-flowing hair and the wild roughness of his beard surpassed that of even a lion's mane, and his hands, bristling with long curved talons, greatly resembled those of eagles,[46] while he ate grass in the customary way of oxen, chewing again and again the pale herb.[47] Yet this punishment commended him to God and restored to him the powers of the kingship, once his own.[48] He at whom men shuddered, God received, blessed as he was through this very calamity of harsh treatment. Behold the surgical cutting which I promised! Whoever shall be able to endure it shall be healed!

10. I will still apply fire from the apostolic cauterizing iron. Let us see whether you can bear it. "I have judged," he says, "when you are gathered together and my spirit is with the power of the Lord Jesus Christ, to deliver such a person to Satan for the destruction of the flesh, so that the spirit may be saved in the day of the Lord."[49] What do you say, penitents? Where is "the destruction of your flesh"? Is it the case that in the very time of penance you always walk along with the air of respectability, stuffed from the feast, smooth from the bath, with fashionable attire?[50] Behold, here is a man who was once frugal, once somewhat poor, once poorly dressed in a coarse cloak. Now he is well-attired and wealthy, and a proper man—as if he would lay the charge against God that he cannot serve him and would restore his dying soul through the pleasure of his members. It is well that we are of moderate means, or else we, too, should be doing those same things of which certain fashionable men and women are not

---

46. I.e., Nebuchadnezzar. Cf. Dan 4.28–33. Also, see Tertullian, *De Paenitentia* 12: "Long did he [Nebuchadnezzar] offer to the Lord a sacrifice of penance, performing his exomologesis for seven squalid years, his nails growing wild like the talons of an eagle, his hair unkempt like the shaggy mane of a lion."

47. Cf. Virgil, *Eclogae* 6.54 (on the bull of Pasiphaë). Also, see Tibullus, *Elegiae* 1.8.17.

48. Cf. Tertullian, *De paenitentia* 12: "Will the sinner knowingly spurn exomologesis, which has been instituted by God for his restoration, that exomologesis which restored the king of Babylon to his royal throne?"

49. 1 Cor 5.3–5.

50. For the section which follows, cf. Tertullian, *De paenitentia* 11.

ashamed: dwelling in marble edifices, weighed down with gold, sweeping along in silk, glowing with scarlet. If dark-purplish powder glistens on their eyebrows, or false color glows upon their cheeks, or artificial ruddiness melts on their lips[51]—these things perhaps you do not have. But still you are not lacking for pleasant retreats at your garden villas or at the sea, wines of more exquisite quality, and rich banquets, as well as old wines well-refined. So you act, so you believe, since you live so!

(2) I can bear it no longer, my brethren. Daniel, with his comrades, covered in sackcloth and ashes and exhausted through fasting, speaks in this fashion, "We have sinned, we have committed iniquity, we have acted wickedly, we have transgressed your orders and your judgments."[52] About Azariah also, the divine Scripture says, "Standing up, Azariah prayed and opening his mouth, he was making confession to God together with his companions."[53] David himself states, "Every night I will bathe my bed, I will drench my couch with my tears."[54] But we—what sort of things do we do? What like this do we do? I am not speaking of those things which we gather together into a pile by trafficking, merchandising, plundering; by snatching at profits abroad and lusts at home; by doing simply nothing, by giving nothing to the poor, by forgiving nothing to brethren. We do not even do those things which also can be seen by the priest and praised by the bishop when he witnesses them; nor do we observe the following daily duties: to weep in the sight of the Church; to mourn our lost life in poor garb; to fast, to pray, to prostrate ourselves; to refuse luxurious delights if someone invites us to the baths; to say, if someone asks us to a feast, "Such things are for the blessed. I have sinned against the Lord and am in danger of perishing eternally. What do I, who have injured the Lord, have to do with feasting?"[55] And in addition to this: to hold the poor man by the

---

51. Cf. Cyprian, *De habitu virginum* 13–14.
52. Dan 9.5.
53. Dan 3.25 (as quoted by Cyprian, *De lapsis* 31).
54. Ps 6.6.
55. Cf. Tertullian, *De paenitentia* 11: "If anyone should ask you why you make good cheer, then say to him, 'I have sinned against the Lord. I am in danger of perishing forever. Therefore am I now weakened and wasted and tormented, so that I may win for myself the pardon of God whom I have injured by my sin!'"

hand; to seek the prayers of the widows; to prostrate oneself before the priests; to beg mercy from the interceding Church; to attempt all these first, rather than to perish.[56]

11. I know that some of your brothers and sisters wrap their chests in hair-cloth, lie in ashes, and practice fasting very extensively, nor yet perhaps have they so gravely sinned. Then why shall I speak of the brethren? The wild goats, so we are told, know what will cure their own kind. I have heard that when pierced by poisoned arrows they traverse the Dictaean[57] countryside until, plucking the stalk of the dittany plant,[58] they with the poisonous liquid of the healing juice, expel from their bodies the impelled darts.[59] Shall we repel the fiery darts of the devil with no juice of penance, with no healing herb of confession? The swallow knows how to give sight to her blinded young by use of swallowwort.[60] Shall we cure the lost vision of the mind by no root of hurtful treatment? Behold man who, like neither the goat nor the swallow, is unwilling to give up his own blindness and malady!

(2) Now consider, my brethren, what we promised in the end, what reward, or on the contrary, what result will follow these actions. The Spirit of the Lord threatens self-indulgent sinners and those who do not perform penance, saying, "They did not receive the love of truth so that they might be saved. And because of this he shall send them the working of delusion so that they should believe a lie: this so all who have not believed the truth but took pleasure in unrighteousness might be condemned."[61]

---

56. Cf. Tertullian, *De paenitentia* 9: "It requires that you habitually nourish prayer by fasting, that you sigh and weep and groan day and night to the Lord your God, that you prostrate yourself at the feet of the priests and kneel before the beloved of God, making all the brethren commissioned ambassadors of your prayer for pardon."

57. I.e., Cretan (poetically named after Mt. Dicte).

58. "The juice [of the dittany plant], drunk with wine, is of benefit to those bitten by venomous animals. But such is the power of the plant, that even its smell will drive away and its touch will destroy venomous animals" (Dioscorides, *De materia medica* 3.34).

59. Cf. Tertullian, *De paenitentia* 12 (where the animal named, however, is a stag). See also Aristotle, *Historia animalium* 9.6; Pliny, *Naturalis historia* 8.97; Virgil, *Aeneis* 12.411–415; Cicero, *De natura deorum* 2.50.126.

60. Cf. Tertullian, *De paenitentia* 12; Jerome, *Commentarii in Ecclesiasten* 7. See also Pliny, *Naturalis historia* 8.27, 25.8.

61. 2 Thess 2.10–11.

Likewise, the Apocalypse speaks in this manner of the harlot: "However much she has glorified herself and indulged in luxury, give her that much torment and sorrow."[62] And the Apostle Paul states, "Do you really not know that the goodness of God leads you to repentance? But in accordance with your hardness, you are storing up wrath for yourself on the day of wrath and revelation of the righteous judgment of God."[63]

(3) Fear therefore, dearly beloved, the righteous judgments. Renounce error. Condemn luxurious living. The final epoch is even now approaching. Tartarus and Gehenna are extending their spacious embrace in welcome for the wicked. After the punishment of souls at the appropriate time, everlasting punishment is reserved also for the revivified bodies. Let no one believe in the story of Tityus's liver or the vulture as told by the poets![64] The eternal fire itself renews for itself the substance of the regenerated bodies.[65] Listen carefully if you do not believe. The force of the waters rages wildly in the fire; it shall be renewed by the punishment which nourishes it.[66] If you recoil from the anguish of confession, just remember Gehenna, which confession will extinguish for you.[67] Estimate its intensity even from the things which are presently visible: some of its chimneys are now wearing away the mightiest mountains with its subterranean fires. Aetna in Sicily and Vesuvius in Campania blaze fiercely with tireless masses of flames. And in order to prove to us the eternity of judgment, they are cleft asunder, they are devoured, and yet they never end.

(4) Consider in the Gospel the rich man, who as yet was

---

62. Rev 18.7.
63. Rom 2.4–5.
64. According to the ancient pagan mythographers, Tityus, one of Zeus's giant descendants, attacked Leto in one of her sacred precincts. Her children, Apollo and Artemis, killed the assailant and sent him to Tartarus, where he was eternally tortured by being stretched upon the ground with his arms and legs spread apart and having two vultures eat at his liver.
65. Cf. Tertullian, *Apologeticus* 48; Minucius Felix, *Octavius* 35.3.
66. Here I have followed the reconstruction of the text established by Rubio Fernández. See Anglada Anfruns's summary of past editorial conjectures in his critical apparatus (p. 69, lines 315–316).
67. Cf. Tertullian, *De paenitentia* 12.

suffering under the punishment of the soul only. What kind of punishment shall there be for the restored bodies? What gnashing of teeth therein? What tears from the eyes?

12. Remember, my brethren, that there is no confession in the grave;[68] nor can penance be granted when the time for repentance is past. Hurry while you are still alive, "while you are on the way with your adversary."[69] Note well that we fear the fires of this world and we take fright at the iron claws of tortures. But compare with these the eternal hands of torturers and the forked flames which never die!

(2) By the faith of the Church, by my own concern, by the souls of all in common, I implore and entreat you not to be ashamed in this work, not to be distressed to grasp as soon as you may the offered remedies of salvation: to lower your souls by mourning, to clothe the body in sackcloth, to sprinkle it with ashes, to mortify yourselves by fasting, to prostrate yourselves with mourning, to be aided by the prayers of many. According to how you have been unsparing in your own chastisements, in the same degree God will spare you.[70] "For he is merciful and patient, of great compassion and one who turns aside the sentence he has imposed against such wicked acts."[71] Behold! I promise, I assure you, if you return to your Father with true penitence, sinning no more, adding nothing to former sins, saying also some humble and sorrowful words, such as "Father, we have sinned in your presence, and we are no more worthy to be called your sons,"[72] then immediately both that filthy herd and the shameful food of pods shall leave you.[73] Immediately on your return also the robe shall be put upon you and the ring will adorn you, and your Father's embrace again shall receive you.[74] Behold, he himself says, "I do not wish the death of the sinner as much as I prefer that he turn about and live."[75] And again he says, "Shall he who has fallen not arise, and shall he who has turned away not

---

68. Literally, "in the lower regions" (*apud inferos*). Cf. Cyprian, *Ep.* 55.29. Also see Ps 6.5; Eccl 9.10; Sir 14.16–17.
69. Mt 5.25.   70. Cf. Tertullian, *De paenitentia* 9.
71. Joel 2.13. Cf. Cyprian, *Ep.* 55.23.   72. Lk 15.18–19.
73. Cf. Lk 15.15–16.   74. Cf. Lk 15.20–22.
75. Ezek 33.11. Cf. Ezek 18.23, 18.32; 2 Pet 3.9.

return?"⁷⁶ And the Apostle states, "God has the power to make him stand."⁷⁷

(3) The Apocalypse also threatens the seven Churches unless they should repent. Nor would he, indeed, threaten the impenitent unless he pardoned the penitent. God himself also says, "Remember then from where you have fallen, and repent."⁷⁸ And again, "When, having returned, you shall mourn, then shall you be saved and know where you have been."⁷⁹ Let no one so despair of the vileness of a sinful soul that he believe that God has no need for him any more. The Lord wishes that not one of us should perish. Even those of little worth and the humblest are sought after. If you do not believe it, consider this. Behold, in the Gospel the single piece of silver is sought after, and when found is shown to the neighbors.⁸⁰ The little sheep, although it has to be carried back on his supporting shoulders, is not burdensome to the Shepherd.⁸¹ Over a single sinner who repents, the angels in heaven rejoice and the celestial choir exults. Come then, you sinner. Do not cease from making your entreaties. You see where there is rejoicing over your return! Amen.⁸²

76. Jer 8.4.
77. Rom 14.4.
78. Rev 2.5.
79. Isa 30.15 [LXX version].
80. Cf. Lk 15.8–9.
81. Cf. Lk 15.4–7.
82. Deleted by Anglada Anfruns.

ON BAPTISM

IT IS MY DESIRE to reveal in what way we are born in baptism and in what way we are renewed. I shall speak sensibly, my brethren, in the same words of Scripture[1] lest, because of the elegance of my words, you should perhaps believe that I have taken pleasure in my own style, and also so that you may be able to understand such a mysterious subject. And indeed, how I wish I could impress this upon you. I do not seek glory; for glory belongs to God alone. My only prompting is my concern for you and especially for those candidates for baptism; and I ask myself if we are able truly to comprehend the estimation of so great a happiness. I shall therefore show the original state of paganism, what the faith offers, and what indulgence baptism grants. And if such in this manner finds its way into your hearts, as I think it will, then you will judge, my brethren, that no preaching has ever yielded you more. Hear then, dearly beloved, what kind of death man was subjected to before the coming of baptism.

(2) You certainly know how, long ago, Adam was returned to his earthly place of origin; this condemnation imposed upon him the decree of everlasting death, and that this one decree held sway over all of his descendants. "Death had dominion" over the whole human race, "from Adam to Moses."[2] But through Moses one people only was chosen, namely the seed of Abraham, if they had been able to keep the commandments of righteousness. Meanwhile, we were all held under the bondage of sin, so that we might eat of the fruits of death: destined for feeding on pods and for keeping swine.[3] That is, for impure acts under

---

1. *Verbis sane ipsius loquar. Ipsius* almost certainly refers to the Bible since a scriptural reading normally preceded sermons of this kind. Cf. Rubio Fernández, "El texto," p. 365–66.
2. Rom 5.14.
3. Cf. Lk 15.15–16.

the influence of wicked angels, whose dominion allowed us neither to do nor to know righteousness. For our very servitude compelled us to obey such masters. As for how we were delivered from these powers and from this death, listen now.

2. After Adam sinned, as I have noted before, he was condemned to death when the Lord said, "Earth you are, and to earth you shall return."[4] This condemnation was transmitted to the whole human race. For all sinned, with nature itself now impelling them to it, as the Apostle states, "Since through one man sin entered into the world, and through sin, death; and so it came down to all men, because all have sinned."[5] Sin therefore reigned, in whose bonds we were dragged, as it were, like captives to death, a death that would last forever. But this sin, before the times of the Law, was not even understood, as the Apostle states, "For until the Law was established, sin in the world was not accounted."[6] That is, it was not apparent. With the coming of the Law it revived. Now it was clearly seen, yet to no avail since no one came close to keeping it. For the Law said, "You shall not commit adultery, you shall not kill, you shall not covet."[7] Yet covetousness with all its attendant vices still continued. So it was that before the Law sin slew man with a sheathed sword, and under the Law, with a drawn sword. What hope therefore did man have? Without the Law he perished because he could not recognize sin; and under the Law he perished because he rushed into that very sin which he saw. Who could free him from death? Hear the Apostle! "O most wretched man that I am! Who shall deliver me from the body of this death? Grace," he says, "through our Lord Jesus Christ."[8]

3. What is grace? It is the remission of sin; that is, a gift. For

---

4. Gen 3.19.
5. Rom 5.12. Pacian's quotation of this noteworthy passage is: *Quia per unum hominem in mundum peccatum introivit et per delictum mors, et sic in omnes homines devenit, in quo omnes peccaverunt.* I have rendered the key phrase, *in quo*, to reflect the precise meaning of the Greek original. It is, of course, clear from this passage and its context that Pacian regarded the sin of Adam as having been passed down to all of his descendants.
6. Rom 5.13.
7. Cf. Deut 5.18, 5.17, 5.21.
8. Rom 7.24–25.

grace is a gift. Christ, therefore, in coming and taking upon himself the nature of man, first presented before God this very human nature, pure from the power of sin and innocent. "Behold," Isaiah says, "a virgin shall receive in her womb and bear a son, and you shall call his name Emmanuel. Butter and honey he shall eat by the time he may know to defer the evil and choose the good."[9] And again it is written about him, "This one committed no sin, nor was there deceit found in his mouth."[10]

(2) Under this protection of innocence, Christ first undertook the defense of man in the very flesh of sin. Immediately that father of sin and disobedience, who had once deceived the first human beings, began to be impatient, agitated, and anxious. For he was destined to be vanquished by the abrogation of that law of sin by which alone he had kept man in his power or could maintain it. He armed himself therefore for a spiritual contest with the Immaculate One. At first, under a pretense of respect, he attacked our Lord with the stratagem with which he had overcome Adam in Paradise. As if he were perplexed about Christ's heavenly power, he said, "If you are the Son of God, command that these stones become bread."[11] He hoped that Christ, out of shame or an unwillingness to conceal that he was the Son of God, might fulfill the tempting commands. And behold that even then he was not silent, suggesting that if our Lord would cast himself down from on high, he would be received on the hands of angels, to whom the Father had entrusted that "on their shoulders they will bear him up, lest it happen that he should dash his foot against a stone."[12] All this so that, while the Lord wished to prove that it was he concerning whom the Father had commanded these precautions, he might do what the tempter urged. Finally, the serpent, having been crushed again, acted as if he were now giving up and promised those same kingdoms of the world which he had seized from the first man.[13] He did this so that, while the advocate of man believed that he had triumphed, he might, by accepting the realm which he was

9. Isa 7.14–15.
10. Isa 53.9; 1 Pet 2.22.
11. Mt 4.3. Cf. Lk 4.3.
12. Mt 4.6; Lk 4.11.
13. Cf. Mt 4.8–9; Lk 4.5–7.

defending, look favorably upon the position offered by the evil one, and so at long last, sin. But in all these attacks the enemy was overcome and destroyed by the heavenly power, just as the inspired poet[14] says to the Lord: "That you may suppress the enemy and the avenger. For I shall behold the heavens, the work of your fingers."[15]

4. The devil ought to have yielded. But nevertheless he did not yet cease. He enticed with his familiar snares and stirred up with rage the scribes and Pharisees and all that company of wicked men. They, in turn, after using various tricks and deceits of the heart through which they like serpents thought to deceive the Lord by false yielding, and after accomplishing nothing, at last attacked him with open lawlessness and the most cruel kind of suffering. They hoped that either through the indignity of such matters or the pain of such punishments, he might do or say something unrighteous and thus destroy the human nature which he bore, and that his soul might be left in hell, which domain had one law to retain the sinner within it. For "the sting of death is sin."[16] But Christ stood firm and "committed no sin, nor was guile found in his mouth,"[17] as we have noted, not even when he was led away as a victim.[18] This was what it was to conquer, to be condemned without sin! For the devil had received over sinners the power which he claimed for himself over the Immaculate One, and so the devil himself was conquered, that is, by declaring against the Righteous One that which was not allowed him by the decree he had received. Whence the prophet says to the Lord, "So that you may be justified in your words, and may prevail when you are judged."[19] And thus, as the Apostle states, "Having led the authorities as captives in a triumphal procession, Christ condemned sin in the flesh, nailing it to his cross and blotting out the handwriting of death."[20] That is why God

---

14. The word used here is *vates*, which in both classical and early Christian usage can mean a "prophet, seer, or divinely-inspired poet." It is in this last sense that Pacian appears to use the term to designate David, as do other patristic writers. Cf. Prudentius, *Hamartigenia* 575: *rex summus atque Dei vates* (referring to David).

15. Ps 8.2–3.
16. 1 Cor 15.56.
17. Isa 53.9; 1 Pet 2.22.
18. Cf. Isa 53.7; Acts 8.32.
19. Ps 51.4.
20. Col 2.14–15.

"did not abandon his [i.e., Christ's] soul in hell, nor give up his Holy One to see destruction."[21] That is why, having trampled underfoot the stings of death, he rose again on the third day in the flesh, reconciling flesh to God and restoring it to immortality, having overcome and blotted out sin.

5. But if he alone conquered, what did he bestow on others? Hear this in a few words. The sin of Adam had passed on to the whole human race. "For through one man," as the Apostle says, "sin entered in, and through sin, death. And so it came to all men."[22] Therefore, the righteousness of Christ must pass on to the whole human race. And just as Adam by sin had caused the destruction of his own descendants, so Christ by his righteousness would give life to his whole race. This the Apostle emphasizes, saying, "Just as by the disobedience of one man, many were made sinners, so, by the attention, by the word of the one, many shall be made righteous. So that just as sin has reigned unto death, so also grace might reign by righteousness unto life everlasting."[23]

6. Someone will say to me, "But the sin of Adam deservedly passed on to his posterity, because they were born of him. Can it be said then that we are born of Christ, that we can be saved because of him?" Do not think of these things in a carnal manner and then you will see how we are born of Christ, our parent. In these last times Christ certainly received a soul together with the flesh from Mary. It is this flesh which he has come to save. It is this flesh which he has freed from sin. It is this flesh which he did not abandon in hell. It is this flesh which he joined to his spirit and made his own. And this represents the marriage of the Lord, joined together in one flesh, so that according to "that great mystery" they might become "two in one flesh, Christ and the Church."[24] From this marriage is born the Christian people, with the Spirit of the Lord coming from above. And at once, with the heavenly seed being spread upon and mingled with the substance of our souls, we develop in the womb of our [spiritual] mother, and once we come forth from her womb, we are made

---

21. Ps 16.10.
23. Rom 5.19, 5.21.
22. Rom 5.12.
24. Eph 5.31–32.

alive in Christ. And so the Apostle says, "The first Adam [became] a living soul; the last Adam [became] a life-giving spirit."[25]

(2) Thus Christ engenders life in the Church through his priests, as the same Apostle states, "And indeed, in Christ I have begotten you."[26] And so the seed of Christ, that is, the Spirit of God, produces through the hands of the priests the new man, conceived in the womb of our [spiritual] mother and received at birth at the baptismal font, with faith still attending as the nuptial protectress. For neither will someone appear attached to the Church who has not believed, nor will someone be born from Christ who has not received his Spirit. We must believe therefore that we can be born again. For Philip asserts thus, "If you believe, it is possible."[27] Christ must be received so that he may beget, for so says the apostle John, "As many as received him, to them he gave the power to become sons of God."[28] But these things cannot otherwise be fulfilled, except by the sacraments of baptism and chrism at the hands of the bishop.[29] For by baptism sins are washed away; by chrism the Holy Spirit is poured out upon [the individual]. Yet both of these are obtained through the action and words of the bishop. And so it is that the whole man is born again and renewed in Christ, "so that just as Christ was resurrected from the dead, so we, too, may walk in the newness of life."[30] In other words, having put aside the errors of our former life—namely, servitude to idols, cruelty, fornication, licentiousness, and the other vices of flesh and blood—we should, through the Spirit, follow new ways in Christ: faith, modesty, innocence, and chastity. And "just as we have borne the image of earthly man, let us also bear his, who is from heaven,"[31] because "the first man was of the earth, the earthly one; the second, from heaven, the heavenly one."[32] If we act in this manner, dearly beloved, we

---

25. 1 Cor 15.45. Cf. Gen 2.7.   26. 1 Cor 4.15.
27. Acts 8.37.   28. Jn 1.12.
29. The word used here is *antistitis*, which in early Christian writings can mean either "priest" or "bishop." In Pacian's time and place the right to consecrate the chrism and administer the second anointing (consignation) was generally restricted to bishops (cf. second Council of Carthage, canon 3, etc.). Hence, the translation as "bishop."
30. Rom 6.4.   31. 1 Cor 15.49.
32. 1 Cor 15.47.

shall die no more. For even if we die in this body, we shall live in Christ, as he himself says, "He who believes in me, although he were dead, shall live."[33] We are assured, in fact, on the testimony of the Lord himself that Abraham, Isaac, and Jacob, and all the saints live for God. Indeed, concerning these very men the Lord states, "But they all live for him, for he is the God of the living, not of the dead."[34] And the Apostle says about himself, "To me, to live is Christ; and to die is gain; I would wish to be set free and to be with Christ."[35] And furthermore, "But while we are in this body, we are absent from the Lord; for we walk by faith, not by sight."[36]

7. This is what we believe, dearly beloved brethren. But "if in this lifetime we are the ones who entertain hope, we among all people are the most wretched."[37] Cattle, wild beasts, and birds, as you yourselves see, share the life of this world with us, or have even longer lives. That which Christ has given through his Spirit belongs to humans alone: namely, eternal life, but only if we now sin no more. For just as death is obtained by wickedness, it is avoided by goodness. Thus life is lost by wickedness, and it is retained by goodness. "So the wages of sin is death; but the gift of God is eternal life through Jesus Christ our Lord."[38]

(2) Remember above all else, my children, that just as we have said above, all peoples who were once given over to the princes and powers of darkness are now set free through the victory of our Lord Jesus Christ. It is he, he indeed, who has redeemed us, "forgiving us all our sins," as the Apostle says, "and blotting out the handwriting of disobedience that was against us. For he also has taken it out of the way, nailing it to his cross, divesting himself of the flesh. He exposed the powers [of darkness] openly, triumphing over them in himself."[39] He set free those who were bound, and burst asunder our chains, just as David had said, "The Lord lifts up those who are fallen. The Lord sets free those who are bound. The Lord opens the eyes of the blind."[40] And again, "You have burst asunder my chains. I will offer to you a

33. Jn 11.25.
34. Lk 20.38. Cf. Mt 22.32.
35. Phil 1.21, 1.23.
36. 2 Cor 5.6–7.
37. 1 Cor 15.19.
38. Rom 6.23.
39. Col 2.13–15.
40. Ps 146.7–8.

sacrifice of praise."[41] Freed therefore from our chains, when through the sacrament of baptism we come unto the sign of the Lord, we renounce the devil and all his angels whom we served in the past, so that we should now not serve them any longer, having been liberated by the blood and name of Christ. But if after this anyone, by forgetting himself and ignoring his redemption, returns again to "the servitude of angels"[42] and to "those weak and beggarly elements of the world,"[43] he shall be bound once more by his old fetters and chains—that is, by the chains of sin—"and his last state shall be worse than his first."[44] For the devil will bind him even more tightly, as if he were caught while fleeing, and Christ will no more be able to suffer for him because "he who was resurrected from the dead will now not die again."[45]

(3) Therefore, dearly beloved, only once are we washed; only once are we set free; only once are we admitted into the eternal kingdom; just once is it that "happy are they whose transgressions are forgiven and whose sins are covered."[46] Hold firmly what you have received, keep it happily, and do not sin anymore. Keep yourselves pure and unblemished from that time until the day of the Lord. Great and boundless are the rewards granted to the faithful, rewards "which no eye has seen," he says, "nor ear heard, nor have they entered into the heart of man."[47] Strive to secure by labors of righteousness and spiritual supplications that you may be able to receive these rewards! Amen.

41. Ps 116.16–17.
42. Col 2.18.
43. Gal 4.9.
44. Lk 11.26.
45. Rom 6.9.
46. Ps 32.1.
47. 1 Cor 2.9. Cf. Isa 64.4.

OROSIUS OF BRAGA

INTRODUCTION

Like Pacian of Barcelona, Orosius was an active and prominent participant in the ecclesiastical affairs of his time, but like Pacian, too, his life's story is known only in its most basic features. Orosius himself provides few autobiographical details in his extant writings, and there are only scattered references to him in the contemporary sources.[1] Even the surname "Paulus" traditionally attributed to him is possibly inauthentic. From all indications Orosius was born sometime between 380 and 390 at Bracara Augusta in Hispania Citerior (now Braga, in northern Portugal). This city was the capital of the province of Gallaecia (Galicia) and after the Germanic invasions of the early fifth century, capital of the Suevian kingdom.[2] Although our first explicit reference to a Christian presence in Braga does not come until the middle of the fourth century, we know of flourishing Church communities in nearby cities at least a century before that. By the time of Orosius, Braga and Galicia were deeply involved in the Priscillianist dispute. Indeed, Braga's Bishop Paternus (fl. ca. 400), Orosius's contemporary, had actually been consecrated originally by the Priscillianist Symposius, bishop of nearby Astorga, but had later returned to orthodoxy after reading works of Ambrose.

(2) Judging by Orosius's own writings and the literary evaluations of his contemporaries, he received a good classical and Christian education as a youth. Whether he was schooled formally by professional teachers or informally at home by family members is not known. As a young man he entered the priesthood,[3] and

---

1. By far the most thorough modern biography is by Paul A. Onica, "Orosius" (Ph.D. dissertation, University of Toronto, 1987).

2. On Christian Braga, see José Augusto Ferreira, *Fastos episcopales de Igrejia primacial de Braga* (Braga: Edicão de Mitra Bracerense, 1950).

3. He is called *compresbyter meus* by Avitus of Braga, *iuvenis presbyter* by Augustine of Hippo, and *presbyter hispanus genere* by Gennadius.

soon was actively involved in both the orthodox Church's struggle against Priscillianism and, possibly, Roman resistance to the Germanic invaders who swept into the Iberian peninsula in the autumn of 409.[4] The Priscillianists were a force to be reckoned with in Spain, especially in Orosius's native province of Galicia where they dominated the Church hierarchy—this despite numerous conciliar and imperial injunctions issued against them.[5] Even Orosius in his early career is said to have been attracted to this heresy, according to one late source.[6] Origenist ideas, too, were seen by some as a growing threat to the integrity of teachings of the Church in Spain. Indeed, it is clear from the text as well as the title of Orosius's first polemical treatise, *Consultatio sive commonitorium Orosii ad Augustinum de errore Priscillianistarum et Origenistarum*,[7] that Orosius regarded the Origenist influence as equally pernicious in his homeland.

(3) When in 414 Orosius left Spain for North Africa he was perhaps a man in his early thirties.[8] Although Orosius would have us believe from his testimony in the *Commonitorium* that his departure from Spain and his arrival on the shores of North Africa in the latter part of 414 was entirely miraculous and providential,[9] a more likely scenario is that which he himself

---

4. Orosius's account of his own escape from the invaders perhaps hints at his own active opposition to their takeover: "And yet, if I may speak of my own story, how for the first time I saw the strange barbarians, how I avoided my enemies and flattered those in authority, how I guarded myself against the pagans, fled from those who lay in wait for me, and how finally, enveloped by a sudden mist, I slipped through the clutches of those who with stones and spears pursued me over the seas, I would wish that I could move all my audience to tears" (*Historia* 3.20).

5. For example, Fabrizio Fabbrini, *Paolo Orosio, uno storico* (Rome: Edizione di storia e letteratura, 1979), 84–85, notes that at the close of the fourth century all the Galician bishops except one were Priscillianists.

6. Braulio, bishop of Saragossa (631–51), writes, "Beware, moreover, of the poisonous doctrine of Priscillian of that country in former times, by which we found both Dictinius and many others to have been infected—the blessed Orosius himself, also, although he was corrected by the blessed Augustine" (*Ep.* 44).

7. Hereafter, *Commonitorium*.

8. Augustine in 415 characterizes Orosius as "a religious young man, a brother in the Catholic fold, in age a son, in dignity a fellow priest" and "a certain very pious and studious young priest" (*Ep.* 166.2, 169.13). Since the bishop of Hippo was sixty-one years of age at that time, Orosius was probably in his early thirties.

9. "I do recognize why I have come. It was not by choice, not by necessity, and not by common agreement that I departed from my native land. Rather, I was

later provides in his *Historia* (3.20). Here he indicates that the dangers presented by the Germanic takeover of his homeland prompted his flight.[10] It is certainly understandable that Orosius, in his initial contact with Augustine, would not want the revered bishop of Hippo to think that he had fled Spain—and deserted his flock—because of personal danger. For his part, Augustine became convinced of the Spanish priest's sincerity and veracity, and in 415 offered the following testimonies: "Orosius, . . . prompted only by burning zeal in regard to the Holy Scriptures, came to us from the most remote part of Spain, namely from the shore of the ocean;"[11] and, "For from the remote western coast of Spain he has come with eager haste to us, having been prompted to do this by the report that from me he could learn whatever he wished on the subjects concerning which he desired information."[12] Whatever Orosius's true motivation—personal safety, theological training and enlightenment, career advancement, or a combination thereof—he was warmly received by the bishop. Orosius's stay in Hippo Regius (now Annaba, Algeria) was to be a short one. By the spring of 415 he would set off on a journey farther east, to Palestine and Jerome. But during his brief time with Augustine, Orosius quickly demonstrated the characteristics which he would reveal both in his writings and in his personal actions in the future. Augustine describes him as "a man of quick understanding, ready speech, and burning zeal, desiring to be in the Lord's house a vessel rendering useful service in refuting those false and pernicious doctrines, through which the souls of people in Spain have suffered much more grievous wounds than have

---

prompted by some hidden force, until I was delivered to the shores of this land. Here, at last, I have come to the realization that I was being ordered to come to you" (*Commonitorium* 1).

10. See note 4 above. Henry Chadwick, *Priscillian of Avila: The Occult and the Charismatic in the Early Church* (Oxford: Clarendon, 1976), 190, relating Orosius's situation in 414 to his later literary activity, rightly observes, "Several passages in the *History* indicate that, while Orosius's apologetic and imperial policy necessitated a friendly and favourable portrait of the barbarian invaders, his personal and private prejudices were unsympathetic to them."

11. *Ep.* 169.13.

12. *Ep.* 166.1.

been inflicted on their bodies by the sword of the barbarians."[13] While Orosius resided at Hippo he wrote a short treatise on the twin dangers which Priscillianism and Origenism posed for his co-religionists in Spain. This *Commonitorium* he dedicated and offered to Augustine. In it he requests that the bishop, with his superior learning and experience with schismatics and heretics, respond with a tract of his own, thus providing spiritual and theological assistance in the struggle with such groups. Augustine did so, and his *Ad Orosium contra Priscillianistas et Origenistas* is the result. Shortly thereafter the bishop proposed that Orosius journey to Bethlehem in Palestine to study further with Jerome, Augustine's esteemed (if not always cordial) colleague.[14] Such an arrangement also provided Augustine the opportunity to correspond with the biblical scholar by means of a trusted messenger.[15] No doubt there was much to report concerning the ecclesiastical situation in North Africa, particularly the threat of the recently-departed Pelagius and his supporters.[16] Accordingly, Augustine furnished the young Spanish priest with various messages and letters to Jerome, two of them virtual treatises in themselves.[17] It is probable, too, that Orosius carried with him copies of Augustine's earliest anti-Pelagian tracts, including his *De natura et gratia*, completed early in 415. Since Pelagius was then residing at Jerusalem in the sympathetic company of the

13. *Ep.* 166.1.
14. In Augustine's words, "And he [Orosius] did gain something from his coming: first, not to put too much faith in what he heard from me; then, I instructed the man as far as I could. I pointed out to him where he could learn what I could not give him, and encouraged him to go to you" (*Ep* 166.2).
15. "I was looking around for someone to send to you, but it was not easy to find anyone endowed with reliability of conduct, readiness to obey, and experience in traveling; so, when I found this young man, I did not doubt that he was just the one I had been asking of the Lord" (*Ep.* 166.2). Cf. *Ep.* 169.13: "I wrote these to Jerome because I did not wish to lose an opportunity of correspondence afforded by a certain very pious and studious young priest, Orosius ... whom I persuaded to go on from us to Jerome."
16. Of great importance would be the news that Pelagius's chief lieutenant, Caelestius, had been condemned by a North African synod at Carthage in 411.
17. *Ep.* 166 and *Ep.* 167 in Augustine's collection (131 and 132 in Jerome's). For a description of these letters and their implications vis-à-vis Orosius's journey, see John N. D. Kelly, *Jerome: His Life, Writings and Controversies* (New York: Harper and Row, 1975), 317–18.

INTRODUCTION   101

bishop, John, modern scholars have theorized that Orosius's eventual appearance in Palestine was more than a coincidence. In the words of J. N. D. Kelly, "Augustine's sending of Orosius 'to sit at Jerome's feet' was thus a deliberate move in the controversy; we need not doubt that he was anxious to alert the church at Jerusalem, where Pelagius was being hospitably entertained, and Jerome in particular to the dangers of the new movement."[18] Orosius's journey to Palestine took him first to Egypt where he paid his respects at Christian shrines and observed first-hand the bleak remnants of the great libraries of Alexandria.[19] Upon his arrival in Palestine he made himself known to the resident bishop, John, at Jerusalem and then traveled to Bethlehem. There he met Jerome. From all accounts the two saw each other as kindred spirits,[20] an unbending adherence to orthodox doctrine coupled with a fierce, impetuous nature. To the young Orosius, his acceptance by the famous biblical scholar, theologian, and ascetic must have been almost overwhelming. He at once took up residence at Bethlehem, most probably in Jerome's own monastic hospice, and prepared to serve his new master as student, messenger, and spiritual soldier.[21] Jerome was then, characteristically, quarreling with the local prelate, in this case John of Jerusalem. The stage was thus set for a confrontation which would bring together several of the key players in the simmering Pelagian controversy.

(4) We can only speculate about the exact circumstances which led to the convening by John of a diocesan conference[22] to

18. Kelly, 318.
19. *Historia* 1.10 (reference to chariot-wheel tracks left by the army of the Pharaoh on the shore of the Red Sea); 6.15 (reference to the destruction of the great libraries at Alexandria in the time of Julius Caesar and of the Serapeum in 391).
20. Jerome in his return letter to Augustine calls the young visitor "that honorable man, my brother and your excellency's son, the priest Orosius [whom] I have, both on his account and in obedience to your request, made welcome . . ." (*Ep.* 122 in Augustine's correspondence).
21. It is unlikely that Orosius "lay in obscurity at Bethlehem, a foreigner, penniless and unknown" for any length of time before taking up the anti-Pelagian struggle. Cf. Orosius, *Liber apologeticus contra Pelagianos* 3. This work is commonly referred to as the *Liber apologeticus*.
22. Although Orosius throughout his *Liber apologeticus* seems to stress the offi-

investigate various charges leveled against Pelagius. But we can be sure that both Jerome and Orosius were very much involved in creating the appropriate climate for such an investigation. The conference was duly held on 28 July 415 at Jerusalem, with John presiding. Perhaps it is not surprising that Jerome himself did not attend. His poor relationship with John would not have helped his side, and in any case, Orosius was only too eager to serve as his surrogate and spokesman. According to Orosius's own *Liber apologeticus,* he was summoned by John to the meeting to testify about his knowledge of Pelagian activities in North Africa.[23] As a recent arrival from that region he was in a position to provide details (albeit from Augustine) about the difficulties which both Pelagius and Caelestius had created there. Apparently Orosius, too, had already met Pelagius at some point during his stay in Palestine, and this personal encounter only served to confirm Augustine's opinion in his mind and reinforce his opposition to the man and his teachings.[24] Orosius told the assembled group of the trial and condemnation of Caelestius at Carthage in 411; read a letter of Augustine to Hilary, bishop of Syracuse, attacking the Pelagians in Sicily;[25] and announced that Augustine was, even as they were meeting, composing another treatise refuting the ideas of Pelagius. Early on Bishop John had determined that the presence of Pelagius himself was warranted,

---

cial "synodal" nature of the meeting, most modern scholars view it as an informal, preliminary, investigatory conference—this, because of the circumstances of its calling, the nature of the participants (local Greek clergy, visitors, outside witnesses, Latin exiles, translators, and others), and the fact that an official synod was later held at Diospolis (December 415) on the basis of formal charges filed against Pelagius.

23. *Liber apologeticus* 3: "It was you who wanted me to be a participant in your struggle, to come as a helper, not as the champion. . . . From there I traveled to Jerusalem, called by your summons. After this I came up to your assembly, together with you, on the orders of Bishop John. There all of you requested from my insignificant person that I disclose truthfully and simply whether I knew anything that had occurred in Africa concerning that heresy which Pelagius and Caelestius have sown."

24. *Liber apologeticus* 4: "'Pelagius told me that he was teaching that a person could be without sin and could easily observe God's commandments if he so wished.' Pelagius replied to you who were listening, 'I cannot deny that I both said this and still am saying it.'"

25. *Ep.* 157.

INTRODUCTION   103

and accordingly he was called in to testify on his own behalf. When asked whether he had indeed taught such things as Augustine had objected to, he replied, "And who is Augustine to me?" This elicited a shocked and angry response from at least a part of those gathered.[26] John then was able to restore only some semblance of order by his own rejoinder, "I am Augustine!" Orosius proudly reports that he and others responded to this by declaring, "If you are going to assume the role of Augustine, then follow the sentiments of Augustine!"[27] The tone was thus set for the remainder of the session. Orosius and his supporters[28] declared that a central theme of Pelagius's teaching—that a person could, if he wished, live a life without sin and easily keep God's commandments—was heretical and that it had been declared so by the Council of Carthage, by Augustine, and by Jerome. It soon became clear, however, that the anti-Pelagian faction (the majority of whom were perhaps visiting and exiled Latin clerics) would not carry the day, especially in the face of the presiding bishop's intransigence. The situation of Orosius and other western witnesses who did not speak Greek was made even more precarious through the inattention and willful mistranslation on the part of assigned interpreters.[29] Pelagius asserted his innocence, maintaining that he preached the necessity of God's help in the cultivation of human virtue, and John soon turned the tables on Orosius by asking, "Now, however, when he [Pelagius] adds that a person can be without sin, but not without God's assistance, what

---

26. Orosius claims somewhat more, "Even though *everyone* shouted that he was blaspheming against the bishop from whose mouth the Lord has bestowed the healing medicine of unity to all Africa, and that he ought to be expelled not merely from the present assembly but also from the Church as a whole, ..." (*Liber apologeticus* 4).

27. Gerald Bonner, *St Augustine of Hippo: Life and Controversies* (Philadelphia: Westminster, 1963), 333, wryly observes that this final remark "at least ensured that Pelagius would receive a fair hearing before the indignant Bishop John."

28. Passerius, Avitus, Domnus, and Vitalis are named as principal allies of Orosius at the conference (*Liber apologeticus* 6–7).

29. Orosius does not tell us whether Pelagius attempted to speak to the gathering in Greek. But it can be noted that at the Council of Diospolis held in December of that year Pelagius spoke through an interpreter (cf. Augustine, *De gestis Pelagii* 1.2). The general issue of the extent of Pelagius's knowledge of Greek has aroused much scholarly debate in recent years; on this see B. R. Rees, *Pelagius: A Reluctant Heretic* (Woodbridge: Boydell, 1988), 76, n. 96.

do you say to that? Or do you perhaps deny God's assistance?"[30] Orosius was forced to acquiesce in this "clarification" of Pelagius's position, but undoubtedly took some solace in the fact that the assembly finally decided to refer the matter, raised as it were by Latins, to a Latin authority: Pope Innocent I. In the meantime, Pelagius was to keep to himself, and Orosius and his faction were to refrain from criticizing Bishop John. Thus the situation stood until 12 September when, at the annual dedicatory festival of the Church of the Resurrection at Jerusalem, Bishop John confronted Orosius and accused him of blasphemy. The shocked priest inquired when, where, and how he had done this, and John replied that he himself had heard Orosius say at the diocesan conference that it was impossible for a person to live without sin, even with God's help. Orosius, of course, vehemently denied the charge and went on to write shortly thereafter his *Liber apologeticus*, a treatise which was publicly circulated and intended both as a rebuttal of John's allegation and as an attack upon Pelagius, his ideas, and his supporters and defenders, including John. Neither Orosius nor Jerome attended the subsequent church council held at Diospolis (Lydda) in December of the same year, at which time Pelagius was called to defend himself against formal charges brought by two exiled Latin bishops: Heros of Arles and Lazarus of Aix. Although the presiding bishop this time was different (the primate of Palestine, Eulogius of Caesarea), the result was the same. Pelagius managed to extricate himself cleverly, if not always gracefully, from the snares his writings would seem to have cast for him. At the council's close, Pelagius was pronounced to be in full communion with the Catholic Church. For Orosius and Jerome both ecclesiastical assemblies must have been bitter disappointments.[31]

(5) Before departing Palestine in the spring of 416 Orosius was to be involved in one final notable episode. In December 415 the ancient tomb of St. Stephen was located at the village of

30. *Liber apologeticus* 6.
31. Indeed, in a letter to Augustine (dated to early 416) Jerome remarks that this was "an extremely trying time, when it was better for me to keep silence than to speak, so much so that serious study had to cease and speech degenerated (in Appius's phrase) into the snarling of dogs" (*Ep.* 134.1).

INTRODUCTION

Caphar-Gamala. As the first Christian martyr Stephen was greatly revered by the faithful, and the discovery of his tomb and especially his remains created a sensation. Orosius was chosen by Avitus, his fellow priest from Braga, to return with a portion of the relics to Bishop Balconius of Braga and his congregation. Avitus, for his part, had secretly acquired the relics from the local village priest who had actually unearthed them.[32] Also given to Orosius was a first-hand account by the Greek priest (translated by Avitus into Latin) of the discovery, as well as a brief explanatory letter by Avitus addressed to Balconius.

(6) Orosius returned, as he had been instructed,[33] to Augustine in the summer of 416 bearing the sacred and protective relics of Stephen (together with the two writings by Avitus), minutes of the Council of Diospolis, and several letters from Jerome. However, Braga was never to receive the precious cargo. After a brief stopover at Hippo, Orosius did set out for his homeland, sailing first to the island of Minorca (late summer or autumn 416) and intending then to make the crossing to Spain. But on Minorca he learned of renewed warfare and dangers on the mainland and, unwilling to continue his journey, returned once more to North Africa, leaving to the Christians of the island the remains of Stephen.[34] The relics were to become an object of great veneration and were soon employed by local Christians as a miraculous evangelical instrument to convert their Jewish neighbors.[35] Orosius took up residence at Hippo and possibly it was at this point that he began work on his most famous book, the *Historia*. Certainly he had the requisite time since he was now a refugee with no other major commitments. According to all indications he finished the lengthy volume, dedicated to his sometime host and teacher Augustine, in about a year and a half—

---

32. This secrecy may have been essential since John of Jerusalem certainly would have opposed such a translation of relics to Spain by two of his opponents.

33. *Ep.* 166.2: "As he [Orosius] received this counsel or rather injunction of mine with pleasure, and with intention to comply with it, I asked him to visit us on his way home to his own country when he comes from you."

34. They were duly deposited at a church outside Magona, the town at the eastern end of Minorca.

35. On this, see the thorough study by Scott Bradbury, *Severus of Minorca: Letter on the Conversion of the Jews* (Oxford: Clarendon, 1996).

that is, in late 417 or early 418. After the completion of this task, he disappears from the view of history. We have only Augustine's brief and perhaps somewhat cool notice in the *Retractiones* (2.44) where he notes that his *Ad Orosium contra Priscillianistas et Origenistas* was composed in response to an inquiry from "a certain Spanish priest, Orosius." No other reference is made to Orosius, his *Liber apologeticus*, or his specially commissioned *Historia* in Augustine's voluminous later writings. A growing consensus of scholars holds that Augustine was not pleased with the end result of Orosius's researches and speculations.[36] Whether he remained in North Africa, traveled again to Minorca or Palestine, or was finally successful in his return to Spain is not known.

(7) We possess three works by Orosius. Earliest in date (late 414 or early 415) is the *Commonitorium*. This brief memorandum, dedicated and addressed to Augustine, was written by Orosius both to provide his host with an account of the dangers of Priscillianism[37] and Origenism[38] in his homeland and to invite the bishop's refutation of these heresies. The work is markedly deferential in tone, not surprising considering Augustine's reputation in the West and his role then as host and mentor to Orosius. The first chapter, containing much flattery of the bishop, promises a detailed exposition of the heresies and requests Augustine's urgent response to the memorandum, since the Christians of the Iberian peninsula are said to have been "more

---

36. See especially Paul Onica, *Orosius*; Theodore E. Mommsen, "Orosius and Augustine," in Eugene F. Rice, Jr., ed., *Medieval and Renaissance Studies* (Ithaca: Cornell University, 1966), 299–324; and Eugenio Corsini, *Introduzione alle "Storie" di Orosio* (Turin: Universita di Torino, 1968).

37. On Priscillian and his movement, see Chadwick, *Priscillian of Avila*; Virginia Burrus, *The Making of a Heretic: Gender, Authority, and the Priscillianist Controversy* (Berkeley: University of California, 1995); Raymond Van Dam, *Leadership and Community in Late Antique Gaul* (Berkeley: University of California, 1985), 88–114; and Joyce Salisbury, *Iberian Popular Religion 600 B.C. to 700 A.D.: Celts, Romans and Visigoths* (New York: Mellen, 1985), 191–226.

38. Excellent analyses of Origen's life, thought, and legacy include Henri Crouzel, *Origen*, trans. A. S. Worrall (San Francisco: Harper and Row, 1989), and Charles Kannengiesser and W. L. Peterson, eds., *Origen of Alexandria: His World and His Legacy* (Notre Dame: Notre Dame University, 1988). For the later debate over Origenist theology in the West, see B. Studer, "Zur Frage des westlichen Origenismus," in *Studia Patristica* 10.3 [*Texte und Untersuchungen* 94], ed. F. L. Cross (Berlin: Akademie, 1966): 270–87.

gravely wounded by evil teachers than by the most bloodthirsty of enemies." In chapter two Orosius treats Priscillian and his teachings, especially those concerning the human soul.[39] Much of his information seems to have come from an earlier anti-Priscillianist work, the *Apologia* of Bishop Ithacius of Ossonuba, who was a contemporary and implacable foe of Priscillian. Orosius offers Priscillian's curious exposition on the names of the Hebrew patriarchs, refers to the apocryphal *Memoria apostolorum*, defines the sect's Manichaean affinities, and outlines Priscillian's own Trinitarian viewpoint. Orosius sees the Priscillianist denial of divine providence and grace as decisive in human affairs, as well as the sect's refusal to accept the union of soul and body as determined by divine mandate, as the defining features of the heresy. Chapter three relates, among other things, the story of two Spanish priests named Avitus who departed Spain to find help in combatting this heresy. One went to Rome, the other to Jerusalem; the former returned with writings of (Marius) Victorinus, the latter with works by Origen. Eventually the champion of Origen won over the partisan of Victorinus and the two spread Origenist ideas throughout Spain. Orosius goes on to outline the Alexandrian's teachings on creation, eternity and universalism, the nature of the soul (angelic, human, demonic), divine judgment, the devil, Christ's redemption, passion, and resurrection (and future role), as well as his speculations on the rationality of the sun, moon, and stars. In the last chapter Orosius again deferentially implores Augustine to respond to his urgent invitation, declaring that he has been both truthful in his recounting and specially sent by God to request spiritual assistance from the bishop. Augustine's response was favorable and his own brief treatise, *Ad Orosium contra Priscillianistas et Origenistas*, was the result.[40] Here Augustine does not address systematically each major issue concerning Priscillianism raised in the Spanish priest's memorandum, but instead refers the visitor to his previously written treatises on Manichaeism, wherein he refutes the theory of

39. For an insightful analysis of key elements of Orosius's discussion of Priscillianism, see Chadwick, *Priscillian of Avila*, 191–206.
40. Daur's critical edition of this work is included in the same volume [CCL 49] as that of Orosius's *Commonitorium*.

the soul's divine nature. In the case of Origen, Augustine is more cautious, judging particular Origenist doctrines to be mistaken but always treating the great Alexandrian and his basic theology with respect.

(8) Orosius's *Liber apologeticus* (probably written in the autumn of 415) represents our sole source of information for the diocesan conference held at Jerusalem in late July 415. In addition to furnishing valuable testimony as to the background and circumstances of the meeting itself, this work affords a view of Orosius's and, perhaps, a more generalized Latin (especially North African) understanding of Pelagian doctrines. Despite Orosius's personal stake in the outcome of the controversy, his vehement opposition to Pelagius and Pelagian ideas, and his use of traditional techniques of rhetorical polemic in the *Liber apologeticus*, it is to his credit that he in general faithfully represents the positions of his opponents. The picture he leaves of the contemporary debate is an accurate and vivid one. Since the treatise is addressed throughout to "the most reverend fathers,"[41] it is likely that it was composed as a kind of apologetic pamphlet intended for the participants of the Jerusalem conference. It is written in the form of a speech and owes much in its overall structure, internal features, and modes of argumentation to guidelines set out by the Roman rhetorician Quintilian in his *Institutio oratoria*.[42] Orosius's purpose here is threefold: to defend his reputation against the charge of blasphemy (and, by implication, heresy) made by Bishop John of Jerusalem; to reaffirm his and the orthodox party's correct beliefs in contrast to those of Pelagius; and to attack and destroy the doctrines of Pelagius and his associates. The work is divided into two main sections. Chapters 1–9 treat the Jerusalem conference and Orosius's defense of his own actions and statements; chapters 10–33 offer a detailed exposition and refutation of Pelagian ideas (especially those drawn from Pelagius's own *Testimonia* and *Epistula ad Demetriadem*). In the first two chapters, Orosius addresses his audience

---

41. See *Liber apologeticus* 1, 3, 8, 33.
42. On this topic, see Ruth M. Gover, "The *Liber Apologeticus* of Paulus Orosius," (Master's thesis, Queens College, 1969).

and complains of the injustice done to him by John and others. His struggle is likened to that of the young David, forced to confront the giant Goliath. As such it also represents the struggle of good and evil, the spiritual and the carnal. In addition, the names, characters, and reputations of the combatants behind the scenes, Pelagius and Caelestius, are contrasted with those of Jerome and Augustine. Chapters 3-6 offer Orosius's fascinating, straightforward account of the Jerusalem conference itself. Following the advice of Quintilian, his narrative is written clearly and, for the most part, is "free from any taint of meanness."[43] Chapters 7-9, which relate the crucial confrontation of John and Orosius at Jerusalem on 12 September and Orosius's indignant reaction to the allegation made against him, form a transition, linking the preceding simple narrative with the later, polemical sections focused on Pelagius. By far the greater portion of the work (chapters 10-33) is, indeed, an attack by Orosius upon the person, activities, and teachings of Pelagius. The author emphasizes the moral shortcomings of his opponent and portrays him as merely another leader (albeit a dangerous one) of the latest heresy, which is akin to both Priscillianism and Origenism. In particular he argues that Pelagius has misunderstood and subverted the crucial Christian concept of divine grace. Such attendant issues as original sin, the weakness of human nature, and the necessity of God's assistance in the world are carefully examined. It is in this lengthy section that Orosius displays his rhetorical training most openly. He carefully follows most of the guidelines set out by Quintilian, but supplements them with elaborate scriptural proofs, patristic citations, and lengthy digressions, mixed with occasional personal invective. In the end, the case he builds against Pelagianism is impressive in its scope and volume, if not in its originality, consistency, and clarity.

(9) The best known of Orosius's works, the *Historia* (completed late 417 or early 418) was written, according to author's own testimony, at the request of Augustine of Hippo.[44] The

---

43. *Institutio oratoria* 4.2.36.
44. "You [Augustine] bade me speak out in opposition to the empty perver-

North African was then working on his *De civitate Dei*. In response to pagan critics who charged that the calamities the Empire had undergone in the recent past were the result of the abandonment of the ancient pagan religion and the adoption of Christianity, Augustine argued that the pre-Christian world had suffered far more by way of catastrophes and misfortunes than the contemporary world. To document this contention, Orosius says, Augustine chose him to write a tract which would complement and support his own.[45] The result is the earliest universal Christian history. Divided into seven books (as the week is into seven days), it treats the history of the world, as seen from Orosius's perspective, from Adam to A.D. 417. As its full title indicates, the work is strongly apologetic in tone. To Orosius the actions of divine providence through the ages clearly reveal God's designs for all of humanity. The last book, dedicated to the imperial epoch of Rome and markedly more optimistic in tone than the others, expresses the belief that from the time of the emperor Augustus good began to triumph over evil and that the formation of the Christian Empire only served to strengthen this tendency. This viewpoint does not accord especially well with Augustine's own researches and conclusions in his *De civitate Dei*. As a result a number of modern scholars speculate that a rift possibly developed between the two men in 417–18.[46] This

---

sity of those who, aliens to the City of God, are called 'pagans' from the crossroads and villages of country places or 'heathen' because of their knowledge of earthly things.... You bade me set forth from all the records available of histories and annals whatever instances I have found recorded from the past of the burdens of war or ravages of disease or sorrows of famine or horrors of earthquakes or of unusual floods or dreadful outbreaks of fire or cruel strokes of lightning and storms of hail or even the miseries caused by parricides and shameful deeds, and unfold them systematically and briefly in the context of this book" (*Historia*, preface).

45. "Since you [Augustine] should not be concerned with a trifling work (such as this), while your reverence is especially intent on finishing the eleventh book of your work against those same pagans, . . . and since your holy son, Julian of Carthage, servant of God, demanded that his petition be satisfied in this matter with the same confidence as that with which he asked for it, I gave myself to the task . . ." (*Historia*, preface).

46. The concluding passage in the *Historia* (7.43) is perhaps something more than a traditional rhetorical flourish and may reveal a certain feeling of insecurity on Orosius's part: "So now I enjoy the certain and only reward of my obedi-

would explain the virtual lack of later references to Orosius in Augustine's own writings. In the Middle Ages Orosius's *Historia* was immensely popular (as the more than 200 extant manuscripts testify) and served as a model for many of the universal histories composed in Western Europe.

(10) Like Pacian, Orosius is demonstrably a competent writer, well-versed both in classical pagan and Christian literature and in rhetorical techniques and usages. But unlike Pacian, whose compositions possess a certain originality of thought, clarity of argument, balance, and rhythm, Orosius is an author who provides many challenges and not a few difficulties for the reader. His writings often show signs of haste, carelessness, and lack of focus. Lengthy digressions, lost threads of arguments, and obscurities abound. Nevertheless, he is an author who can and often does tell a fascinating story and is able to provide a unique and valuable perspective on his own turbulent times.

(11) The *editio princeps* of Orosius's works was published by J. Coster in 1558. The anticipated critical edition by Guy Fink never appeared.[47] For the present translation of the *Liber apologeticus*, the modern critical text of Karl Zangemeister has been used;[48] for the *Commonitorium*, the recent edition of Klaus Daur has been consulted.[49]

---

ence, which I ought to have desired. But as for the quality of my books, you who bade me write them shall see; if you publish them, they shall be approved by you; if you destroy them, they shall be condemned by you." Also, see note 36 above.

47. Cf. CPL (2nd ed., 1961), 130.

48. Karl Zangemeister, *Pauli Orosii historiarum adversum paganos libri vii; accedit eiusdem liber apologeticus* [CSEL 5] (Vienna: Gerold, 1882). Cf. CPL, 200 (no. 572).

49. Klaus D. Daur, *Commonitorium Orosii et sancti Aurelii Augustini contra Priscillianistas et Origenistas* [CCL 49] (Turnhout: Brepols, 1985). Daur includes helpful patristic citations. Also, see the earlier critical edition by Georg Schepss, *Orosii commonitorium de errore Priscillianistarum et Origenistarum* [CSEL 18] (Vienna: Tempsky, 1889). Cf. CPL, 200 (no. 573).

SELECT BIBLIOGRAPHY

Altaner, Berthold. "Augustinus und Origenes." In *Kleine patristische Schriften*, 224–52. Berlin: Akademie Verlag, 1967.
Barbero de Aguilera, A. "El priscilianismo, ¿herejia o movimiento social?" *Cuadernos de Historia de Espāna* 37/38 (1963): 5–41.
Bartalucci, Aldo. "Lingua e stile in Paolo Orosio." *Studi Classici e Orientali* 25 (1976): 213–53.
Bonner, Gerald. *St Augustine of Hippo: Life and Controversies*. Philadelphia: Westminster, 1963.
Bradbury, Scott. *Severus of Minorca: Letter on the Conversion of the Jews*. Oxford: Clarendon, 1996.
Brown, Peter. *Augustine of Hippo: A Biography*. Berkeley: University of California, 1969.
Burrus, Virginia. *The Making of a Heretic: Gender, Authority, and the Priscillianist Controversy*. Berkeley: University of California, 1995.
Chadwick, Henry. *Priscillian of Avila: The Occult and the Charismatic in the Early Church*. Oxford: Clarendon, 1976.
Coffin, Harrison C. "Vergil and Orosius." *Classical Journal* 31 (1935/1936): 235–41.
Corsini, Eugenio. *Introduzione alle "Storie" di Orosio*. Turin: Università di Torino, 1968.
Crouzel, Henri. *Origen: The Life and Thought of the First Great Theologian*. Translated by A. S. Worrall. San Francisco: Harper and Row, 1989.
Daur, Klaus D. *Commonitorium Orosii et sancti Aurelii Augustini contra Priscillianistas et Origenistas*. [CCL 49] Turnhout: Brepols, 1985.
Davids, Johannes A. *De Orosio et Sancto Augustino Priscillianistarum adversariis. Commentatio historica et philologica*. The Hague: Govers, 1930.
De Bruyn, Theodore. *Pelagius's Commentary on St Paul's Epistle to the Romans*. Oxford: Clarendon, 1993.
De Castro, Rafael García y García. "Paulo Orosio, discípulo de San Agustín." *Boletín de la Universidad de Granada* 3 (1931): 3–28.
Diesner, Hans-Joachim. "Orosius und Augustinus." *Acta Antiqua Academiae Scientiarum Hungaricae* 11 (1963): 89–102.
Evans, Robert F. *Four Letters of Pelagius*. New York: Seabury, 1968.
———. *Pelagius: Inquiries and Reappraisals*. New York: Seabury, 1968.
Fabbrini, Fabrizio. *Paolo Orosio, uno storico*. Rome: Edizione di storia e letteratura, 1979.

Ferguson, John. *Pelagius: A Historical and Theological Study.* Cambridge: Heffer and Sons, 1956.
Ferreira, José Augusto. *Fastos episcopales de Igrejia primacial de Braga.* Braga: Edicão da Mitra Bracerense, 1950.
Fink, Guy. "Recherches bibliographiques sur Paul Orose." *Revista de Archivos, Bibliotecas y Museos* 58 (1952): 271–322.
Fink-Errera, Guy. "San Agustín y Orosio. Esquema para un estudio de las fuentes del *De civitate Dei.*" *La Ciudad de Dios* 167 (1955): 455–549.
Frend, William H. C. "Augustine and Orosius on the Fall of the Roman Empire in the West." *Augustinian Studies* 20 (1989): 1–38.
Goetz, Hans-Werner, *Die Geschichtstheologie des Orosius.* Darmstadt: Wissenschaftliche Buchgesellschaft, 1980.
Gover, Ruth M. "The *Liber Apologeticus* of Paulus Orosius." Master's thesis, Queens College, 1969.
Green, Tamara Marcus. "Zosimus, Orosius and Their Traditions: Comparative Studies in Pagan and Christian Historiography." Ph.D. dissertation, New York University, 1974.
Haight, Roger. *The Experience and Language of Grace.* New York: Paulist, 1979.
Hamman, A. "Orosius de Braga et le pélagianisme." *Bracara Augusta* 21 (1967): 346–55.
Hunt, E. D. "St. Stephen in Minorca: An Episode in Jewish-Christian Relations in the Early 5th Century AD." *Journal of Theological Studies* 33 (1982): 106–23.
Kannengiesser, Charles, and William Petersen, eds. *Origen of Alexandria: His World and His Legacy.* Notre Dame: Notre Dame University, 1988.
Kelly, John N. D. *Jerome: His Life, Writings and Controversies.* New York: Harper and Row, 1975.
Koch-Peters, Dorothea. *Ansichten des Orosius zur Geschichte seiner Zeit.* Frankfurt: Lang, 1984.
Lacroix, Benoit. "La importancia de Orosio." *Augustinus* 2 (1957): 5–13.
———. *Orose et ses idées.* Montreal: Université de Montréal, 1965.
Lippold, Adolf. "Orosius, christlicher Apologet und römischer Bürger." *Philologus* 113 (1969): 92–105.
López Caneda, Ramón. *Prisciliano. Su pensamiento y su problema histórico.* Santiago de Compostela: Instituo P. Sarmiento de Estudios Gallegos, 1966.
Madoz, José. "Arianism and Priscillianism in Galicia." *Folia* 5 (1951): 5–25.
Marrou, Henri I. "Saint Augustin, Orose et l'augustinisme historique." *La Storiografia Altomedievale* 1 (1970): 59–87.

Mommsen, Theodore E. "Orosius and Augustine." In *Medieval and Renaissance Studies*, 325–48. Edited by Eugene F. Rice, Jr. Ithaca: Cornell University Press, 1959.
Nelson, L. H. and C. A. S. "Orosius' Commentary on the Fall of Roman Spain." *Classical Folia* 31 (1977): 85–104.
O'Connell, Robert. "St. Augustine's Criticism of Origen in the *To Orosius*." *Revue des Études Augustiniennes* 30 (1984): 84–99.
Onica, Paul A. "Orosius." Ph.D. dissertation, University of Toronto, 1987.
Plinval, Georges de. *Pélage: ses écrits, sa vie et sa réforme*. Lausanne: Payot, 1943.
Prieto, S. *Paolo Orosio e o "Liber Apologeticus."* Braga: Cruz, 1951.
Rees, B. R. *The Letters of Pelagius and his Followers*. Woodbridge: Boydell, 1991.
———. *Pelagius: A Reluctant Heretic*. Woodbridge: Boydell, 1988.
Robles, Laureano. "El origen y la espiritualidad del alma: S. Isidoro de Sevilla, S. Agustín y la cuestión priscilianista." *Estudios de Vedat* 1 (1971): 407–88.
Salisbury, Joyce E. *Iberian Popular Religion 600 B.C. to 700 A.D.: Celts, Romans and Visigoths*. New York: Mellen, 1985.
Schepss, Georg. *Orosii commonitorium de errore Priscillianistarum et Origenistarum*. [CSEL 18] Vienna: Tempsky, 1889.
Studer, Basil "Zur Frage des westlichen Origenismus." In *Studia Patristica* 10.3 [*Texte und Untersuchungen*]. Edited by F. L. Cross. Berlin: Akademie, 1966.
Svennung, Josef. *Orosiana. Syntaktische, semasiologische und kritische Studien zu Orosius*. Uppsala: Uppsala Universitet, 1922.
———. "Zur Textkritik des *Apologeticus Orosii*." *Arctos* 5 (1967): 135–39.
Theiler, Willy. "Augustin und Origenes." *Augustinus* 13 (1968): 423–32.
Trape, Agostino. "Nota su giudizio di S. Agostino su Origene." *Augustinianum* 26 (1986): 223–27.
Van Dam, Raymond. *Leadership and Community in Late Antique Gaul*. Berkeley: University of California, 1985.
Vollmann, Benedikt. *Studien zum Priscillianismus*. St. Ottilien: Eos, 1965.
Wermelinger, Otto. *Rom und Pelagius: Die theologische Position der römischen Bischöfe im pelagianischen Streit in den Jahren 411–432*. Stuttgart: Hiersemann, 1975.
Zangemeister, Karl. *Pauli Orosii liber apologeticus*. [CSEL 5] Vienna: Gerold, 1882.

BOOK IN DEFENSE AGAINST THE PELAGIANS

OST REVEREND FATHERS,[1] this is not something which I have instigated nor is it a mark of my own presumption, but rather, as you yourselves recognize, it is of the most dire and even desperate necessity that I now appear. Indeed, I have been forced to do this because of an injustice done to me, and now I stand not only as a defender of my faith but also as a witness to another's faithlessness. For just as I should strive to exonerate myself out of good conscience—I mean, not my own conscience, but that of another person—so, too, am I forced out of faith and zeal—not my own zeal, but that for Christ—to call your attention to the wolves[2] caught within the flock of sheep. Yet I do not presume anything recklessly, since I am the most insignificant of all persons.[3] It is a matter of necessity for me to make known the injustice which I have suffered. Let it be evident to all those who have inflicted it. For it is both God's will and his command that an evil which was patiently endured be necessarily disclosed, and that there occur not only the censure of the most wicked doctrines but also the identification of the individuals who ought to be reproached, as they themselves by their pursuit of madness receive the proper reward for their error—as is fitting! For the Fathers—both those who have already found eternal rest as martyrs and confessors, Cyprian, Hilary, and Ambrose, as well as those for whom it is still necessary to remain in the flesh and who are the pillars and foundations of the Catholic

---

1. Literally, "most blessed priests" (*beatissimi sacerdotes*).
2. The image of the heretic as a wolf menacing the Christian flock, based on biblical precedents (esp. Acts 20.29) and common in patristic polemics, is applied to the Pelagians also by Augustine in his later treatise, *Contra duas epistolas pelagianorum* 4.34.
3. An early Christian formula expressing modesty, derived from earlier pagan and biblical usages. Cf., for example, Pope Gelasius, *Ep.* 3.4: *Ego quidem sum omnium hominum minimus*.

Church, Aurelius Augustine and Jerome—have already published much in their most admirable writings against this wicked heresy without specifying the names of the heretics. And yet this abomination of the most poisonous doctrines even turns people now living into the dead and the dead into the living! For Origen, Priscillian, and Jovinian, who for their part have been dead for some time, now live in them and not only live, but also speak through them. And behold! As if those who are dead have continued to live in them, Pelagius and Caelestius now in fact hiss against the Church—which is contemptible—and hiss openly from within the Church—which is even more contemptible; and these impious serpents, licking their putrid mouths with their darting tongues while taking up residence at the holy and inviolable episcopal see unto which they stealthily crept,[4] terrify all the faithful with the fear that we may not come one day with each other to that unshakable refuge on Zion. Since the stench from their mouths is spreading far and wide, it turns the fragrance of life into death for all those to whom the fragrance of life used to be for life everlasting.

2. Against this serpent and its suffocating stench, those most blessed men, whom we have mentioned above, have undoubtedly furnished the many and varied fragrant perfumes of the Scriptures and set alight the most sweet-smelling incense with their offering of prayer, so that the hearts of people agitated by doubt might be calmed. But it is not enough merely to argue against a virtually hidden opponent, trading charges for countercharges in order to moderate an atmosphere tainted by such a pernicious stench, if the serpents themselves are not dragged out into the light and trampled underfoot. When, for the purpose of protecting only their head, they expose the rest of their body to mutilation and injury, judging that it is no loss even if all of their parts are cut off—leaving only that portion which contains the various poisonous tongues within them free from danger—does it then seem sufficient for us merely to moderate the

---

4. Although this passage can be interpreted in other ways, Orosius here seems to be contrasting contemporary Jerusalem, the current place of refuge and support (by Bishop John) for the heretic Pelagius, with the eternal, incorruptible, heavenly Zion.

putrid odor without dislodging the serpents themselves from their innermost sanctuaries? As if there were ever an end to a foul stench without the elimination of its source! And in this regard, does not that adage of Solomon come to mind, "When one person is building up [and] another is tearing down, which one of them will avail, if not the toil itself?"[5] Yet there stands Goliath, monstrous in his pride, swollen with his earthly power, confident that he can do everything by himself, with his head, hands, and entire body clad in much bronze, having his own armor-bearer behind him who, though he does not himself fight, nevertheless furnishes this Goliath with all kinds of aid in bronze and iron.[6] And it is not surprising if Scripture, foreseeing our present situation, comments appropriately when it says, "The Philistines were standing on top of the mountain on this side,"[7] since the individual who is attacking the heresy is now being banished from the Church, while the heretic is found to be nourished at its very breast! Because of this, it is so stated by the Holy Spirit that on the other side Israel was standing, while on this side, the enemy.[8] And such is often the way. For even King David, who was always the righteous father towards his unrighteous son, having laid aside his royal robes, was forced to flee from Jerusalem, whereupon the tyrant Absalom immediately entered.[9] There now stands Goliath—oh, what sorrow!—on this side, that is, within the Church; and he not only stands but even offers challenges.[10] And at the same time, over the course of many days, he reproaches holy Israel for its well-known fear of God.[11]

3. I implore you, most reverend fathers, let no one think that under the pretext of the figure of Goliath I am boasting of the

---

5. Sir 34.28.
6. Cf. 1 Sam 17.4–7. G. de Plinval, *Pélage: ses écrits, sa vie et sa réforme* (Lausanne: Payot, 1943), 213, identifies this "armor-bearer" as one of Jerome's correspondents, a certain wealthy layman, Ctesiphon, who does not fight openly for Pelagius, but provides his "Goliath" with financial support. V. Grossi, in A. Di Berardino and J. Quasten, *Patrology*, English tr. by Solari, (Westminster: Christian Classics, 1986), 4.493, on the other hand, offers an identification with Anianus, the deacon of Celeda, himself possibly a member of the powerful Roman Anician family. Finally, it may be that Orosius has in mind here Bishop John himself.
7. 1 Sam 17.3.   8. Cf. 1 Sam 17.3.
9. Cf. 2 Sam 15.16–17, 16.15.   10. Cf. 1 Sam 17.8–10.
11. Cf. 1 Sam 17.16.

name David. It was you who wanted me to be a participant in your struggle, to come as a helper, not as the champion. Inasmuch as I lay in obscurity at Bethlehem, a foreigner, penniless and unknown, why am I, an unfortunate man speaking this way, perhaps to be reprimanded again for boasting? Indeed, David himself was also such a man and he, too, came from that place. So, I lay in obscurity at Bethlehem, having been instructed by father Augustine to learn the fear of the Lord by sitting at the feet of Jerome. From there I traveled to Jerusalem, called by your summons. After this I came up to your assembly, together with you, on the orders of Bishop John. There all of you requested from my insignificant person that I disclose truthfully and simply whether I knew anything that had occurred in Africa concerning that heresy which Pelagius and Caelestius have sown. I explained as briefly as I could to your gathering that Caelestius, who was by this time stealthily advancing towards the office of the priesthood,[12] had been given a hearing at Carthage before a great number of bishops sitting in judgment, been found guilty, confessed, been denounced by the Church, and made his escape from Africa.[13] I went on to say that the blessed Augustine wrote a most detailed response, indeed, to the book of Pelagius, addressed to Pelagius's own disciples who were appearing in public and making attacks.[14] I stated that I also had in my possession a letter by the above-named bishop, which he not long ago had arranged to send on to Sicily and in which he refuted the many arguments of the heretics.[15] You instructed me to read that letter then and there, and I did so. In response to this, Bishop John demanded that Pelagius be admitted in person. In deference to his

12. Cf. Augustine's account in his *Ep.* 157, addressed to Hilary (dated to 414): "One of them, named Caelestius, had begun a stealthy approach to the dignity of priesthood in a church of that same city, but the free and faithful action of the brothers brought him before the bishop's tribunal because of his arguments against the grace of Christ."

13. Note the rhetorical figure of homoioteleuton: "proditum auditum convictum confessum destestatumque . . ."

14. Augustine's *De natura et gratia* was a response to Pelagius's own *De natura* which had been sent to the bishop by two of Pelagius's disciples, Timasius and James. Cf. *De natura et gratia* 1.1.

15. Augustine, *Ep.* 157 (to Hilary, bishop of Syracuse).

position as patriarch and for the good of the proceedings, since you believed that it would be more proper for Pelagius to be condemned to his face by the bishop, approval for his admission was granted.

4. After Pelagius had been admitted, all of you with one mind asked whether he realized that he taught things against which Bishop Augustine had responded. He answered at once, "And who is Augustine to me?" Even though everyone shouted that he was blaspheming against the bishop from whose mouth the Lord has bestowed the healing medicine of unity to all Africa, and that he ought to be expelled not merely from the present assembly but also from the Church as a whole, Bishop John immediately ordered Pelagius, who was clearly a layman in a gathering of priests and a culprit guilty of flagrant heresy in the midst of Catholics, to be seated, and then said, "I am Augustine!" so that naturally, by assuming the role of Augustine as if he were present, he might pardon Pelagius more freely from the authority of the very one who was being injured and restrain the passions of those feeling aggrieved. Thereupon it was said by us to John, "If you are going to assume the role of Augustine, then follow the sentiments of Augustine!" Then this bishop said to all of us, "The words which have been said here have been spoken against other individuals; do you think it should be suggested that these words have been said concerning Pelagius? Therefore, if you have anything to say against Pelagius himself, disclose it." But I, with your approval, said, "Pelagius told me that he was teaching that a person could be without sin and could easily observe God's commandments if he so wished." Pelagius replied to you who were listening, "I cannot deny that I both said this and still am saying it." I immediately followed up, "This is the very doctrine which the African synod denounced in the case of Caelestius. This is the doctrine, as you have heard, to which Bishop Augustine reacted with horror in his treatises. This is the doctrine which he now condemns in the writings of Pelagius himself by his own refutation.[16] This is the doctrine which the blessed Jerome has also condemned in his letter recently addressed to

16. That is, in his *De natura et gratia*.

Ctesiphon[17]—Jerome, whose pronouncement the entire West awaits, just as the dew upon the fleece[18]—for already by his attack many heretics together with their teachings have been confounded. In a similar way, Jerome is also refuting this doctrine in the book he is writing even now, with the whole dispute set in the form of a dialogue.[19] For it is a difficult thing to catch a serpent on a fishhook, lest he be able to escape."[20]

5. But Bishop John, listening to none of these words, tried next to extract from us an admission that we were the accusers while he was the judge. The reply, given over and over by all of us, was, "We are not this man's accusers, but we do communicate what your brothers, our fathers, have thought and decreed concerning this heresy which this layman now publicly proclaims; we do this so that Pelagius may not throw into disorder, above all, your Church in whose bosom we have found refuge." But Bishop John kept trying to entice us into some semblance of a formal declaration by pretending to instruct us, saying that it had been said by the Lord to Abraham, "Walk before me and be without sin";[21] and that Zechariah and also Elizabeth had been declared to be "both righteous before the Lord, walking in all of the just commandments of the Lord without blame."[22] And indeed, it was known by many of us that the pronouncements cited by Bishop John had been made by Origen.[23] My response to him was, "We are the sons of the Catholic Church. Do not demand from us, father, that we dare to act as teachers over teachers or judges over judges. The fathers who are approved of by the universal Church throughout the world and to whose communion

---

17. *Ep.* 133. This letter, written sometime in 414, contains a scathing attack on the ideas Pelagius was then teaching at Jerusalem.
18. Cf. Deut 32.2; Judg 6.36–40.
19. Jerome's *Contra Pelagianos dialogus* was composed in the period between the diocesan conference of Jerusalem (July 415) and the Council of Diospolis (December 415). It is interesting to note that at the close of the dialogue the Pelagian spokesman merely departs, without admitting defeat.
20. Cf. Job 40.25 [40.20 (Vulgate version)].
21. Gen 17.1.
22. Lk 1.6.
23. Like his mentor in Bethlehem, Orosius purposely and ungraciously links the bishop not only with the present perceived threat of Pelagianism, but also with the recent revival of Origenism in Palestine.

you joyfully adhere have decreed that these doctrines are deserving of condemnation. When they render their judgment, it is fitting for us to obey them. Why do you ask the sons what they think when you hear what the fathers decree?"

6. He debated this for a considerable time and when, because of the inexperience of an interpreter unknown to us—an interpreter whom such leading citizens and devout individuals as the priests Passerius and Avitus,[24] and Domnus, a former notable, had proven time and again either to be giving an erroneous translation or to be withholding much of what was being said or suggesting different implications for various statements made[25] —and when, as I said, because of this our statements had been either altered on most occasions or passed over in silence, Bishop John said, "If Pelagius were to say that a person could do this without God's assistance, then that would be most wicked and deserving of condemnation; now, however, when he adds that a person can be without sin, but not without God's assistance, what do you say to that? Or do you perhaps deny God's assistance?" In answer to this, I replied, "As you and the previously named men have witnessed and are even now testifying to, a person who denies God's assistance should be anathematized. Certainly I do not deny this, especially since, on the contrary, I have refuted the heretics." Then, once this "judge" had been exposed and the interpreter betrayed, when we shouted that the heretic was a Latin-speaking individual, that we were Latin-speaking, that the heresy was more widely known to the Latin-speaking parts of the Empire and ought to be discussed by Latin-speaking judges, and when that one person in particular [Pelagius], the very suspect, kept forcing himself upon us as judge in an all but shameless manner—although we were not the accusers—it was necessary for most of us to say, "The same person cannot be heretic, advocate, and judge." After many other issues had been dealt with, Bishop John pronounced a new decision, confirming

---

24. Avitus, like Orosius, hailed from Braga and had journeyed to the Holy Land and become an associate of Jerome before Orosius arrived in Palestine.

25. Orosius himself, like many of the recent western visitors to Palestine, was not competent in Greek. This put him and his supporters at a distinct disadvantage in such a situation as the present one.

at long last our demands and purpose: namely, that certain brothers and correspondence be sent to the blessed Innocent, the Roman pope,[26] with everyone agreeing to obey that which he would decree; that the heretic Pelagius, having silence imposed upon him, would in the meantime keep to himself; and that we would cease our mockery of John, who had been proven to be wrong and who had admitted as much. All of us concurred in this decision. After the ritual of thanksgiving was celebrated, peace was made and a final prayer was said as a token of reconciliation; then we adjourned.

7. However, forty-seven days later, when I approached Bishop John on the first day of the Festival of Dedication[27] to pay my respects, as I have been accustomed to do ever since my arrival, in response to my greeting I immediately received from him the brand of a false accusation. For he said to me, "Why do you, as a man who has blasphemed, come before me?"—wishing, I believe, to be understood as meaning, "Do not touch me because I am pure and without sin."[28] But since I was not conscious of any guilt, I asked, "When did anyone hear anything or what kind of thing was said that it could be regarded as blasphemy?" The bishop replied, "I myself heard you say that not even with God's assistance can a person be without sin." Now, most reverend fathers, as you are my witnesses, and as it has been witnessed by all of our brothers and those saintly men as well who are standing as my supporters in this testimony out of their love for the truth, I responded immediately, saying that such a declaration as now has been asserted by the bishop to have been made by me, never in the past came out of my mouth. Admittedly, by dwelling too often on the ridiculous nature of this contemptible falsehood, making frequent use of declarations, it may appear not so much that I have proven my case, but rather, that I have betrayed another

---

26. Innocent I was bishop of Rome from 402 until 417. On the role the papacy played in the Pelagian controversies, see Otto Wermelinger, *Rom und Pelagius: Die theologische Position der römischen Bischöfe im pelagianischen Streit in den Jahren 411–432* (Stuttgart: Hiersemann, 1975).

27. That is, 12 September 415. The feast celebrated the dedication of the Church of the Resurrection in Jerusalem.

28. Cf. Job 33.9; Isa 65.5.

DEFENSE AGAINST THE PELAGIANS 123

individual. For I concede that whatever the nature of that statement, I would have asked, "How did a Greek who lacks knowledge of the Latin language understand a Latin-speaking person?" Or, "If he heard a sacrilegious statement, why did he not immediately refute the blasphemer or, to act more leniently, why did he not as a devoted father warn his incautious son about the necessity of controlling the urge to engage in dangerous speech?" But, on the contrary, when much had been forgotten due to this long interval of time, Bishop John himself, all by himself, brought forth the accusation; he provided the testimony; and he alone pronounced the verdict,[29] assuming under the authority of his own person the responsibilities for all offenses, in spite of the fact that he had been well instructed by the reading of the Gospels that our Lord Jesus would not have been condemned had it not been for the testimony of the chief priest![30] On the one side my brothers took me under their protection, on the other side there were false brothers. And then there is the fact that in that same assembly the priests Avitus and Vitalis sat together with me on one side; on the other side sat that "unknown" interpreter; and next to him were men esteemed by both the world and God, Passerius the priest and Domnus, the former notable.[31] Both of these last two were considered worthy to be present as interpreters because of their skill and their faith, and met with us after being invited and brought there by your circle of clerics with the agreement of Bishop John himself. Indeed, in your midst was the very one who in that situation was not less heard than seen. Considering this, it is amazing how his words, once spoken, could have passed by so many opponents, colleagues, and listeners, and entered the unwary ears of an experienced listener!

8. But driven on by the fire of truth, I press my case far enough; I am exceeding the limits of my intended declaration. It should be conceded, instead, that the interpreter seems to have

---

29. This charge parallels that made against Pelagius in chapter 6 above.
30. Cf. Matt 26.57–68; Mk 14.53–65; Lk 22.54, 22.63–71; Jn 18.13–14, 18.19–24.
31. It is probable that these four allies of Orosius, like him, did not attend the Council of Diospolis held later that year. Cf. Augustine, *De gestis Pelagii* 16.39.

erred in his translation rather than that the bishop should appear to have misrepresented what he heard and should now be seeking false witnesses to come to his aid instead of demanding back that prize which he has awarded the heretics. Of course, no one should be surprised at this point that there are false witnesses in Jerusalem and that they are being sought out by priests and senior clerics.[32] The blood of St. Stephen was once proclaiming this;[33] the standards of our Lord's cross demonstrate this;[34] the injustice that is now aroused by them also reveals this. But whether it is supposed that these statements have been recklessly believed by the bishop, or maliciously misrepresented, or understood through simple ignorance, I leave it for Christ the judge to dispel them. Since I am a poor and unknown sinner, far be it from me ever to be so bold as to challenge a bishop, and particularly the bishop of Jerusalem, in front of other bishops. As for me, my simple faith and approval before the most eminent Trinity of God's omnipotence and before all of his Catholic servants is sufficient. While you, most reverend fathers, have knowledge of this same matter and are now testifying with me, I here call upon God as my soul's witness, that in your aforementioned assembly I did not pronounce any blasphemy from my mouth and did not make any such statement as the one Bishop John has accused me of: namely, that even with God's assistance a person cannot be without sin. I also want for that reason satisfaction in this dispute over a belief—one which is unknown to us—lest you, in thinking that you did not hear what I nevertheless said, should fall prey perhaps to untrustworthy testimony; therefore, be it publicly reported or by way of a rumor, one should not believe that, as long as the bishop could not be telling a lie, someone who is innocent is sinning because he easily believes something. And who does not know of the persons

---

32. Orosius's choice of words here (*a sacerdotibus atque senioribus*) seems intentionally reminiscent of the language of Mt 26.47 (*a principibus sacerdotum et senioribus*) and Mk 14.43 (*a summis sacerdotibus et a scribis et a senioribus*) [Vulgate version].

33. Cf. Acts 6.11–13. Orosius certainly might be expected to bring up the martyrdom of St. Stephen, given his recent and continuing association with the protomartyr's relics. See introduction.

34. Cf. Mt 26.47–50; Mk 14.43–46; Lk 22.47–48; Jn 18.3–9.

responsible either in the indictment of Susanna[35] or in the stoning of Naboth?[36]

9. And lest someone perhaps not know that there has never been in Jerusalem a lack of support from silver[37] nor a lack of soldiers' whips[38] for the purpose of shedding Christian blood, now let him know that I believe that I am free from this or any such statement: free by your faith, free by my conscience. And after first examining the ambiguous meaning of the statement itself, I will attempt to discover how those who allege that I spoke thus seem to have brought this action against me. Perhaps through this mode of inquiry, the secret of their doctrine will be exposed, so that by trading blow for blow, as it were, the missiles, when returned with greater accuracy, may punish the original attacker. For Bishop John says that I made the following response: "Not even with God's assistance can a person be without sin." If anyone at all thinks that this should be stated in such a manner in order to prove that God, subject to the infirmity of the human being, has no power and in order to suggest that, in the matter of every creature residing in the heavens, the earth, and the infernal regions, something is impossible for the omnipotence of God, then that kind of blasphemer, I should say, not only ought to be anathematized in my view, but also punished after the example of Nadab and Abihu[39] by divine fire, or as in the destruction of Dathan and Abiram[40] by the earth opening up, receiving him, and plunging him alive into hell. For each of these pairs, by their obstinacy of heart, disparaged God's power: the former by offering an unhallowed fire,[41] as if God needed it; the latter, in their opposition to Moses, by not believing that they could be brought to the promised land. God can do all things, and is always able to do what he wishes. And just as he is capable of creating something out of nothing, so he can easily perfect what he

---

35. Cf. Dan 13 [*Historia Susannae*].
36. Cf. 1 Kings 21.1–16.
37. Cf. Mt 26.14–15; Mk 14.10–11; Lk 22.3–6.
38. Cf. Mt 27.26; Mk 15.15; Jn 19.1.
39. Cf. Ex 6.23, 24.1, 24.9, 28.1; Lev 10.1–2; Num 3.2, 3.4, 26.60–61; 1 Chr 6.3, 24.1–2.
40. Cf. Num 16.1–33, 26.9–10; Deut 11.6; Ps 106.17.
41. Literally, "strange/foreign fire" (*ignem alienum*).

has created. For he has the power at hand when he wishes.⁴² Grace which has been freely granted according to the Spirit reveals this; conventional law according to its literal sense attests to this; natural law in all places recognizes this; the most well-ordered operation of the universe demonstrates this. For who among the pagans, in whose view there always exist the distinct components of sky, land, and sea, would dare deny this? Who among the Jews, to whom an understanding, however limited, of the Law has come, handed down by Moses, can mistrust this when he both recognizes and believes what has been written? Namely, that the waters of the Erythraean Sea were parted, laying bare its depths and offering a safe journey in the seabed to anyone traveling by foot on land;⁴³ and that the river Jordan divided its waters and, swirling, turned and flowed back unto its source.⁴⁴ Or that a mortal man, Elijah, in bodily form was carried up [to heaven] in a fiery chariot and yet was not harmed by the fire.⁴⁵ Or that Habakkuk, though burdened with a large amount of prepared food, is said to have been transported in merely one day's time directly from Judaea to Babylonia, in order to serve a meal to that just man [Daniel] who was going hungry among the ravenous beasts, as the common [Latin] text has it.⁴⁶ And what Christian does not admit this in his own heart within a split second of thought? The Christian who knows that Lazarus, dead for four days, and with his whole body stinking and wasting away and his skin already becoming fluid within him, sprang forth because of his devoted service to the Lord?⁴⁷ The Christian who has read that a certain man, blind from birth and already in old age, became vigorous because his vision was suddenly either created or restored to him?⁴⁸ The Christian who has learned how the winds, waves, and storms—forces clashing simultaneously among themselves—were tamed by the heeded order of the Lord's reproach?⁴⁹ The Christian who believes that Peter, though burdened with the weight of his carnal body and destined to deny

---

42. Cf. Wis 12.18.
43. Cf. Ex 14.
44. Cf. Josh 3.
45. Cf. 2 Kgs 2.11.
46. Cf. Dan 14.32–38 [Vulgate version].
47. Cf. Jn 11.
48. Cf. Jn 9.
49. Cf. Mt 8.23–27.

the Lord three times in succession,[50] walked with hesitant footsteps upon the swollen waves?[51]

10. Accordingly, I think that all persons who are endowed with outstanding faith and wisdom or who in another way hold this belief—namely, that God can do all things— do revere it, believe it, confess it. Therefore, he is generally called "omnipotent" by the whole of creation because he can do all things. And it is the one God who says, "These things are impossible for humans."[52] In another passage he teaches us, saying, "Without me, you can do nothing."[53] Therefore, he who can do everything can do all things as regards a human being. And yet, why does mere dust and ashes[54] [i.e., Pelagius] hold himself so proud as to say, "A human being is able," when only God is. The Apostle[55] proclaims, "By his grace I am what I am, and his grace has not been lacking in me. On the contrary, I have worked more abundantly than all of them; not I, however, but the grace of God with me."[56] You imprudent, presumptuous man, why do you think that Paul said "with me"? Observe that he prefaced this by "not I." Hence, between these two expressions, "not I" and "with me," there is situated "the grace of God." Truly it is God's prerogative both to wish and to accomplish things according to a will which is good, in spite of human will.[57] Whence, Paul confessed that he was saying "with me" because he had said "not I." Thus, there operates in the will of a human being the grace of divine virtue which has given him that very will. Just as the conscience of a human being professes to say, "not I," so the grace of God generously allows, "with me." The Apostle proclaims, "By the grace of God I am what I am." For he was mindful of the Lord's announcement, "No one comes to me unless the Father has drawn him."[58] And

---

50. Cf. Mt 26.69–75. 51. Cf. Mt 14.25–32.
52. Lk 18.27. 53. Jn 15.5.
54. Cf. Gen 18.27; Job 34.15; Augustine, *De Genesi ad litteram* 10.8.14, *De divinatione daemonum* 80.2.

55. Like Pacian, Orosius in his writings identifies Paul solely by the word *apostolus* (i.e., the Apostle). Hereafter, when this identification is intended by Orosius, *apostolus* will be rendered as "the Apostle." Cf. Pacian, *Ep.* 1, n. 8 above.

56. 1 Cor 15.10.
57. Cf. Augustine's discussion in *De civitate Dei* 12.8–9.
58. Jn 6.44.

again, in another passage, "I am with you for all of your days, right up to the end of the world."[59] And in yet another place, the Lord says concerning the Holy Spirit, "It is advantageous for you that I depart; for if I do not go away, the Comforter[60] will not come to you; but if I go, I will send him to you."[61]

11. O you wretched man, according to the truth of God's judgment! The Father draws you, the Son is with you, and the Spirit is your comforter; and in the face of such great, divine majesty you dare to say, "With the grace of God assisting me, admittedly, but by my own power, I am what I am." For now, after this "correction" was placed with your earlier error, you maintain the following, "A person is able to be without sin—with the assistance of God." But yet, in your own treatise which you entitled *Book of Testimonies*[62] this very statement was written in the following way: "A person is able to be without sin and can easily observe God's commandments if he so wishes." There is no "grace of God," no "assistance" mentioned, however often you talk about the "grace of God." I did not deny it [i.e., the alleged assertion that "not even with God's assistance can a person be without sin"] because I did not say it; but for that very reason, because I did not deny it, I am assumed to have said it. It is as if, indeed, it ought to be believed that Susanna confessed adultery because she did not deny it when others were accusing her,[63] or that the Lord Jesus assented to the testimony of false witnesses because he was silent. But among your kind, if it is the case that not to have denied it means to have said it, and to have kept silent means to have proclaimed it, then David asks in vain, "Station, O Lord, a guard over my mouth and a gate round about my lips."[64] Also, if another person was able to hear what my words did not say, then in vain am I proving, through witnesses and testimony, that I did not say what I am accused of. However, I do concede that in your case you think that what you did not say at all ought

---

59. Mt 28.20.
60. Orosius's text reads *consolator*. Cf. Vulgate *Paraclitus*.
61. Jn 16.7.
62. For Jerome's reply to Pelagius's now lost *Liber testimoniorum*, see his *Adversus Pelagianos dialogus* 1.25–32.
63. Cf. Dan 13.42–43 [*Historia Susannae*].
64. Ps 141.3.

to be interpreted as said. What do we do then, when we discover a contradiction of statements on the basis of sense, seeing that they are not coherent in their discordant links and seeing that on the page itself the words do not harmonize with each other? For you write that a person is able to be without sin and can easily observe God's commandments if he wishes. And as the most blessed father Jerome has explained regarding this very idea, in a letter which he wrote to Ctesiphon, you are now adding at the last minute, as if you are just awaking from a deep sleep, "not without the assistance of God."[65] In this regard, truth itself contends against you and protests. Why do you, through your haughty arrogance and nauseating humility, keep mouthing that the assistance of God is necessary for you when you judge that all things are easy for you?[66] "You honor me superficially with your lips, but your heart is far from me."[67] There is no need for two to be working in a task which is easy for one; and vainly does the grace of divinity insert itself where man declares that he can easily do things if he wishes. You have said that for a person who wishes it, the commandments are easy; but I also assert this: you say that even difficult things can be completed. Yet, whenever you promise that things can be done by man in this manner, you accuse the Lord of envy, since in that case God is trying to ascribe to his own assistance that which man could have accomplished alone through his will. Either remove "if he wishes" from man and attribute what he can do to grace or, since you give credit to man for being able to do things when he wishes, remove your pretended flattery of grace which does not belong there, and out of the fullness of your heart state your undisguised blasphemy.

12. But it is not my function to investigate such notions to any great extent, especially since the most blessed fathers, Augustine and Jerome, have delivered to the western provinces [of the Roman Empire] a most detailed examination of this convicted heresy. I would return, rather, to the issue which I raised previously, not roused to action by a boldness of temperament, but

---

65. *Ep.* 133.8: *post gravissimum somnum . . . conaris adiungere.*
66. See Augustine's critical comments on Pelagius's addition of the word *facile* ("easily") in the context of his testimony before the bishops gathered at Diospolis (December 415) in the *De gestis Pelagii* 30.54.
67. Cf. Isa 29.13.

moved by the injustice that has been done. You say that a person is able to be without sin in this world with God's assistance. You say, "a person is able"; I say, "God is able." The raging flames inside the fiery furnace did not harm the three young men in it.[68] Which one of them could accomplish what was done contrary to nature? The three themselves or a fourth figure in their midst who is likened to "the Son of God"?[69] The leper exclaims, "Lord, if you wish, you can make me clean";[70] here the Lord is revealing his will through his power and affirming his will by his power. For he himself is the only one for whom such an ability exists when he wills it. Blind men approached him, begging that sight be given to them. And to them Jesus said, "Do you believe that I am able to do this?"[71] The Lord Christ judges it to be worthy of the highest reward of faith if someone believes that the Son of God can do such things; and yet our man from Britain[72] is confident that he can accomplish it as soon as he has willed it! To the paralytic man who had faith, the Lord declares, "Son, be of firm resolve, your sins are forgiven you."[73] And now this new teacher[74] and attendant of tables[75] has dared to presume the remission of sins on the basis of his own power—he does not even wait to hear from God! The [Jewish] scribes, not understanding the truth, grumble and say [to Jesus], "Who is able to forgive sins but God alone?"[76] Yet this man [Pelagius] judges that sins, about which he does not even know that God has forgiven them, are erased.

68. Cf. Dan 3.
69. Cf. Dan 3.25. Orosius's text here is identical to the Vulgate: *similis filio Dei*—with a similar range of interpretations open to the author. In verse 28 this figure is identified as an angel of God.
70. Mt 8.2.
71. Mt 9.28.
72. Most modern scholars agree that Pelagius was born in Britain, despite Jerome's designation of him as *Scotus* (*Commentarius in Ieremiam* 3, preface). Rees, *Pelagius*, xiii, ventures that this may well be a contemporary term of abuse employed by Jerome.
73. Mt 9.2.
74. Pelagius is described here as a *novus magister*, which may imply, in Orosius's view, inexperience, theological "innovation" (always a dangerous charge), or a contrast with the original "Christian" teacher, Jesus.
75. *Minister mensarum*. Orosius in this instance may be referring to Pelagius's alleged obesity or rumored attraction to wealthy patrons such as the Anicii.
76. Mk 2.7.

13. Behold, puffed up by your carnal spirit, as though there is nothing higher, and glorying in your "free will," you boast and say, "I am a sinner because I wish; I sin when I wish. But, on the other hand, when I wish I can be without sin." What you say—"I sin when I wish"—is true, because even what you have not committed by deed you have committed by thought. Also, your statement, "When I wish, I do not sin," which is shameless, indeed, and troublesome, too, is not always applicable to everyone; nevertheless, there is no doubt that at times it can be realized. However, truly to be able to be without sin, for someone who has sinned at one time or another, is imposssible without the sole grace of baptism, when, in conformity with the person of the Lord, it is stated, "Your sins are forgiven you." I am urged to believe this because I am allowed to hear, "I am able, therefore, to be without sin." I do not embrace this, I do not presume it, nor do I venture to say this, at least in this corrupt state in which we live. For if David is praying to God, "Against you alone I have sinned and I have done evil in your presence,"[77] and if, according to the Apocalypse of John, the dead are to be judged on the basis of their sins committed in God's presence, receiving afterwards from these what has been recorded in the books [of judgment] according to their own deeds,[78] why then do I presume beforehand my own judgment if I know that I must also be judged by God? Or, if those holy books, which are never to be opened except in judgment, receive the good and evil acts of our life in equal measure and if they are going to put forth the process of judgment in sum, how do we know that our sins have been forgiven without the process in this life and before death—sins which we read are to be revealed not only after death, but also after the resurrection? I have had it within my power to sin; I do not have it within my power to be freed from sin. To offer prayer is up to me; to be absolved is not up to me. When, in fact, I have given myself over to sin I have become a slave of the accuser, a guilty party answerable to the Judge.[79] Thanks to the intercessions

77. Ps 51.4.
78. Cf. Rev 20.12.
79. Here Orosius employs traditional Roman juridical terminology (*accus-*

sent ahead by constant prayers, I can have hope of a kind judge. I cannot lay claim to an innocent conscience without fear before the official proclamation of the sentence. For the Apostle says, "Do not judge anything before the time, until the Lord should come, who will both bring to light[80] the hidden things of the darkness and make manifest the purposes of the hearts. And then shall each and every person have praise from God."[81] Otherwise, if it is within a person's power to make himself free from his own sin, then either Christ is not judge or he is it in vain.

14. But you say, "I said that a person is without sin according to the following sense: once a sinner has lamented his sin, then he will be saved, that is, he will begin just then to take the first step toward salvation." Yet that person will not immediately be without sin. For the Lord, when he entered the house of Zacchaeus, a man who believed, said, "Today salvation has come to this house."[82] Is it really possible that if a single member believed, immediately the entire family of the house was without sin at that exact time when the head of the household who believed entered into the initial stage of salvation? For David also lamented when he had sinned and, however much he deserved to hear that his transgression had been forgiven, nevertheless much later atoned for this very transgression by his exile and great disgrace, so that it would clearly appear that his punishment had been exacted in the present, and that forgiveness had been promised for the future. Through this God bestowed a great act of mercy upon the lamenting sinner so that by means of a temporary reprimand he would remove a sin which merited death. It was said to Ananias concerning Paul, as he was fearfully complaining of Paul's persecution [of Christians], "I shall show him how much he must suffer for the sake of my name,"[83] so that when Paul was saved there where he had bound Christ by persecuting him, he would be afflicted with suffering for Christ, right

---

atoris, reus, iudicis) in the context of Christian judgment. The term *accusator* was often used by Christian writers as an epithet of the devil.

80. The editor has preferred the manuscript reading *inluminabat*.
81. 1 Cor 4.5.   82. Lk 19.9.
83. Acts 9.16.

up to his own death, but be glorified in the resurrection. So it is, because "mercy and truth go always before the face of God";[84] so that if a voluntary sacrifice of an afflicted spirit and a contrite heart is offered in time by the lamenting person, truth arises in mercy and in the end mercy is exalted over judgment.

15. It is believed and it is hoped that Christ the Lord, "who is to come in the glory of God the Father, shall judge the living and the dead";[85] Christ, "from whose presence heaven and earth will flee,"[86] as Scripture attests. And there are people who, because of their ignorance, in order that I do not say because of their conscience, neither consider that they are subject to the forthcoming judgment nor tremble at the coming of the Lord and the apparition of his brilliance amidst the blazing of the elements and the destruction of the world.[87] I fear that they will be among those concerning whom the Lord forewarns us, "For many will say on that day,"—persons, obviously, of that earthly arrogance by which they used to corrupt others, and so-called "just" ones, not so much before God as among themselves!—"'Lord, Lord, did we not prophesy in your name and accomplish many deeds of power in your name?' And then I will declare to them and say, 'I do not know you; go away from me, evil-doers.'"[88] It is said by the prophet David in the person of Christ, "O Lord, who shall dwell in your tent, and who shall find rest on your holy mountain? He who walks without stain and practices justice."[89] This is, in fact, to say: who can be and is without sin? For the very Lord says about himself, "The prince of this world is coming, and he finds nothing of his own in me."[90] What is that of the devil's own? Without a doubt, it is sin. "For from the beginning the devil is a liar,"[91] and, in contrast, my Lord is "he who speaks the truth in his heart and who has not practiced treachery with his tongue."[92] The mighty and powerful angel, so Scripture affirms, proclaims in heaven, "'Who is worthy to open the book and to break its seals?' No one in heaven, nor on earth, nor under the earth was

84. Ps 89.14.
85. Mt 16.27; 2 Tim 4.1.
86. Rev 20.11.
87. Cf. 2 Pet 3.10.
88. Mt 7.22–23.
89. Ps 15.1–2.
90. Jn 14.30.
91. Cf. 1 Jn 3.8; Jn 8.44.
92. Ps 15.2–3.

able to open the book or to look through it."[93] John wept and lamented greatly that of all the rational creatures, no one was found worthy to open the book and examine it. One of the elders consoled John as he was weeping, and said, "Do not weep, John. Behold, the Lion of the tribe of Judah, the Root of David, has prevailed to open the book and to break its seals."[94] What, I ask, is that book which no one except "he who walks without stain and practices justice"[95] was to receive from the hand of the one who lives forever? It is not enough to say "without stain"; it is too little to say "a lamb" unless he was also slaughtered,[96] unless he crowned the purity of his life with the testimony of his suffering, "having seven horns and seven eyes which are the seven spirits of God,"[97] and without doubt having "the spirit of wisdom and understanding, the spirit of counsel and might, the spirit of knowledge and piety, the spirit of the fear of the Lord."[98] What, therefore, is that book? As far as I believe, it is the book of judgment. "For the Father does not judge anyone, but has given all judgment to the Son."[99]

16. What sorrow! I am forced to say what I have shuddered to think. Behold! Pelagius, who has dared to declare that he himself is without stain and sin, now consequently imagines that he is worthy to receive even the book and the judgment. And it is most likely that he is saying to himself, "I have the power of setting aside my life and of taking it up once more," and that he is preparing himself to be the future colleague of Christ on the throne. Wretched man, who does not understand that he is, on the contrary, preparing himself as the harbinger of the coming of the Antichrist! This is the man who "when he has been revealed, exalts himself above everything that is called God or that is worshipped as God,"[100] and who, according to this, is even now readying himself for this attempt at equality with the one and only Son of God! The Lamb of God, the Son of God, in order to receive the book from the hand of his Father, offers the marks of

---

93. Rev 5.2–3.
94. Rev 5.5.
95. Ps 15.2.
96. Cf. Rev 5.6.
97. Rev 5.6.
98. Isa 11.2–3.
99. Jn 5.22.
100. 2 Thess 2.3–4.

his sufferings,[101] not considering his victory as complete except as embodied in his death and resurrection. And yet my "fellow without sin"[102] claims that the achievement of a pure life can come to him as he is eating, drinking, and sleeping! When the devil tempted our Lord Jesus on three occasions after forty days of fasting, and when he had been defeated three times, he left him.[103] Yet he did not leave him forever, but only temporarily until Jesus' death on the cross, to reappear even more dangerously[104] with an apostate apostle.[105] And our "untroubled man"[106] has obviously conquered his temptations, so it seems to him, as well as the agent of the temptations, and he believes that he cannot be tempted or disturbed thereafter. That perfect Lamb, that one, who not only does not possess sins but also "takes away the sins of the world"[107] and "who has seven horns and seven eyes,"[108] was not capable of flinging the tempter into the air so that he would not return. Yet, our man without horns, smooth on the forehead[109] and having only two eyes,[110] considers that this defense for his head is not necessary for him, as he presumes such a

---

101. *Praefert stigmata passionis.* It is interesting to note that the verb *praefero* has strong historical associations with traditional Roman cultic formulae.

102. The Latin (from the Greek original) reads: *anamartetus.* The word, meaning "sinless," was properly applied to only God and Christ. But some patristic writers accused various rigorist sects, including the Pelagians, of a heretical application of the term. Cf., for example, Sozomen, *Historia ecclesiastica* 1.22.3 (on the Novatianists).

103. Cf. Mt 4.1–11; Lk 4.1–13; Mk 1.12–13.

104. Cf. Lk 4.13.

105. Almost certainly Judas is meant, since the word used here, *praevaricante*, corresponds with the traditional Latin rendering of Acts 1.25: *apostolatus de quo praevaricatus est Iudas.*

106. The Latin (from the Greek original) reads: *apathes.* Perhaps Orosius here is sarcastically using a term which in early Christian writings could denote a person of superior spiritual qualities, or perhaps he is pointedly asserting that Pelagius has claimed for himself another of the attributes of God. For it is especially in chapters 16–18 that Orosius ascribes to Pelagius a teaching which equates human sinlessness with that of God, thus leading to an extreme form of the doctrine of deification.

107. Jn 1.29.

108. Rev 5.6.

109. *Levis in fronte.* It is possible that Orosius intends two meanings here: "smooth on the forehead" (i.e., without the requisite protective horns); and "shallow in the forehead" (i.e., fickle or irresponsible of mind).

110. The Latin (from the Greek original) reads: *dyoptalmus.*

power in the flesh! Wretched man, who according to the Gospel, would not have more sin even if he were blind! But perhaps because the seven eyes are the seven spirits [of God], he brags about having plenty of all of these and boasts, so to speak, that his own "inner man" is flourishing by means of the sevenfold powers of grace which have been conferred upon him—especially since he is glorying in the same number of titles for his doctrines! Whence, it can happen that Pelagius in his own judgment thinks that he has been filled with the spirit of wisdom, particularly since he says that the commandments of God are easy to keep. He imagines that he is well-endowed with the spirit of understanding, by which he knows in advance and foretells that all sinners together with the wicked are to be condemned to the eternal flames. He thinks that he is rich with the spirit of counsel, by which he warns that evil is not even to be contemplated. He considers that he is powerful through the spirit of might, by which he claims that a person can be without sin. He imagines that he is inflated with the spirit of knowledge when he hopes that, unless someone has knowledge of God's law, he cannot be without sin. He considers that he is abounding in the spirit of piety, by which he teaches that an enemy ought to be loved as a friend—having forgotten that he himself said an enemy is not to be believed in any possible way. He imagines that he has been honored with the spirit of the fear of God, by which, after a great amount of intoxication,[111] he was very recently awakened and now adds, "it is possible for a person to be without sin—but not without the assistance of God." As a result of these "spirits," as I think, he does not shrink from ascending to such a height of presumption, that he says that, by his own perfect power, the fullness of the Holy Spirit descended upon him after the manner of Christ and remained in him completely. But this has been given by God the Father to that one only, "upon whom God also gave the name which is above every name,"[112] and "who alone is without sin and walks without stain,"[113] and in whom abides "the very

---

111. This seems to be another pointed reference to Pelagius's alleged overindulgence in food and drink.
112. Phil 2.9.   113. Cf. Ps 15.2.

ointment of sanctification."[114] We, on the other hand, hasten into the fragrance of his ointments and, while inhaling the life-giving odor above us, try to breathe in the sweet breaths of life with the Lord showing us the way.[115]

17. But you say, "Why do you assail me so injustly? Why do you so aggravate the situation with the malevolence of your arrogant words? Would I, a mere servant, dare to compare myself with my Lord? Would I, mere dust and ashes, compare myself with the Word of God? Should I, who am subject to death, be mentioned as an equal to the victor over death?" O what damned evil! Well, indeed, are you bearing witness to God, rendering yourself humble by your words, but your meaning declares something different from within the pages! You say that a person can be without sin. I repeat over and over: the person who can do this is Christ. Either assume the name Christ, or abandon your boldness. God has given that power to only one and to no one else except his "firstborn among many brothers."[116] Such is passed down by the Catholic faith, such we maintain. Certainly our Lord has admonished unbelievers, "I have come in my Father's name and you have not received me. Another will come in his own name; perhaps you will receive him."[117] Either follow, together with us, him in whom we sinners believe, the one without sin, the one who is only-begotten; or, if you are the other one, admit it! That very person is the Lord Jesus who, after subduing death and triumphing over the devil, "ascending on high, made captivity itself a captive and gave the gifts to people,"[118] and "from whose fullness we all have received."[119] The Apostle teaches likewise, "But to each one of us grace was given according to the measure of Christ's giving."[120] And the same teacher of the gentiles writes to the Romans, "For by the grace given to me, I say to all who are among you not to be wiser than you ought to be wise, but to be wise with prudence, each according to the measure of faith that God has apportioned."[121] Next he proclaims to the Corinthians, "Truly there are varieties of spiritual gifts, but the same Spirit.

114. Ex 37.29.
116. Rom 8.29.
118. Eph 4.8. Cf. Ps 68.18.
120. Eph 4.7.
115. Cf. Song 1.3.
117. Jn 5.43.
119. Jn 1.16.
121. Rom 12.3.

And there are varieties of activities, but the same Lord. And there are varieties of ministries, yet it is the same God who activates all of them in everyone."[122] After many enumerations of spiritual gifts and powers,[123] he adds, "But all of these things are activated by one and the same Spirit, who allots to each one just as he wishes."[124] Then, through a comparison of members in the human body, he shows that the body of Church unity comes to a single harmony of perfection as a result of different kinds of works,[125] demonstrating decisively that there is no intrinsic member of that body which does not require the aid or company of another, with the Lord himself as designated head, the Lord "in whom are hidden all the senses and treasures of wisdom and knowledge."[126] Hence, "And he has given us understanding by which we may know"[127] that the Word is in Christ Jesus, "in whom the whole fullness of divinity exists corporeally."[128] And when, according to the testimony of John, the Holy Spirit was descending upon Christ and was remaining on him, John the Baptist declared him to be the Lord.[129] Accordingly, if no one has anything except "if he asks it of you"[130] and if no one receives anything except in keeping with such apportionment and measurement, and if he who has received needs the assistance of another for preserving it, then I ask: by what madness does such a man make guarantees to himself from the fullness [of divinity] when he is unable to maintain himself even in his individual state? The evangelist attests concerning the Lord, "But he was the true light which illuminates every person coming into this world."[131] Moreover, the Lord declares to his apostles, "You are the light of this world."[132] There, in the Lord alone, is light in its entirety, because it is the true light. Here, in all of the apostles there is light, to be sure, but only from out of the light which is whole. If this is the case for the apostles, in whose selection the universal body of the Church has been taken on, what are we—I say, we who are

---

122. 1 Cor 12.4–6.
123. Cf. 1 Cor 12.8–10.
124. 1 Cor 12.11.
125. Cf. 1 Cor 12.12–30.
126. Col 2.3.
127. 1 Jn 5.20.
128. Col 2.9.
129. Cf. Jn 1.29–34.
130. Mt 5.42.
131. Jn 1.9.
132. Mt 5.14.

mere individuals—what can we appear to be after them except ignorant people, according to the apostle Peter, who believe only through faith in the words of the Gospels and in "the prophetic message"[133] as though "by a lamp shining in a dark place"?[134] For just as we are illuminated, so to speak, we ourselves are convinced that in good works there have been prepared "lighted lamps"[135] in our hands which, assailed by many kinds of tribulations, are put at risk always by their own failings and by blows from others. Therefore, the Lord also says in the Gospel, "And if that very light which is in us is darkness, how great will be the darkness itself!"[136]

18. But I concede that, however little that light is, it continues to shine with unfailing vitality to the very end; that is, it does not lose that gift which is one's portion of special grace. Moreover, the fullness of light is present throughout; darkness does not abide—here I mean the darkness of folly which arises from the impurities of sin. And what if there exists a corresponding ratio, so that however much light is lacking, to such an extent darkness has ascendancy? But at the same time, it is a very difficult situation since darkness has nothing to hold it back. It is necessary for a human being, constituted of a quantity of light with the remaining part from darkness, who wishes good but does not succeed in avoiding evil, that assistance continues and sin is not missing. But if this appears to anyone to be stated obscurely, let him accept an example from human experience. Two individuals have different gifts: one has the ability to be humble in silence; the other, the ability to be persuasive in teaching. If, of that one to whom silence is dear, it is demanded that he render an account concerning his faith, do you think that he would suffer no discomfort in speaking? Or, if that one whose skill in teaching has been brought forth for approval should be chastised for arrogance, do you think that he employs no deception in his humility? Or do you willingly believe that a person can be simple-minded without buffoonery, outwardly joyful without a word, anxious without anger, long-suffering without carelessness,

133. 2 Pet 1.19.
135. Lk 12.35.
134. 2 Pet 1.19.
136. Mt 6.23.

placid without laziness, learned without boastfulness, and submissive without jealousy—this quite apart from that desire for illusory fame which is the common blindness of all good deeds? Therefore, if this is piously and religiously understood, let each one of us accept the comparison, so that in his preference for what is morally better each individual condemns himself rather than represents himself as righteous in contempt for what is morally worse. Then, only in this way, if he in turn will unite the members by a single love—just as the skin surrounding bones requires sinews joined together—can man, conscious of what is his, understand that this very grace which he has is not something owed to him, but rather, a gift. And, on the basis of this, let him glory in the Lord from whom he receives this grace, instead of being angry that he did not originally acquire it. For, although "we were by nature children of wrath"[137] because of our sin and thus deserving of nothing except damnation, we have been made children of mercy because of the Lord's clemency. Let us not burden the Lord with a complaint about not "acquiring," but rather, let us respond with gratitude for "receiving" and glorify that sole Creator and Redeemer, our Lord Jesus Christ, "whom God has set forth as one who atones by his blood, so that at his name every knee should bend, of those in heaven, on earth, and under the earth";[138] whom "all flesh in that aforesaid power should see"[139] as judge; and to whom "every tongue should confess."[140] Hence the Apostle also says, "Therefore we strive, whether we are absent or present, to please him. For we must all be manifested before the judgment seat of Christ, so that each may bear the appropriate things for what he has done in the body, whether it be good or evil."[141] And in another passage he states, "For we shall all stand before the judgment seat of God."[142] The Apostle Paul has said that even he will stand before the judgment seat of God and give back the appropriate things for what he has done in the body, together with everyone else. But Pelagius, on the other hand, boldly dares to say, "I am achiev-

---

137. Eph 2.3.
138. Rom 3.25; Phil 2.10.
139. Cf. Isa 40.5.
140. Phil 2.11.
141. 2 Cor 5.9–10.
142. Rom 14.10.

ing such complete perfection in the flesh that I hope for no generosity whatsoever from the Judge." On that day of the Judge, the righteous, when they hear the praises of their deeds, will nevertheless still ask as if they are ignorant, "Lord, when did we see you and do these things for you?"[143] And now this person, our man so very knowledgeable in God's law, discerns on what day, at what hour, and at what moment he will enter into that final resting place, beyond which there is no other dwelling of the fullest sanctity!

19. Or it may be that he objects and declares, "These insults about my folly, not to speak of pride, would have been justifiably heaped on me if I were to say that without assistance a person is able to be without sin. Now, however, I assert, 'with the assistance of God,' for whom nothing is difficult.[144] Or do you, perhaps, deny God's assistance?"[145] I do defer briefly to your fallacious claim so that, while I may seem to reveal in myself that which I wish to expose in you, I might be found to be more cleared of blame in my defense and you might be found to be more obvious in your confusion. My faithful and undoubted opinion has always been this: God not only provides his assistance in his body, which is the Church, to whom he bestows his special gifts of grace on account of the faith of believers. He also grants it to all the peoples in this world because of the patient and everlasting generosity which is his own; and not, as you claim, together with your disciple, Caelestius, for whom already at the African synod the hidden character of your impious doctrines was crushed, that in natural good alone and in free choice one grace is commonly bestowed on all people. Rather, it is the case that God supplies it specially to all and each individually, in season and out, on every day, at every minute, and in every smallest moment of time. For Scripture states, "Who makes his sun to rise upon the good and the evil."[146] But maybe you reply, "Nature, which is well-ordered, preserves its own pattern, and because of this the courses of the heavenly bodies have been established once for all

143. Cf. Mt 25.37.
144. Cf. Gen 18.14.
145. An echo of Bishop John's accusation. Cf. chapters 7–9 above.
146. Mt 5.45.

times. God causes it every day because he has caused it once." What, then, is your opinion about that section of the statement which follows, "He brings about rain upon the just and the unjust"?[147] Surely he who gives, gives when he wishes and gives where he wishes, either by arranging the well-ordered nature or by lavishly bestowing his own munificence. And in case you contemplate also casting aside this statement, in keeping with the madness of your impiety, listen to the prophet testifying about this truth: "He who calls for the waters of the sea and pours them out upon the face of the earth: the Lord is his name."[148] What should I in fact say about the true hope of the human race, seeing that "everyone who plows, plows in hope"?[149] However, to hope is not a matter of one's own powers, but rather of another's munificence. When, moreover, someone has planted the scattered seed and has buried it within the bosom of the earth, this cultivator has, beyond that, nothing more to do except turn his eyes toward heaven and pray, not to the land to which he has entrusted the seed, but to God in whom he believes, so that he will make his labors fruitful through early and late rain. And, that I may employ a spiritual precept to common practices, "Neither he who plants nor he who waters is anyone whatsoever, but God who gives the growth."[150] How much, therefore, should I rejoice about God's assistance! Judge, through this, the fact that I demonstrate that assistance is provided to all individually and to all people, so that it may be clear to us that we ought to take heed of him up to our very ends and that we ought to call upon him unceasingly.

20. The devil is asked by the Lord, "'From what place do you come?' And he answers, 'I come from visiting the earth and from traversing those regions which are under the heavens.'"[151] I ask you: is that solicitude on the part of the devil an indication of good intention or of evil intention? You would be forced to admit, "Of course, of evil intention." For also his subsequent demand shows this.[152] That particular appearance of the devil took

147. Mt 5.45.
149. 1 Cor 9.10.
151. Job 1.7.
148. Am 5.8, 9.6.
150. 1 Cor 3.7.
152. Cf. Job 1.11, 2.5.

place in the time of Job, which is to say, in the time of Moses. Certainly there was no Judaea in those days, no Jerusalem, no Church spread across the world. Up to that point in time all nations had no knowledge of God and yet, the devil was already visiting the earth and traversing all those regions which are under the heavens, driven to corrupt and utterly destroy the human race by the unceasing anxiety of his wickedness. Accordingly, when you see that such great evil of the devil befell people unacquainted with God for the purpose of destroying them, do you believe that nothing of God's grace was present to protect them? Or do you perhaps think it has been said mistakenly, "The earth is the Lord's and the fullness thereof, the world and all who dwell in it."[153] But indeed, in order that you may judge more clearly that God's assistance is present on every single occasion and for each individual person, observe that the devil himself, while testifying about the universe, is questioned about a single individual! "Have you observed," says God, "my son Job, that there is not anyone like him on the earth?"[154] The Lord knows every single person individually; the devil also knows each one. God has such knowledge through the power of his nature; the devil, through the exertion of his wickedness. The devil knows in order to tempt man; God knows in order to test him. When the adversary is speaking against him, Job is being praised by his Creator. For the Lord wishes to judge the deeds of a human being because he himself works within that one. But truly the devil also admits God's assistance, for he says, "Have you not walled in those things which are outside his house and inside his house?"[155] At the enemy's request, God disarms his servant for trials but does not leave him altogether unprotected; he removes Job's worldly goods, but bestows grace upon him. "Behold," he says, "I place in your hand all that he has, but do not touch him."[156] But this is not enough! In hatred the devil rages, and he tries to bring about Job's death. But on the contrary, he is controlled by God's providence; grace is not removed. The victim sought by the

153. Ps 24.1. Cf. Ps 50.12, 89.11. Also, see Ex 19.5; 1 Cor 10.26.
154. Job 1.8.   155. Job 1.10.
156. Job 1.12.

hunter is allowed him, but once again the devil is called upon to be the protector of his own victim![157] For it is said to him, "Behold, I am handing him over to you; only protect his life."[158] From this, no one would think that the devil was just contriving to corrupt the soul in Job's body unless he was also contriving to tear it from the body itself, if the guardianship of the compassionate God did not safeguard the afflicted and frail man and if that guardianship, so placed, did not always counteract every attempt of the devil's crafty devices!

21. You now have, to my way of thinking, sufficient evidence of God's grace which operates among the peoples. Accept in the same way the obvious meaning of that special gift which is generously conferred upon the Church and its body. The Apostle Paul writes to the Corinthians, "I give thanks to my God always for you in the grace of God that has been given to you in Christ Jesus; because in all things you have been enriched in him, in all speech and in all knowledge, just as the testimony of Christ has been confirmed among you, so that, accordingly, you are not lacking in any grace."[159] And again, "Therefore, since we have been justified by faith, let us have peace with God through our Lord Jesus Christ: through him we have access to faith in that grace, through which we stand and glory."[160] Hence, the apostle Peter also reminds us, saying, "Receiving the object of your faith, the salvation of your souls. Concerning this salvation, the prophets who prophesied about the future grace of God in us searched and inquired."[161] On this basis, it has been declared most clearly that God's assistance is not lacking for any person, and above all, when the deceiver pursues us and our weakness is present.

(2) The fallacy of this blind, accusatory man who says, "Perhaps you deny the assistance of God?" has been refuted and destroyed. But since we have already made mention of Job, let also earlier testimony concerning Job be reviewed, who in the words of the Lord is "a man without blame, a truthful worshipper of

---

157. Note the typical Orosian alliteration and cadence: *expetita praedoni praeda permittitur et rursus praedae suae custos adhibetur.*
158. Job 2.6.
159. 1 Cor 1.4–7.
160. Rom 5.1–2.
161. 1 Pet 1.9–10.

God, restraining himself from all evil."[162] For to prove that a person can be without sin, it is usual for you to state very frequently that a person has been without blame,[163] that is, that Job by means of God's testimony has been called "a man without blame," and "truthful," and that Zechariah, too, is shown in the Gospel as an esteemed individual "without reproach."[164] The Lord said concerning Job, "a man without blame." Surely he did not say, "without sin"? For it is the thought which conceives sin. Blame, however, is only shown by an act. In addition, to be "without reproach" is attributed to someone according to the acquaintance and judgment of those for whom there is a readiness to see the gentleness in one's face but not to know the turbulence in one's heart. Hence, too, Paul decrees with assurance these words, "For a bishop must be without blame";[165] and in another passage he gives a testimony of universal application to the Corinthians, and asserts, "Thus, so that you are not lacking in any grace as you await the revelation of our Lord, Jesus Christ, who will also strengthen you to the very end without blame."[166] Observe this! Paul a little later rebukes in the same letter those very people whom he assures by his testimony that they are "without blame to the very end" when he writes, "Now, to be sure, there is fault in you because you have lawsuits with one another."[167] Thus, lo and behold, here we find under one title and referring to the very same persons the words "without blame" and "fault." Hence, he declares that those whom you would perceive to be designated "without blame" are not immediately asserted to be "without fault." For the Lord Jesus has also said, "John came neither eating nor drinking."[168] And again it has been written, "His nourishment was locusts and wild honey."[169] Are we really to believe on the basis of one or the other of these statements either that John had not eaten or that the Lord was mistaken? On the contrary, in both statements there is truth because

162. Job 1.8.
163. On the subject generally, see the interesting analysis by Augustine, *Contra duas epistolas Pelagianorum* 1.28.14.
164. Lk 1.6.
165. Tit 1.7.
166. 1 Cor 1.7–8.
167. 1 Cor 6.7.
168. Lk 7.33.
169. Mt 3.4.

John had taken some nourishment into the substance of his body, and, on the other hand, the Lord had spoken truly about John that he had not eaten what the rest had eaten nor with the rest. This proves that he and the Holy Scriptures reveal men's sentiments when the knowledge of God has often been hidden. Therefore it is obediently accepted that whenever Scripture mentions someone as "just and without blame," he is called so only within the confines of temporality and according to the judgments of men, not according to that final judgment of God, to whom the conscience of the entire world is subjected and "who should be confessed by every tongue."[170]

22. Lastly, understand this clearly: the justification of Job and the permission for afflictions to attack his body has, through the provident design of God, brought about the confusion of the insolent devil, so that, while man is being praised for honoring his Creator, with the Lord himself sanctioning it, the angel was punished while avoiding the stigma of faithlessness. On the other hand, however, in order not to do more serious injury to his servant while saving him and not to inflict a wound upon his soul while caring for his body—that is to say, in order not to allow the blessed Job to fall under the devil's judgment after he had overcome such a great trial, and after he had stood forth exalted and proud, when all of his possessions had been doubled and restored to him—Job is warned by his secret sins that he should know from within that, even if he was being praised from the outside for his righteousness, he ought to be submissive to him by whom he was being protected. For the Lord says to him, "Who is this who conceals counsel from me, confining words in his heart, and thinks to conceal them from me? Gird up your loins like a man! I shall question you, and you, answer me! Where were you when I established the earth? Tell me, if you have the knowledge."[171] And after much admonishment by instruction and much instruction by admonishment, Job, in response, said to the Lord, "Why am I judged, having been admonished and rebuked by the Lord: I hear such things, although I am nothing?"[172]

---

170. Rom 14.11. Cf. Isa 45.23; Phil 2.11.
171. Job 38.2–4 [LXX version].
172. Job 39.34 [LXX version].

(2) So also was the case of Zechariah, a man "without reproach," worthy of being honored by men, worthy, too, in the testimony of the Scriptures, who, as a result of this, as I think, was already being titillated by his swollen pride and was beginning to believe his fame more than his conscience, and therefore was reproved with the stigma of faithlessness by a chastising angel and punished with a temporary inability to speak.[173] Hence also Paul says, "Therefore, let him who thinks that he is standing take heed lest he fall."[174] And serving, so to speak, as a model for men, the same one proclaims about himself, saying, "I chastise my body and bring it into subjugation lest perhaps, when I have preached to others, I myself should become valueless."[175] Thus, to call anyone "without blame" and "without reproach" is not evidence of perfection, but an example of outward conduct.

23. Moreover, Scripture everywhere makes pronouncements concerning the "undefiled" person. As David says, "Blessed are the ones who are undefiled on the Way, who walk in the law of the Lord."[176] I am of the opinion that this has been stated through a sound doctrine because truly blessed are those who are undefiled in the Way; that is to say, those walking in truth with a perfect faith, not straying through heretical depravity, turning neither to the right nor to the left. Christ is the Way who leads us, through the Holy Spirit, to the Father. Therefore he who is without blemish and leprosy and who has not been desecrated by those "whose talk spreads like a cancer"[177] hears, believes, and understands the glory of the venerable Trinity and stands blessed and undefiled in his faith. For this reason also it is said to Abraham, "Walk before me and be without blemish."[178] For Abraham—"who believed God, and it was reckoned to him as righteousness"[179] so that he might be in him whom he believed, saw, and [in whom he] rejoiced—was necessarily exhorted to be perfect and without blemish, and was made "father of many nations"[180] in faith and also "bosom of the faithful,"[181] in order that we who, together with the

---

173. Cf. Lk 1.20, 1.22.
174. 1 Cor 10.12.
175. 1 Cor 9.27.
176. Ps 119.1.
177. 2 Tim 2.17.
178. Gen 17.1.
179. Gen 15.6. Cf. Rom 4.3, 4.22–23; Gal 3.6; Jas 2.23.
180. Gen 17.4–5; Rom 4.17–18.
181. Cf. Lk 16.22.

faithful Abraham, place our hopes in God may all be at rest. It is written, "Blessed are those undefiled in the Way."[182] For we walk by faith, not by sight."[183] But if you truly wish to hear about an undefiled individual, such as is sought by David when he is praying, put aside your vain reliance on your own power and, having prostrated yourself, join in prayers along with the entreaty of the prophet, lamenting side by side with him, saying, "Who understands sins? Cleanse me, Lord, of my secret ones and spare your servant from those of others. For if they do not take dominion over me, then shall I be undefiled."[184] When will I, a miserable man, avoid the sins which I as yet do not understand? Peter loved Christ and never turned away from this love. Now at one time, by the evidence of his love for the Lord, he was designated as the "rock" of the foundation of the Church;[185] but at another time he was disfigured by the name "Satan."[186] And on one occasion it was said to him, as he was invariably devoting himself to one and the same thing, "Flesh and blood has not revealed this to you, but my Father who is in heaven."[187] But then the following charge was leveled against him, "You do not comprehend the things which are of God, but rather those things which are of men."[188] Because of his love Peter was chosen as an apostle; because of his love he was refuted, sinning due to too great a love. For it was due to the impatience of his love that he said to the Lord, when the Lord was making known his suffering, "Be merciful to yourself, Lord; such a thing will not happen to you."[189]

24. O misery of wretched humans! If Peter sinned in his loving of Christ, then "who understands sins?"[190] The prophet cries out and cries out in the Holy Spirit; he cries out, the same man about whom the Lord has said, "My hand shall give him aid and my arm shall strengthen him, and the enemy shall accomplish nothing against him."[191] And pay close attention to what David cries out! "Cleanse me, Lord, of my secret ones."[192] That David,

---

182. Ps 119.1.
183. 2 Cor 5.7.
184. Ps 19.12–13.
185. Cf. Mt 16.18.
186. Cf. Mt 16.23.
187. Mt 16.17.
188. Mt 16.23.
189. Mt 16.22.
190. Ps 19.12.
191. Ps 89.21–22.
192. Ps 19.12.

who was chosen "after the heart"[193] [of God], to whom God promised that "he would fulfill all of God's wishes,"[194] whom God consecrated as king, upon whom he bestowed the blessing of a prophetic spirit; that man, stunned by the perverse surprise of his sins, cries out to the Lord and implores him that he might be cleansed of his secret sins. And in another passage, the Lord says to him, "You shall not build a house to my name because you are a man of war and have shed blood,"[195] as if God were indeed unable to cleanse him by the abolition of all of his stains in order to make him deserving of this worthy undertaking! Even up to his death, David was not cleansed, and, with his son having been preferred over him for the construction of the Temple, he condemned himself. And now this "Goliath" together with his armorbearer falsely accuses me[196] that the Lord does not do in his particular case what he has never done before in the world! And Ecclesiastes says, "There is nothing new under the sun, nor is anyone able to say, 'Behold, this is a new thing.' For it has occurred already in the ages which were before us."[197] And this teacher of new doctrines maintains that what has never happened can happen! You do not inquire whether something has been, because you have no doubt that it can! God wished that a house be built to his name and that it be well-constructed by no one except an upright and undefiled person. Two kings with all virtues were chosen for this end: each one for the purpose of helping, and to each a promise was made concerning his responsibility. On the subject of David, God indeed says, "My truth and my mercy are with him."[198] And about Solomon it is truly affirmed, "I have chosen him to be a son to me, and I will be a father to him."[199] Of these two, one made preparations for the Temple of the Lord; the other built it. The older man made the preparations; the younger carried them through.[200] For it is fitting that a holy individual should build the

---

193. 1 Sam 13.14. Cf. Acts 13.22.   194. Acts 13.22.
195. 1 Chr 28.3.
196. Again, a reference to Pelagius and one of his chief supporters (see chapter 2 above).
197. Eccl 1.9–10.   198. Ps 89.24.
199. 1 Chr 28.6.
200. Orosius employs the words *senex* and *puer*. Although I have translated them here as "older man" and "younger man" to denote the chronological rela-

holy Temple of the Lord. The older man made the preparations, as I have said, but ceased to sin, as it were, only from that point onwards; the younger carried the preparations through, but one might say it was only at that time that he did not begin to sin. The older man sinned previous to his task; the younger, following his task. David did not deserve to build the Temple because of his great sin, while Solomon neglected what he had built because of his great sinning. And during this time God's holy ordinance miraculously arranged that what could not be permanent in man would be found between these two lifetimes by virtue of God's seizing hold of time itself. Each of these two did not sin at a particular time; nevertheless, each was not able to be without sin. "Let God be true, though every man is a liar, as it is written."[201] "The sons of men are but illusions; the sons of men are but liars in the balances."[202]

25. Although they certainly possessed the grace and the assistance of God, nevertheless, neither could David attain a state of being sinless nor was Solomon strong enough to keep it. And this "son of Jovinian"[203] hopes that the omnipotent God will change such a great order of things for him and his followers! And if such, perhaps, should not happen, would he then accuse God of being impotent? "A person is able," Pelagius says, "to be without sin, yet with the assistance of God." What am I to do? I, for my part, will tolerate for the time being this new scrap garment sewn together from an old rag[204] until a worse tear discloses the falsity of this wretched emendation. For I concede that when

---

tionships subsequently emphasized by the author, the former clearly has the connotation of "father" or "head of the family" while the latter can mean "son."

201. Rom 3.4. Cf. Jn 3.33; Ps 116.11.

202. Ps 62.9.

203. A monk from Milan and erstwhile opponent of Orosius's mentors, Jerome and Augustine, Jovinian aroused controversy in the late fourth century by arguing for a spiritual equality of Christians regardless of one's sexual and matrimonial status. He was eventually condemned by church councils at Rome and Milan. Orosius's pointed reference here, unfortunately, does not reveal what link he hoped to establish between Pelagius and Jovinian. Cf. also the reference in chapter 1.

204. Cf. Tertullian's use of this language vis-à-vis Marcion: *Adversus Marcionem* 4.11.

he said, "A person is able if he wishes"—in opposition to our guide of spoken truth—Pelagius appeared to have said, "A person is able with the assistance of God." Now at last, I must return to the beginning of my proposition, just as in a sermon, and for a short time, having put aside the distress caused by the injustice done to me, we must with reverence in the disputing have recourse to the very height of authority. For our authority is Christ Jesus, "whom," as the Apostle says, "God has set forth as an atonement through faith in his blood to show his righteousness, for the remission of previous sins, through the forbearance of God and the showing of his righteousness in this time, so that he himself may be righteous and be justifying the one who is of the faith of Jesus."[205] Thus, the one who atones through faith by his blood, who is placed to show and represent righteousness, that very one is "mediator between God and humans, the man Christ Jesus!"[206] About him John, after he has been brought into that all but "inaccessible light,"[207] proclaims, "In the beginning was the Word, and the Word was with God, and the Word was God. He was in the beginning with God. All things were made through him."[208] And after that, following a brief section explaining the truth of divine operation, he adds, "And the Word was made flesh and dwelt among us, and we have seen his glory, the glory as it were of the one and only Son of the Father, full of grace and truth."[209] He "who did not commit sin, nor was deceit found in his mouth";[210] who, "like the lamb in the presence of its shearer, not opening its mouth"[211] when he was scourged, crucified, and died; who conquered the sting of death; who arose from the dead; "who, making captivity itself a captive, ascended into heaven":[212] this one is the only-begotten Son in the Father, "the first-born amongst many brothers,[213] in whom the whole fullness of divinity exists corporeally."[214] This one, therefore, is the Lord Christ. This one, I say, is the Son of God, in the

---

205. Rom 3.25–26.
206. 1 Tim 2.5.
207. 1 Tim 6.16.
208. Jn 1.1–3.
209. Jn 1.14.
210. 1 Pet 2.22. Cf. Isa 53.9.
211. Isa 53.7; Acts 8.32. Cf. Mt 26.63.
212. Eph 4.8.
213. Rom 8.29.
214. Col 2.9.

power and the glory of the Father. And that which he established in the beginning and redeemed in the midst of time he will also judge in the end.

26. And so, after the foundation of the universe, which came into existence according to his will, God imposed certain limits on the elements of his well-ordered creation so that what had been created as a rational thing should abide by reason, and what he had endowed with free will would be restrained by the command of his law lest it should rush into ruinous, uncontrolled liberty. And when the created human being was recognizing its Creator and appreciating the stability of his order as the gift of the Lord, having fallen into slavery [to sin] and looking ahead to freedom, he would wish to use this very freedom only for this: that through this servitude by which he was reined in, he might choose through a judgment worthy of his nature, that he might merit a defense out of his experience of servitude and a reward by reason of his free will. This is confirmed by the Apostle who says, "For if I do this willingly, I have a reward."[215] The almighty God said, "Let there be two great lights,"[216] and they came into existence. And he ordered that they separate day from night and that they serve as signs for seasons, for days, and for years. And once this demarcation had been decreed, has it not persisted to the present day? And yet, the very things which were being carried out through this ordained plan the Creator had the power to change when he wished, provided that reason did not prevent him; since in all things, reason is linked to the power of God. For, if an alteration in his works was effected by the Creator, how could it be possible to expect observance of his commands from his creature? It was ordered by God that "the earth should bring forth grass, hay, and the fruit-bearing tree."[217] This is even now regularly observed each year through unceasing labor. And yet, God, having been angered very frequently, diminished the fruits of the earth by denying an abundance of rain; he preferred to punish that which he could totally destroy, in order that this stroke might demonstrate his reproach and that nature

---

215. 1 Cor 9.17.
217. Gen 1.11.

216. Gen 1.14, 1.16.

might maintain its orderliness. "God made man from the mud of the earth,"[218] made him come alive by breathing life-giving spirit into him, and placed him in "a paradise of delights."[219] In addition, God endowed him with freedom of will and confined him by his command between death and everlasting life. Yet your followers, who have sucked forth vast amounts of poison from your breast, claim that man was created mortal and that no harm had touched him as a result of his transgression of the command. But, in fact, because of man's sinning, the earth is cursed and man himself is heavily burdened with toils and sorrows, so that he is ordered to obtain his bread by the sweat of his face and is constrained by the stigma of death until he returns to that earth from which he was taken.[220] Adam was expelled from Paradise and he begat sons[221] who still carry with them the original sin of their unfaithful progenitor. And so the human race sins. God even regretted that he had made mankind on the earth.[222]

27. O Lord, sustain for a short while my folly until he who appears to himself as wise and thoughtful feels shame and becomes aware of his thoughtlessness! As a result of one man's sin, from which a dreadful contagion was carried to all generations and the rule of death prevailed over all, you have sorrow, you feel anger, you are afflicted by grief, and you are moved by emotion as long as the Word made flesh still had before him the passion, the cross, and death. Perhaps it would have been better for that one sinner to be destroyed then and there, and for another one to be substituted shortly thereafter through a second creation, from whom the offspring would descend free from every stain and undefiled! Almighty God, are we to believe that because we know you did not do this, you were not able to do it? You, O Peter, that rock upon which Christ founded his Church,[223] and you, O Paul, who has laid the foundation, which is Christ, beyond which no one can lay any other:[224] you, O blessed apostles, the pillars and mainstays of truth, you at least respond with holy words to this man [Pelagius], who is God's counselor and mediator! Peter

---

218. Gen 2.7.
219. Gen 2.8.
220. Cf. Gen 3.17–19.
221. Cf. Gen 3.23–24, 4.
222. Cf. Gen 6.6.
223. Cf. Mt 16.18.
224. Cf. 1 Cor 3.11.

says, "Blessed be the God and Father of our Lord Jesus Christ, who, by his great mercy, has given us a new birth into the hope of life through the resurrection from the dead of our Lord Jesus Christ, to an inheritance that cannot be corrupted and defiled, reserved in heaven for you who are being protected by the power of God through faith for a salvation ready to be revealed in the last time."[225] Then Paul, "the vessel of election,"[226] offers the treasures of salvation, and says, "Blessed be the God and Father of our Lord Jesus Christ, who has blessed us with every spiritual blessing in the heavenly places, in Christ, just as he chose us in him before the foundation of the world, so that we should be holy and undefiled in his sight in love; by this he predestined us for adoption as children through Jesus Christ to himself, according to the purpose of his will; to the praise of his glory in which he has accorded grace to us in the Beloved, in whom we have redemption through his blood, the remission of sins, according to the riches of his grace, which he lavished upon us in all wisdom and prudence so that he might make known to us the mystery of his will, according to his good pleasure, which he arranged in him in the dispensation of the fullness of time, to restore in Christ all things which are in heaven and which are on earth."[227]

28. Peter says, "for a salvation ready to be revealed in the last time"; and Paul testifies, "which he offered in him to the dispensation of the fullness of time, to renew all things in Christ." And now a certain someone emerges like a frog from out of the mud and loudly croaks, "Why should I wait for the proper time? Why should I wait for the Judgment? If God is able, he is always able; if he is always able, then he does not have unjust regard of people." He, therefore, does have the power and in a certain way is able, and truly ought to be esteemed by you as someone who has unjust regard of people if what he can do in the case of all and what he is inevitably going to do in his own time, God did in your case alone before the allotted time what he did not do in the case of Moses, who was reproached for what was merely a single sin in this life. And yet, only before his death was he forgiven; and this

225. 1 Pet 1.3–5.
226. Acts 9.15.
227. Eph 1.3–10.

was the man who, because of this guilt, was ordered to die lest he enter the Promised Land.[228] Let him therefore listen to Solomon who is testifying concerning the orderly regulation of the seasons and God's arrangement of them, "All things have a season, and everything under heaven proceeds in its own time: a time to be born, and a time to die; a time to plant and a time to pluck out what has been planted; a time to kill and a time to heal."[229] Then, in another passage, he says, "I saw under the sun in place of justice, wickedness; and in place of righteousness, iniquity. And I said in my heart, 'God shall judge both the righteous and the wicked and then there shall be a time for every matter.'"[230] Therefore, O vain man, if you have such confidence, patiently await the order of God which was considered worthy and for which the Lord himself, who made it, waited. "He was made subject to the law,"[231] who had made the law. Listen to him speaking to you, "It is not for you to know the times which the Father has set in his own power."[232] Or, if you are willing to accept a more open testimony, that when God has the power, nevertheless, he does not act on his own behalf, he says to Peter, "Do you really think that I cannot just ask my Father, and he will furnish me with more than twelve legions of angels? But how then shall the Scriptures be fulfilled, that it must be thus?"[233] You see, therefore, that he who created time restrains his powers, and the principle of his plan for the world allows him to mix patience with power. Next the Lord says, "Put your sword back in the sheath. For it cannot be that I shall not drink that cup which the Father has given to me."[234] And yet there is nothing God cannot do, nor is there anything that God does not do, unless perhaps that which he does not wish to do, or that which it is not proper to do, or that which he does not propose to do. Paul speaks to the Thessalonians, pointing out the coming of the Antichrist: "Do you

---

228. It is probable that Orosius, after the fashion of other patristic authors (Origen, Basil, Augustine, et al.), here attributes the death of Moses outside the Promised Land to the lack of faith shown at Meribah (cf. Num 20.10–12). Also, cf. Deut 34.4.
229. Eccl 3.1–3. 230. Eccl 3.16–17.
231. Gal 4.4.   232. Acts 1.7.
233. Mt 26.53–54. 234. Jn 18.11.

not remember that when I was still with you, I used to tell you these things? And now you know what is restraining him, so that he may be revealed in his proper time."[235] Such is the power of God's decree, and so irrevocable is the order of things which have been instituted, each one in its own circumstance and its own time, that the Lord said for the sake of his own elect that the days of the present age were shortened, but not taken away altogether, so that he might bring to pass the fullness of established time in accordance with his majesty and this shortening of time in accordance with his goodness, and so that, simultaneously, he by his mercy might undertake the abridgment of the days and the world might complete its number of days.[236] And now you want—alas, I speak with the anguish of pity!—I repeat, you, a man as I am, want people in this present age to respond to something never before found stated in the holy writings: that any person is without sin. And if, by chance, they have agreed on this point, you want them to endorse such on this very day and at this very moment! You are constructing here a new stratagem of sophistry, in order that we appear to have said that what we say does not happen, could not happen. And by this we proclaim that his omnipotence is especially operative in that arrangement which he established, lest we in our impatience be judged to be indicting God with impotence.[237] Cast aside, I beg you, that vain madness, since this very thing contributes to sin, and by abolishing the authority of time, you seem not to have been thinking of the clemency of the Judge!

(2) Let this, which has been said so far about the power of God, power which we proclaim and honor, and also about the predetermination of times which have been set by the most profound design of God himself, suffice. Concerning this, even if there were no more writings of the saints, at least the response of the demons alone, who cry out to the Lord from their consciousness of being condemned, would suffice: "What have you to do with us, Son of God? Why have you come to harm us before the

---

235. 2 Thess 2.5–6.
236. Cf. Mt 24.22.
237. Again, note the alliteration: *ne inpatienter infamare inpotentiam iudicemur.*

DEFENSE AGAINST THE PELAGIANS   157

time?"[238] When you acknowledge that they are admitting that judgment has been determined by God, then take this most unambiguous illustration of that judgment against yourself. If you realize that those were caught in the midst of oppressing the wretched man and then condemned to final judgment,[239] then accept the fact that even you yourself have to be cleansed by that imperturbable cleansing. If, however, as one reads, God's sufferance grants people free will up to this very day, believe that also you must be tested up to this very day!

29. Now I move on briefly to another argument which you are said to hurl often against all Catholics. For even now in that letter of yours,[240] contrived, so it would seem, very late at night,[241] there are things that we can scarcely understand! For I say that you, "a most honorable man," did not blush to write such things to a girl, Demetrias, who I hear is consecrated to God and saintly, teaching her, so I believe, a reverence for chastity as depicted in the story of Joseph and his lustful mistress.[242] When you said, "Having been rebuffed several times, his mistress now sets her traps even nearer to the young man; in secret and with no witnesses she lays her hands upon him shamelessly,"[243] you were weaving an inappropriate tale with most obscene wording![244] And yet, we ought not to hold against you this tale, which is here expressed neither appropriately nor properly in manner, since

---

238. Mt 8.29.
239. Here Orosius appears to incorporate elements of the parallel stories found in Mk 5.1–17 and Lk 8.26–37 where one man, not two, is possessed by demons.
240. Pelagius's well-known *Epistula ad Demetriadem*, written in late 413 or early 414, was the famed teacher's response to the young Demetrias's consecration as a Christian virgin. Beyond that, it represented a sort of manual of instruction for consecrated virgins everywhere; indeed, it was later circulated anonymously and eventually aroused the concern of Augustine. Composed in a rather florid style (at least for Pelagius), it proposed central tenets of asceticism appropriate for such a clientele. Moreover, for the modern scholar, it provides valuable insight into Pelagius's doctrines of nature and grace.
241. *Lucubratissima.* This can be taken either as a compliment or, as is more common in rhetoric usage (and here), an insult.
242. Cf. Gen 39.
243. *Ep. ad Demetriadem* 5.
244. It may be noted that the story, as recorded by Pelagius, is no more risqué than this in either its later or earlier sections.

the circumstances of your birth have not made it possible for you to be enlightened through more honorable studies,[245] nor does it turn out that you have good sense naturally. We should rather lay the charge against those scribes of yours who commit to writing such pitiful thoughts in most pitiful language and put you in the position of being read with derisive laughter, as if creating a reputation for confusion. Meanwhile, then, in that same letter with undigested language, you disgorged[246] the following kind of sentiment: that the majority of us [Catholics] assert that God has constructed an evil nature for man.[247] This is also the charge that your man Phinehas[248] cautiously attempted to lay at our feet. Therefore, I will first briefly make my declaration; then I will reply to this charge. May he not be worthy to stand before Christ's tribunal among the lambs of God at his right hand[249] and may he not deserve to see either the Lord "in the land of the living,"[250] or, in the glory of the resurrection, "the life of Jesus made manifest in his mortal body"[251] who says God has made nature evil, whether of a man or of anything whatsoever, or who eliminates the possibility of free will in anyone, when he has read what has been written, "All that God made at any time is exceedingly good."[252] And it has been written about man's free will, "God created man imperishable"[253] and "left him in the hand of his own counsel."[254] O blind and wicked man—for I am unable to speak to you in any other manner, since you do not have the understanding to perceive the Lord's authority, nor the awareness of

---

245. This is a common charge by the opponents of Pelagius, perhaps based in part on his British provincial origins, in part on his lack of clerical status, and in part on the standard rhetorical usages of the day.

246. Here Orosius almost certainly hopes that his audience will choose the more literal and graphic of the two types of meaning for the language he has chosen. The key words are *indigestis* ("physically undigested" or "confused") and *eructasti* ("vomit/disgorge" or "bring forth/declare").

247. Cf. *Ep. ad Demetriadem* 3.

248. Perhaps an allusion to the supporter of Pelagius described in chapter 2, based on the story of the wicked sons of the priest Eli (cf. 1 Sam 1, 2, 4). In this case, Pelagius would be identified with Hophni, and his supporter with Phinehas.

249. Cf. Mt 25.33–34.
250. Ps 116.9.
251. 2 Cor 4.11.
252. Sir 39.16. Cf. Gen 1.31.
253. Wis 2.23.
254. Sir 15.14.

your own frailty, nor a capacity for common sense!—we say that man's nature is weak, not evil. For if it were evil, it would not be capable of good in any circumstances. But now, since man by his natural disposition ardently longs for the good and clings to this good and flees altogether from evil, where in that nature do we have to say that there is an evil essence? The Lord proclaims, "The spirit indeed is willing, but the flesh is weak."[255] Abraham cries out, "I am but earth and ashes."[256] Job declares, "Man is corruption and the son of man is a worm."[257] Isaiah cries, "Woe is me since I have been afflicted because, since I am a man and have unclean lips, I dwell in the midst also of a people who have unclean lips."[258] Jeremiah exclaims, "The soul in anguish and the troubled spirit cry out to you. See, O Lord, and have mercy."[259] Habakkuk declares, "I have watched myself and my stomach became greatly frightened at the sound of the prayers, and within me my condition was disturbed."[260] David cries, "Hear me in your righteousness and do not enter into judgment with your servant, for in your sight no living thing will be declared righteous."[261] All the apostles, roused by the fear of their frailty, call out, "Lord, save us, we are perishing!"[262] John proclaims, "If we say that we have no sin, we deceive ourselves and the truth is not in us."[263] James declares, "For in many things we all offend."[264] Paul cries forth, "Unhappy man that I am! Who shall deliver me from the body of this death? The grace of God through Jesus Christ our Lord."[265] And just as generally the weakness of all mankind calls out, so the Holy Spirit among the holy ones[266] proclaims, "All flesh is grass and the glory of man is as the flower of the grass. The grass withers, the flower wilts. But the word of the Lord endures into eternity."[267]

255. Mt 26.41.
256. Gen 18.27.
257. Job 25.6.
258. Isa 6.5.
259. Bar 3.1–2.
260. Hab 3.16 [LXX version].
261. Ps 143.1–2.
262. Mt 8.25.
263. 1 Jn 1.8.
264. Jas 3.2.
265. Rom 7.24–25.
266. A reference either to the prophets (such as Isaiah) or the people of Judah whom God calls his own in Isa 40.1.
267. Isa 40.6, 40.8.

30. Against such splendid and lucid clouds of divine testimonies, let the entire world who toil amidst their own lamentations hear Pelagius as he loudly cries out in protest and struggles against the humble truth, not only through the imprudence of his spoken words but also through the red-hot irons of his writings! For he says in that letter which we cited above, "But, on the contrary, with a casual and disdainful spirit, in the manner of good-for-nothing and haughty slaves, we protest and declare in the face of the Lord, 'It is hard, it is difficult, we are not able; we are but men, we are clothed in frail flesh.' What blind insanity! And what impious boldness! We accuse the Lord of a twofold lack of knowledge, so that he appears not to know what he has done, nor know what he has commanded! And, as if forgetful of the human frailty of which he himself is the author, he has imposed on man that which he cannot bear!"[268] What, I ask, is more deadly than this presumption? What is more depraved than this reprimand of God? You are blaming the Catholic Church, of which we are the heart, because it appears as if it is saying in despair that God, the author of man, has imposed on man something which he cannot bear. Nevertheless, the Church professes most faithfully, both by its lips and by its humbleness that God, in the first place, has commanded that all things are possible and yet, for all that, with no one fulfilling those things which may be done—for which reason the entire universe was subject to God—thereafter he lightened the burden of his command by the substitution of the favor of his grace. But even so, you evil and wicked slave, you who attempt to remove from your fellow slaves that which your Lord has forgiven you,[269] first there will be a discussion of your idea; and next, if you please, I will explain mine. You who argue that some have said that the burden of the law cannot be borne—do you, then, have confidence in yourself to be able to bear it? O wretched man, you who say in your heart according to what has been written, "'I am rich, and I have been enriched, and I have need of nothing;' and you do not realize

---

268. *Ep. ad Demetriadem* 16. Pelagius echoes this section on human complaints about the severity of divine law in his *Ep. ad Celantiam* 15.
269. Cf. Mt 18.32–33.

DEFENSE AGAINST THE PELAGIANS   161

that you are wretched and miserable and poor and blind and naked."[270] Has not Christ told you, "Amen, I say to you; flesh and blood has not revealed it to you, but my Father who is in heaven"?[271] Has he not said to you, "You shall be called Cephas"?[272] Has he not promised to you, "Upon this rock I shall found my Church"?[273] Well then, listen carefully to what the apostle Peter, with the Holy Spirit teaching him, counsels, saying, "And now, therefore, why are you tempting God to put on the neck of the disciples a yoke which neither our fathers nor we ourselves have been able to bear. But by the grace of our Lord Jesus Christ we believe that we will be able to be saved, in the same way as they also."[274] Peter, the apostle, says that he who now makes efforts to impose the burden of the law on man truly tempts God. But, unlike Peter, you charge and state menacingly that he is accusing God of injustice who, through confession of his own weakness, takes refuge in the grace of the Spirit from the letter which is crushing him. Samuel, Elijah, Elisha, Isaiah, Jeremiah, Daniel, Zechariah, all the holy ones, either judges or kings or prophets, are without doubt our fathers, and Peter affirms that none of the fathers, not even the apostles themselves when they were Jews, were able to bear the burden of the law, but that they had been saved by faith in Christ, in keeping with the promise of grace.

31. Can it really be possible, as you say, that all of these holy fathers did not have the assistance of God? Look here, Peter rebukes those who were trying to impose a heavy yoke on the neck of the disciples! You, on the contrary, despite the obstacle of Peter, are rebuking those who flee to the constant mercy of God and despair of bearing the burden of the law by themselves as individuals. But perhaps you have some special self-confidence for the carrying of that burden because you have been nurtured on baths and sumptuous feasts.[275] You have broad shoulders and a

---

270. Rev 3.17.
271. Mt 16.17.
272. Jn 1.42.
273. Mt 16.18.
274. Acts 15.10–11.

275. A common mode of attack on Pelagius by enemies such as Jerome and Orosius, since Pelagius's reputation among many Christians, especially those at Rome, was that of an ascetic.

strong neck,[276] even now displaying your portliness before you,[277] as it is written, "For he has stretched out his hand against God and has been strengthened against the Almighty. He has run against him with his neck held up, and is armed with a fat neck. Fatness has covered his face, and the fat hangs down on his sides."[278] But those men, to whom Christ speaks always in their heart, are not able to be of such a character! "Strive to enter through the narrow passage;[279] for it is the wide one which leads to death."[280] And the Apostle Paul advises, "Give no care to the flesh in its desires.[281] The truth of Christ is in me because I suffer much sorrow for you."[282] For, according to my blessed father Augustine, self-confidence is characteristic not of a sane person, but of an insane person. If you consider it worthy, I put a question to you concerning a single precept which is at the same time the first precept. In the law the Lord orders through Moses, what also Christ affirms in the Gospels, "You shall love the Lord your God with all your heart and with all your soul and with all your might;"[283] and a second precept which is similar to this, "You shall love your neighbor as you yourself."[284] I ask you, and answer not to me, but to God; answer not with your voice, but with your conscience! Do you love God with all your heart in such a way that you never admit any thought concerning him which can be understood apart from the fear and love of God? Do you follow him with all your soul in such a way that once the cross has been

---

276. *Robustamque cervicem.* Perhaps Orosius here wishes his readers to associate Pelagius with the more figurative meanings: "haughty head, obstinacy, stubbornness, pride."

277. On the subject of Pelagius's appearance generally, Rees's comment (*Pelagius*, p. xii) is helpful: "The pen-pictures contributed by his contemporaries, who can hardly claim to be objective, leave us with little more than an indication that he must have had a distinct tendency to obesity . . . Due allowance must obviously be made for the extravagance of theological polemic."

278. Job 15.25–27.

279. Lk 13.24. Cf. Mt 7.13–14.

280. Mt 7.13. The implications of these two scriptural precepts for Pelagius, at least from the perspective of Orosius, are obvious.

281. Rom 13.14. Cf. Gal 5.16.   282. Cf. 2 Cor 11.10; Rom 9.1–2.

283. Deut 6.5.

284. Lev 19.18. Together these two precepts represent in the synoptic Gospels the basis for, and a summary of, Mosaic law. Cf. Mt 22.36–40; Mk 12.28–34; Lk 10.25–28.

DEFENSE AGAINST THE PELAGIANS 163

taken up, you do not at all succumb to any delight in having even a temporary pleasure? Do you burn in all your innermost being with such a fever of charity that you do not find comfort at all in passions or desires through any feeble arguments of "necessity," since in that case it has been written, "All which is not of faith is sin"?[285] And, if you have consorted with bishops of famous places[286] or powerful men of the world[287] or if you meet the rich under the pretext of religious observances,[288] do you not indulge at all in any obsequious flattery, or in apprehension, or in anticipation when you have been captivated by the approval of important personages, or anything for which your heart may rebuke you and your conscience may constantly vex you? Or do you not respond to questions with words better suited to the occasion than to the truth?[289] I also ask you this: do you love all Christians as much as you love yourself? For we are all brothers under one head, which is Christ, and under one Church, which is Christ; and we are one body in Christ. Confess, therefore, whether you love as you love yourself all those whom you nevertheless know, those who hope for the mercy of God. For I do not ask you about strangers, whom for that very reason you imagine yourself as loving, because, since you do not know them, you do not hate them. But why do I call for such things from your confession when the populace is acquainted with your conduct? You perfect man without any weakness! You who are capable of enduring the entire burden of the law! I say, you conceit-filled but empty man! Listen, if you deem it worthy, to the Lord Savior calling upon you to return to sanctity if you are still able, "Amen, I say to you, whosoever does not receive the kingdom of God as a little child, shall not enter it."[290] A little child has nothing within himself,

---

285. Rom 14.23.
286. Certainly a reference to Pelagius's "protector," Bishop John of Jerusalem.
287. Pelagius's cordial relations with a number of the leading families of Rome, including the Anicians, were well known.
288. Perhaps a veiled accusation of the type that Jerome himself had endured: that some of his associations with the rich of Rome, especially wealthy women, were improper. Here it is possibly directed toward Pelagius's association with Demetrias and her family.
289. Another common rhetorical insult of the time.
290. Mk 10.15.

except that he loves the person who soothes him, and he obtains his bread not through his own toil, but through his entreaties, hoping for the nourishment of life through a simple request which he does not merit through work which can be trusted. Inasmuch as you have been admonished by this comparison, return to childhood so that you may return to life!

32. And since I have made a statement above concerning the possibility of bearing the burden [of God's law], first there will be a discussion of your ideas and afterwards, if you please, I will explain mine. It is my conviction that we also sin in this: since we are weak, we complain about our weakness.[291] As the Apostle says, "Shall that which has been formed say to him who formed it, 'Why have you formed me in this way?'"[292] For a complaint about weakness represents a striving for one's own strength, since one who strives for his own strength is secretly scorning God's assistance. And now it is this devil who says, "I shall accomplish it through my own powers." But, for my part, following the Apostle, "I will always glory in my weaknesses,"[293] so that my heart may always say to God, "Under the cover of your wings I shall rejoice; my soul clings to you; your right hand has supported me."[294] Whence it is written, "Let your petitions become known before God and may the peace of God which surpasses all understanding guard your hearts and bodies in Christ Jesus."[295] Accordingly, I possess weakness and I rejoice in the recognition of my own weakness. "For when I am weak, then I am powerful"[296] by invoking the powerful God, who hears me who is weak, and has promised us again with every assurance, "I am, indeed, with you all the days until the end of the world."[297] It is the special task of weakness, always and everywhere, to pray that almighty God, who has promised not to desert us, does not cease also from helping us. For, you see, Scripture proclaims to those who are weak, "Seek the Lord and be strengthened; seek his countenance evermore."[298] To this a pious

---

291. At this point in the text, all of the manuscripts insert lengthy passages from Augustine's *De natura et gratia contra Pelagium*. These have been deleted from the Orosian text by most editors, including Zangemeister.

292. Rom 9.20.
293. 2 Cor 12.9.
294. Ps 63.7–8.
295. Phil 4.6–7.
296. 2 Cor 12.10.
297. Mt 28.20.
298. Ps 105.4.

and true confession has answered, "Behold, just as the eyes of servants are on the hands of their lords, so our eyes are toward the Lord our God until he has mercy on us."[299] Great and sure is our confidence based on perfection, when the Almighty does what the weak one prays for. And again, great and sure is our security based on confirmation, when the Almighty preserves and does not destroy those who are weak, just as it is written, "Now to him who is able to accomplish all things more abundantly than we seek and imagine in accordance with the power which he works within us; to him be glory in Christ Jesus."[300] Therefore, the Apostle urges us, "Set your minds on the things which are above, not on the things which are on the earth. For you have died and your life is hidden with Christ in God. When Christ who is your life has appeared, then you also will appear with him in glory."[301] The reward of life is sanctity, and truly sanctity means being without sin. Thus, if the glory of incorruptibility has been hidden from all men in this time, how do you, in this very same age, boast that you are able to be clothed with that very same incorruptibility? For just as sinking into sin has become for man the beginning of corruption, so, not having sin will be the beginning of incorruption. Who, therefore, concealed this prior to the judgment of God, or removed it from the bosom of Christ and handed it over to you? Or do you perhaps think that a person would not merit this in the future from the hand of the Lord? That most distinguished man, Paul, teaches this and says, "But when this mortal thing has put on immortality then shall come to pass the saying which is written, 'Death has been swallowed up in victory. Where, O death, is your victory? Where, O death, is your sting?' Now, the sting of death is sin."[302] Through this the Apostle shows that by no means can anyone so scoff at death and sin, until immortality follows mortality, and incorruption, corruption and when, with the destruction of weakness, perfect virtue succeeds it; when there will not be male and female, but when all will be similar to the angels of God. Furthermore, if someone has already risen to such a great

---

299. Ps 123.2   300. Eph 3.20–21.
301. Col 3.2–4.
302. 1 Cor 15.54–56. For the internal quotations, cf. Isa 25.8 and Hos 13.14.

pinnacle of sanctity that, while living in this flesh, he does not know whether he is a male or a female; if, having already obtained fullest purity for himself, he does not have sin-stained clothing and is similar to the angels of God; and if he is already surrounded by that brightness, like that of the sun, which has been promised to the saints, then he lays claim to that perfection in a fitting manner, not by his words, but by his character. But even so, such a presumption is pure folly. In fact it is more profitable for a man of this kind to listen to and follow, not his own heart, but rather, Paul, the teacher of the nations; and that at the same time he pray together with him so that the Lord may answer his prayer thus: "My grace is sufficient for you; indeed, power is made perfect in weakness."[303]

33. Accordingly, let each one of us offer himself to God as volunteered land, because this alone results in free will and in this alone free will can go forward. "For we are God's husbandry; we are God's edifice."[304] Let him throw into his field the seed, the Word; let it grow[305] in one's heart; let the same one plant, let him water, let him fertilize; but let him who is the true cultivator bestow growth![306] And as for that which voluntary devotion within us can but accomplish, let each one of us faithfully assist by keeping within himself the root of the seed, and by nourishing its abundant offspring; let each of us always awaken the cultivator by our prayers to him, so that an enemy is unable to sow weeds upon the good seed.[307] Let this be each one's collaboration in the work of God, with hope undoubting and love sincere. For the Lord Jesus says, "I am the vine; you are the branches."[308] Whatever anyone has, he has from the vine. The Apostle says, "For you do not support the root, but the root supports you."[309] Why, therefore, does anyone extol himself on the basis of the fruits which seem to be within him, since everything depends on the vine, not only insofar as he is able [to accomplish], but also

---

303. 2 Cor 12.9.
304. 1 Cor 3.9.
305. Here I have adopted the textual variant, *crescat*, (cf. Zangemeister's *credat*) as more in keeping with Orosius's imagery.
306. Cf. 1 Cor 3.6–8.   307. Cf. Mt 13.25.
308. Jn 15.5.   309. Rom 11.18.

insofar as he exists? Otherwise, "it shall be cut down and cast into the fire."[310] For it is not the branch, but the vine that is able, and the branch only shows what the vine is able to do. It is therefore sufficient for each person that he merely possesses; and, to be sure, it is that he knows from what source and when he possesses which lets him both humbly realize and patiently wait, lest "while he does not have, but believes he has, that very thing which he has, be taken away from him."[311] God expelled the first man because of his sinning from Paradise; then, as the first man came to believe in the cross, Christ led him into Paradise. With good cause, therefore, as long as I am not in Paradise and I remain on the earth of Adam's sojourn, I do not believe that I am without sin. If, however, I am brought over into Paradise by God's grace, once also death has been conquered and my sin wiped away, then and there I shall proclaim in my perfection in the presence of God the eternal glory of his power.

(2) Most reverend fathers, I have related these points as best I could in order to promote faith and honesty. Let those who have caused wrongs not be angry at me if they are named during the course of our comparative discussions. Rather, let them bear calmly the examinations and, if they have fear of God, let them rather rejoice that the answer which has been given is that which is true! As Jesus Christ is my witness, I profess that I hate heresy, not the heretic; but, as is proper, for the present I shun the heretic because of the heresy, since I have both convicted and rebuked him. Let him renounce his heresy and condemn it by word as well as by deed, and he will cling[312] to all men by the bond of brotherhood, because it is written, "Bear each other's burdens and in this way you shall fulfill the law of Christ."[313]

---

310. Mt 3.10.
311. Mt 13.12, 25.29.
312. *Haerebit.* Effective contrast with his earlier use of *haeresim* and *haereticum.*
313. Gal 6.2.

OROSIUS'S INQUIRY OR MEMORANDUM[1] TO AUGUSTINE ON THE ERROR OF THE PRISCILLIANISTS AND ORIGENISTS

ROSIUS TO THE MOST BLESSED FATHER Augustine, bishop.

1. I had, indeed, broached the subject to your Holiness earlier, but even then I was intending to present a memorandum on the subject I spoke of—once I was aware that you had been freed from other matters demanding your attention.[2] Since my masters, your sons, the bishops Eutropius and Paul,[3] were motivated by the same concern for the salvation of all people as I, your child, and have already furnished a memorandum concerning several heresies, though they did not indicate them all, it was necessary for me promptly to reveal and gather into a pile all the trees of perdition, with their roots and branches, and offer them to your ardent spirit,[4] so that, after you had seen their array and contemplated their evil, you might measure exactly what disposition of virtue you can employ. You, most blessed father, just remove and cut down the evil plantings[5] or grafts of the

---

1. While Orosius refers to his treatise throughout as a "memorandum" (*commonitorium*), Augustine in his *Retractationes* II.44 (70) terms it an "inquiry" (*consultatio*). The present editor, Daur, includes both in the title.
2. As Daur and others have noted, this was an especially busy time in Augustine's life as a theologian and writer. In his letter to Evodius, dated to 415, he lists several important works with which he was involved during this period. They included *De civitate Dei* and *De Trinitate*.
3. The hierarchy, to Orosius's mind, is here clearly established: he the priest; his fellow Iberians, the bishops Eutropius and Paul; and the eminent, well-known prelate, Augustine. Daur's identification (p. 157) of this Eutropius with Eutropius, author of *Ep. de contemnanda hereditate*, has met with little support. More likely, both Eutropius and Paul were countrymen of Orosius with whom he was familiar, if not well-acquainted, as well as possible recipients of Augustine's treatise *De perfectione iustitiae hominis*.
4. Cf. Mt 3.10, 7.19.
5. Cf. Mt 15.13.

others, and sow the true seed for us who will water them from your fountains.[6] I pledge God as my witness, and I hope for the increase of your work, since that land now produces poor fruits because of improper cultivation. Yet, if you visit it with that hidden manna,[7] entrusted to my keeping and restoring it, the land will bear fruit up to a hundredfold,[8] once your richness has been poured out upon it very profusely. Through you, blessed father, through you, I say, may the Lord our God correct by the word those whom he has chastened by the sword.[9] I have been sent to you by God. Through him I place my hope in you, while I ponder how it happened that I have come here. I do recognize why I have come. It was not by choice, not by necessity, and not by common agreement that I departed from my native land. Rather, I was prompted by some hidden force, until I was delivered to the shores of this land. Here, at last, I have come to the realization that I was being ordered to come to you.[10] Do not judge me impudent, but receive me as I make my confession. Allow me to return to my beloved mistress[11] as a proper merchant who has found the pearl,[12] and not as a runaway servant who has squandered his fortune.[13] We have been more gravely wounded by evil teachers than by the most bloodthirsty of enemies.[14] We, for our part, admit the blow; you, for yours, clearly discern the wound. Dispense, with the help of the Lord, the medicine which is alone sufficient! To this end, I will show briefly what was perniciously planted earlier and has gained strength, and what was, even worse, grafted on later and has now grown strong.

2. First of all, Priscillian is in fact more wretched than the Manichaeans because he supported his heresy by relying on the Old Testament as well.[15] He taught that the soul, which is born of

6. Cf. 1 Cor 3.7.
7. Cf. Rev 2.17; 2 Macc 2.4–8.
8. Cf. Mt 13.8, 13.23.
9. An allusion to the recent upheavals on the Iberian peninsula caused by the invasions, beginning in the autumn of 409, of various Germanic tribes, notably the Vandals, Alans, and Suevi.
10. In contrast to Orosius's rather grandiose, providential claims here is his later declaration in the *Historia* (3.20). See my comments on this in the introduction.
11. Cf. Gen 16.9.
12. Cf. Mt 13.45–46.
13. Cf. Lk 15.19, 15.21.
14. See note 9 above.
15. Contemporary sources agree that while the Manichaeans rejected the Old

God, comes forth from a certain storehouse,[16] declares before God that it is going to do battle, and is instructed by the exhortation of angels. Then, descending from there through certain spheres, it is seized by the powers of evil and, according to the will of the conquering prince, is thrust into various bodies against which is inscribed a decree.[17] Therefore, he was also asserting that astrology[18] prevails against this, stating that Christ destroyed this decree and affixed it to the cross by his passion, just as Priscillian himself says in one of his own letters, "Such is the first wisdom: to recognize in the types of souls the natures of divine powers and the disposition of the body. In this, heaven and earth are seen to be bound and all the powers of the world are seen to have been drawn up to overcome the ranks of the saints. For the first sphere of God and the divine decree of souls to be sent into the flesh are made by the cooperation of the angels and of God and of all souls, and are in the control of the patriarchs. Those on the opposite side who control the force of the zodiacal host . . . and so on."[19] Moreover, he taught that the names of the patriarchs correspond to the parts of the soul, namely: Reuben to the head; Judah to the chest; Levi to the heart; Benjamin to the thighs; and so forth. On the other hand, the signs of the zodiac have been assigned to the parts of the body, namely: Aries [the Ram] to the head; Taurus [the Bull] to the neck; Gemini [the Twins] to the arms; Cancer [the Crab] to the chest; and so forth.[20] He wants these to be understood as eternal darkness and the prince of the world as having emerged from them, supporting this very thing from a certain book which

---

Testament, the followers of Priscillian sought to use it to justify and legitimize their teachings. Cf. Augustine, *De haeresibus* 70.

16. *Promptuario*. Chadwick, *Priscillian of Avila* 191, n. 4 comments that this is "a favorite word in IV Esdras" and that "the concept of a treasury containing souls is Jewish."

17. Cf. Col 2.14. Also, see Augustine's relevant comments in *De haeresibus* 70.

18. *Mathesim*.

19. On this rather obscure passage, see Chadwick's insightful analysis in *Priscillian of Avila* 192–194.

20. Augustine comments in his *De haeresibus* 70: "They also declare that men are bound by the stars controlling their fate and that our very body is composed in accord with the twelve signs of the sky, . . ."

is entitled "Memoir of the Apostles."[21] In it the Savior is seen to be secretly questioned by the disciples and showing from the Gospel parable which begins "The sower went out to sow"[22] that the sower was not good. It claims that, if he had been good, he would not have been negligent, scattering his seed neither beside the path, nor in stony soil, nor on uncultivated ground.[23] It wants this sower to be understood as the one who scatters captured souls in various bodies as he wishes. Also, in this book, many things are said about a prince of wetness and a prince of fire, intending to show that all the good things in this world are done by art, not by the power of God. For it says that there is a certain light-virgin whom God, when he wants to grant rain to humanity, shows to the prince of wetness. As he desires to take her, he sweats with passion and produces rain; and when he is deprived of her, he stirs up thunder by his groaning.[24] Moreover, Priscillian used to speak about the Trinity only in name. For he asserted "unity" without any "existence" or "property,"[25] and by omitting "and" was teaching that Father, Son, Holy Spirit were only one: Christ.[26]

21. The identity of this gnostic gospel, perhaps of Manichaean origin, is still disputed. There is a reference in Theodoret of Cyrrhus's *Haereticorum fabularum compendium* (1.5) to a passage in Irenaeus which describes a heretical group who held that Jesus taught his disciples secretly and requested this "hidden knowledge" to be passed down to worthy descendants.
22. Mt 13.3.
23. Cf. Mt 13.3–5.
24. This myth was apparently passed from Orosius to Jerome who, in turn, transformed it into a Virgilian reference which, he alleged, the Priscillianists used to seduce women: "They shut themselves up alone with little women and sing this to them between intercourse and embraces: 'Then the almighty father, Heaven, descends with fruitful showers into the womb of his fertile wife, and the great one, mingled with her great body, nourishes all offspring.'" Cf. Jerome, *Ep.* 133.3 and Virgil, *Georgica* 2.325–27.
25. *Unionem; existentia; proprietate.* Chadwick, *Priscillian of Avila* 199, n. 1 remarks, "Orosius's rendering of *hypostasis* is of interest as an echo of the terminology of Marius Victorinus."
26. Augustine, *De haeresibus* 70 confirms this observation: "Concerning Christ, they agree with the sect of the Sabellians, saying that he is not only the Son, but also the Father and the Holy Spirit." Chadwick, *Priscillian of Avila* 87 notes that Priscillian's own third tractate "likewise affirms the Christian faith in Father, Son, and Spirit to be belief in one God Christ: he is God, Son of God, Saviour, was born in the flesh, suffered, and rose for the love of mankind."

3. At that time two of my fellow citizens, Avitus and another named Avitus, sought out foreign ideas although the truth alone had already exposed by itself such shameful misunderstanding. One departed for Jerusalem, the other for Rome. Upon their return, the one brought back Origen, the other, Victorinus.[27] Of these two, the second deferred to the first. Both of them, however, condemned Priscillian. We do not know enough about Victorinus, because just at this moment, almost before the publication of the writings, the follower of Victorinus changed over to Origen. Therefore, they began to present many splendid things which they had taken from Origen, but which truth itself would refute on any occasion. On the subject of the Trinity, for instance, we have learned a quite sound doctrine: that all things which have been made have been "made by God,"[28] and that they are all "very good"[29] and are made "out of nothing"—and then there are some rather thoughtful explanations of the Scriptures. All of this was accepted right from the start by the wise individuals after a faithful purging of the earlier teachings. The only obstacle remaining was the issue of "out of nothing." For it was accepted as true that the soul exists, but it could not be accepted that it was made "out of nothing," the argument being made that the will of God could not be "nothing."[30] This issue remains almost to the present time. Now these two Aviti and with them, Saint Basil the Greek,[31] who were most happily[32] teaching these beliefs, transmitted certain opinions taken from the books of Origen himself, incorrect opinions, as I now understand. First of all, they were saying that before all things made became apparent,

---

27. Despite the apparently compelling coincidence, the Avitus who journeyed to Jerusalem and returned with writings by Origen cannot be identified with Avitus of Braga who obtained the relics of St. Stephen and corresponded with Jerome. The Victorinus in question is more likely Marius Victorinus the Neoplatonist than Victorinus of Pettau. Cf. Chadwick, *Priscillian of Avila* 191.

28. Cf. Jn 1.3.

29. Cf. Gen 1.31.

30. Cf. 2 Macc 7.28.

31. It is surprising to see Basil (d. 379) named here, since he was not a contemporary or colleague of the Aviti. Orosius may be reflecting on some aspects of Basil's theology which, like that of Origen, troubled him.

32. The earlier CSEL editor, Schepss, has taken *beatissime* as a vocative (referring to Augustine) and has punctuated the passage accordingly.

they had always existed in God's wisdom as made. They expressed this in the following words: "For whatever God made, he did not begin to make." Next they said that the angels, the principalities, the powers, the souls, and the demons have a single source and a single substance,[33] and that an archangel or a soul or a demon has been assigned a rank according to the quality of its merits. Here they used this expression: "A lesser sin has merited a higher rank." They said that the world was made last of all so that souls who had sinned previously might be purified in it. They taught that the fire, undoubtedly eternal, by which sinners are to be punished, is neither a real fire nor an eternal one, saying that the punishment of the individual conscience was called "fire." They said that "eternal," according to its Greek etymology, does not mean "everlasting,"[34] even adding from the Latin evidence that, in saying "for eternity and age upon age,"[35] something else has been added to "eternal." And thus, they say, all the souls of the sinners will return to the unity of the body of Christ after the purification of their conscience. On the subject of the devil, they also wished to affirm—but here they did not prevail—that, because the substance which is in him was made good, it cannot perish, and that his substance will at some time be saved, once the devil's malice is consumed in its totality. Concerning the body of the Lord, however, they taught that, since the Son of God who came to us after so many thousands of years could not have been idle up to that time, while he was preaching forgiveness to the angels, the powers, and all the higher beings, he took on the nature of the form of those he was visiting, until he had become so dense as to be tangible in the flesh which he had taken on in the form of a human being. And that, finalizing this by his passion and his resurrection, he unburdened himself by ascending until he returned to the Father. Therefore, his body was never put aside and God in his reign has not been confined in any body. They said also that the phrase "the creation unwillingly was subjected to corruption," was to be understood as the

---

33. Cf. Col 1.16.
34. The Greek word apparently under consideration here is *aiônios*, which indeed in its most basic and literal connotation does mean "lasting for an age."
35. *In aeternum et in saeculum saeculi.* Cf. Ps 9.6, 10.16.

sun, the moon, and the stars, and that these were not merely simple lights, but powers endowed with reason, and they rendered servitude to corruption "on account of him who subjected it in hope."[36]

4. This, as far as I have been able to remember it, I have explained briefly so that you may quickly employ the medicine after examining all the illnesses. "The truth of Christ is in me,"[37] because I would not dare to be so impudent before the venerable reverence of your Holiness if I did not know that, according to the clearly visible judgment and plan of God, I was sent to you and you have been chosen to reveal the means of healing such a great people[38]—just as if a sinner has been struck a blow for his sins, then after the blow he has to be cared for. Please, most blessed father, remember me and the many who, along with me, are awaiting to be worthy of your words descending upon them like the dew.[39]

36. Rom 8.20.
38. Cf. Ex 9.14.
37. 2 Cor 11.10.
39. Cf. Deut 32.2.

INDICES

GENERAL INDEX

Aaron (priest), 64n.172
Abihu (priest), 125
Abiram (rebel), 125
Abraham (patriarch): command to, 120, 147; earthliness of, 159; eternal life of, 93; imitators of, 148; seed of, 69, 87
Absalom (son of David), 117
Achan (Judahite), 61
Adam (first man): Christ and, 167; creation of, 92, 153; death of, 87, 88; fall of, 10, 22, 91, 153; Satan vs., 89
adultery, 76
Aetna (volcano), 84
aiônios (the word), 173n.34
Alans, 169n.9
Alexandria, 101
Ambrose, St., 12, 39n.5, 97, 115
anamartetus (the word), 135n.102
Ananias (Damascene Christian), 132
angels: approach to, 77; Christ and, 89, 155; Priscillian on, 170; rank of, 173; rejoicing by, 86; reverence by, 73; servitude of, 94; similarity to, 165, 166; Zechariah and, 147; *see also* devils
Anglada Anfruns, Ángel, 4n.7, 9n.27, 13, 84n.66
Anianus (deacon), 117n.6
Anician family, 117n.6, 130n.75, 163n.287
animals, 63, 93
Annaba (Hippo Regius), 99, 100, 105
anointing, 10, 92
Antichrist, 134, 155–56
Antioch (Syrian), 74
antistitis (the word), 92n.29
Antonianus, Bishop, 44, 66
apathes (the word), 135n.106
Apelles (Marcionite), 17, 21, 39

Apollinarians, 4n.7, 20
Apollo (Greek deity), 84n.64
Apollos (Alexandrian Jew), 47
apostates: Cornelius and, 46; Cyprian and, 28–29, 65, 66; forgiveness of, 44, 45, 47; reception of, 41–42
apostles: appeal by, 159; authority of, 25, 26; as foundation, 54, 67; gentile believers and, 74; heretical contemporaries of, 17; Holy Spirit and, 21; invocation of, 153; light reflected by, 138; repentance of, 50–51; resistance to, 19; warnings by, 76
Appius (Roman statesman), 104n.31
Aratus (poet), 12n.33, 31n.18
Aries (zodiac), 170
Ark of God, 77
Ark of Noah, 63
Arnobius of Sicca, 12
Arnobius the Younger, 31n.17
Artemis (Greek goddess), 84n.64
ascetics, 8on.45, 157n.240
astrology, 170
astronomy, 141–42, 174
Athenians, 32
Augustine of Hippo, St., 105, 116; anti-Pelagian tracts of, 100, 102, 118, 119, 129; Braulio on, 98n.6; conference invocation of, 103, 119; *Epistula ad Demetriadem* and, 157n.240; on heresies, 107–8; historical research by, 109–10; Jerome and, 100, 101, 104n.31; Jovinian and, 150n.203; memorandum to, 100, 168–74; on Moses, 155n.228; on Orosius, 97n.3, 98n.8, 99–100, 106, 111; quotation from, 164n.291; on self-confidence, 162; on "seventy," 31n.17; wolf imagery of, 115n.2

177

GENERAL INDEX

Augustus, Caesar, 110
Aurelius Augustinus, *see* Augustine of Hippo, St.
Aviti (Spanish priests), 107, 172
Avitus of Braga, 121, 172n.27; at Jerusalem conference, 103n.28, 123; on Orosius, 97n.3; relics and, 105
Azariah (Abed-nego), 82

Babylon, 66, 126
Balconius of Braga, 105
baptism, 10, 87–94; authority for, 25, 26; forgiveness and, 131; of Hebrews, 48–49; loosing through, 52–53; remission in, 47–48; symbolism of, 49–50; Sympronian on, 37; *see also* postbaptismal sin
Barcelona, 3
Basil, St., 155n.228, 172
basilisks, 74–75n.20
Bathsheba (wife of David), 23
Beelzebub, *see* Satan
Belial, *see* Satan
Benjamin (patriarch), 170
Bethlehem, 100, 101, 118
binding and loosing, 25, 51, 52–53
bishops: accusation against, 46, 47; authority of, 25, 26, 51; blamelessness of, 145; at Carthage synod, 118; at Diospolis council, 104, 129n.66; inability of, 39; Pelagius and, 163; sacraments and, 92; sexual continence of, 5n.10; of Tarragona, 3
blamelessness, 145, 147; *see also* sinlessness
blasphemy, 56–57
Blastus the Greek, 18
blind men, 130
blood, 74
Body of Christ, *see* Catholic Church
Bonner, Gerald, 103n.27
Braga, 97, 105
Braulio, Bishop, 98n.6

Caelestius, 109, 141; condemnation of, 100n.16, 102, 118, 119; "hissing" by, 116
Caesar, Julius, 101n.19
Caesarius of Arles, St., 11

Cancer (zodiac), 170
Caphar-Gamala, 105
Capitolium (Rome), 29n.7
Carthage, 20n.12, 40nn.10, 11, 46; *see also* Council of Carthage
Cataphrygians, 18, 30; as blemishes, 43; name of, 20, 28; Novatian and, 39
catechumens, 9n.26, 10, 51, 72
Catholic (the word), 6, 18, 20–22, 28, 29
Catholic Christians, 32, 46n.52, 64, 157, 158; *see also* Latin Christians
Catholic Church: character of, 40–41, 42–44, 66–69; departure from, 17, 36, 39, 61; discipline of, 72; division in, 35n.42, 46n.51; faithfulness of, 64; Fathers of, 115–16, 120–21, 155n.228; forgiveness by, 7, 66, 79; foundation of, 153, 161; grace to, 141, 144; harmony with, 19; humbling before, 82, 83; loosing by, 53; mortal sin and, 38, 76; mutual support in, 138; Novatianists vs., 8; parables on, 54, 55; Pelagius and, 104, 116, 117, 119, 120, 160; power passed to, 137; prayers of (*see* prayer); Priscillianism and, 98; sinners entrusted with, 9; souls born to, 91–92; standard of, 35; unrepentant sinners and, 59, 71–72; *see also* Spanish Church
cedar oil, 31
Cerdo (Gnostic), 17
Chadwick, Henry, 99n.10, 107n.39, 170n.16, 171n.26
charisms, 25, 26, 137–38
charity, *see* love
children, 163–64
chrism, 10, 92
Christ Jesus, *see* Jesus Christ
Church, *see* Catholic Church
Church of the Resurrection (Jerusalem), 104, 122n.27
Cicero, Marcus Tullius, 12
Cilicia, 74
civil authorities, 33
clemency, *see* mercy
cobras, 74–75n.20

GENERAL INDEX

commandments, *see* law
confession: Cyprian on, 65; distaste for, 77, 84; healing power of, 83; lost opportunities for, 84, 85; in Old Testament, 82; practice of, 63, 73; *see also* penance
confessors, 65
confirmation, 25
conscience: evil, 77; final judgment and, 133, 146; innocent, 132; purging of, 73, 173; wounded, 79
consignation, 92n.29
contrition, *see* repentance
Cornelius, St., 44; Novatian and, 35, 36, 45, 46; Novatianists and, 40nn. 10, 11, 44n.44
Coster, J., 111
Council of Carthage: 251 C.E., 29n.8; 390 C.E., 92n.29; 411 C.E., 100n. 16, 102, 103, 118, 119, 141
Council of Diospolis (415), 104, 120n.19, 123n.31; *facile* discussed at, 129n.66; interpreter at, 103n. 29; minutes of, 105
Council of Elvira (c. 300–303 or 309), 5n.10
Council of Sardica (342/343), 4n.6
Cretan goats, 83
Cretan persons, 31
crimes, *see* mortal sin
Ctesiphon (Pelagian), 117n.6, 120, 129
Cucuphas, St., 3
Cyprian of Carthage, St., 7, 8; apostates and, 28–29, 65, 66; authority of, 21; on Decian persecution, 46nn.50, 51; election of, 20n.12, 36n.48; on factions, 35n.42; letters of, 34, 36, 41n.23; on Novatian, 35, 44–45; on Novatus, 29n. 10, 46n.50; Orosius on, 115; on O.T. saints, 64–65; pagan authors and, 12; on philosophers, 35n.41

Damasus I, Pope, 4n.7
Daniel (prophet), 161; confession by, 82; Darius and, 32; deliverance of, 42, 65; Habakkuk and, 126; intercession by, 64, 66
Darius I, King of Persia, 32

Dathan (rebel), 125
Daur, Klaus D., 107n.40, 111, 168nn. 1, 2, 3
David, King: appeal by, 159; birthplace of, 118; on confession, 59; confession by, 23, 131; on deliverance, 90, 93–94; on family members, 43; flight of, 117; humbling of, 80; lamentation by, 55, 82; Orosius as, 109; on peaceableness, 62; on praise, 69; punishment of, 132; on queen, 22; on righteous, 133, 147; on secret sins, 148–49; on silence, 128; on sinners, 60; Temple and, 149, 150
death: conquest of, 167; sin and, 87–88, 90, 91, 93, 153, 165; of unworthy communicants, 78
Decian persecution, 29n.6, 45n.45, 46n.50
Decius, Gaius Messius Quintus Trajanus, 38, 39
deification, 135n.106
Demetrias (virgin), 157, 163n.288
devils: appeal by, 156–57; freedom from, 93; influence of, 88; rank of, 173; renunciation of, 94; seizure by, 170; *see also* Satan
Dexter, Nummius Aemilianus, 5
Dictaean countryside, 83
Dictinius, 98n.6
Dioscorides, Pedanius, 83n.58
Diospolis Council, *see* Council of Diospolis (415)
disease, 78, 79
dittany plant, 83
Domnus (anti-Pelagian), 103n.28, 121, 123
Dositheus the Samaritan, 17

Ebion (heretic), 17
Eden, 10, 89, 153, 167
Egypt, 101
Egyptian cobras, 74–75n.20
Eli (priest), 57, 158n.248
Elijah (prophet), 126, 161
Elizabeth (mother of John the Baptist), 120
Elvira Council (c. 300–303 or 309), 5n.10

Elymas (magician), 33
Epaphroditus (Philippian), 25
Ephesian church, 24
Epimenides of Crete, 31n.19
Epiphanius of Salamis, 18n.3
eructasti (the word), 158n.246
Erythraean Sea (Red Sea), 101n.19, 126
Esther (queen consort), 32
eternal (the word), 173
Eucharist, 77n.32, 78
Eulalia, St., 3
Eulogius of Caesarea, 104
Eusebius of Caesarea, 18n.3, 20n.12
Eutropius, Bishop, 168
Evaristus, Bishop, 20n.12, 40, 42, 61
Eve (first woman), 10
evil spirits, *see* devils
Evodius, 168n.2
exomologesis, *see* penance
Ezekiel (prophet), 42

Fabbrini, Fabrizio, 98n.5
Fabian, St., 45n.45
facile (the word), 129n.66
faith: approval of, 130; expression of, 139; gifts and, 141; justification by, 54, 63–64; lack of, 163; loosing by, 52; outstanding, 127; repentance and, 48; salvation by, 10, 161; walk of, 93, 148; wisdom and, 137
fasting, 82, 83, 85
Fawn festival, 71
Felicissimus, 36n.48
Fink, Guy, 111
forgiveness: of apostates, 44, 45, 47; apostolic authority for, 26; availability of, 48, 56, 57; blessedness of, 94; Church grant of, 7, 66, 79; free will and, 131; as loosing, 52; Pelagius on, 130; of sinful Corinthian, 60; *see also* penance; salvation
fornication, 9, 74, 75; *see also* adultery
Fortunatus, 36n.48
free will: endowment of, 152, 153, 157, 158; Pelagius on, 131; voluntary devotion and, 166
freedom, 74, 93–94

Galicia (Gallaecia), 97, 98

Garden of Eden, 10, 89, 153, 167
Gehenna, 84, 90, 91, 125, 136
Gelasius I, Pope, 115n.3
Gemini (zodiac), 170
Gennadius of Marseilles, 97n.3
gentiles, *see* pagan persons
Germanic invasions, 97, 98, 99, 169n.9
Gibeonites, 58
goats, 83
God: Antichrist vs., 134; censure demanded by, 115; creation by, 172, 173; fear of, 117; forbearance of, 77; glory of, 87; grace of (*see* grace); judgment by, 84, 146, 152–53, 155, 157; justification by, 54, 63–64; law of (*see* law); love for, 162–63; "Memoir of the Apostles" on, 171; mercy of (*see* mercy); mortal sin and, 75; natural order and, 141–42, 152–53, 158; power of, 125–26, 127, 155, 156; prayer to (*see* prayer); providence of, 110; remedies of, 22–23; repeated sin and, 49; seven spirits of, 134, 136; universality of, 54; *visitatio* of, 26n.50; *see also* Trinity
God's help, 109, 141, 144; John of Jerusalem on, 103–4, 121, 122, 124, 125; Pelagius on, 128, 129, 130, 136, 150–51
Goliath of Gath, 109, 117, 149
Gordius, 36n.48
grace, 88–89; acknowledgement of, 140; apportionment of, 137; baptism as, 48; blamelessness and, 145; deliverance by, 159; help through, 141; human ability and, 127, 128, 129; law replaced by, 160, 161; loosing by, 52; Pelagius on, 109; power displayed in, 126; protection by, 143–44; reign of, 91; sevenfold powers of, 136; sufficiency of, 166
Greeks, 34, 102n.22
Gregory of Nyssa, St., 5n.9
Grossi, V., 117n.6

Habakkuk (prophet), 126, 159

GENERAL INDEX 181

Ham (son of Noah), 63
heavenly bodies, 141–42, 174
Hebrews, *see* Jews
hell, 84, 90, 91, 125, 136
Heracles (classical mythology), 18n.6
heresies: as adultery, 64; as blemishes, 43; "Catholic" appellation and, 20, 21, 22, 28; lovelessness of, 44; plurality of, 6, 17–18; spiritual barrenness of, 63; *see also* Novatianists; Pelagianism; Priscillianism
Heros of Arles, 104
Hesiod, 12, 32
Hilary of Poitiers, 5n.9, 115
Hilary of Syracuse, 102, 118nn.12, 15
Hippo Regius (Annaba), 99, 100, 105
Holy Spirit: blasphemy against, 56–57; conferring of, 10, 25; Evangelists and, 51; gifts of, 25, 26, 137–38; grace through, 126; injunctions by, 74; languages and, 31; ointments of, 34; Pelagius and, 136; promise of, 128; rebirth through, 40, 41, 44, 92; seven churches and, 24; skill of, 19; souls begotten by, 91, 92; teaching by, 21; threat by, 83
Honorius, Flavius, 5
Hophni (priest), 158n.248
Horace, 12
hypostasis (the word), 171n.25

idolatry, 9, 58, 65, 74, 76; *see also* pagan religion
illness, 78, 79
indigestis (the word), 158n.246
iniquity, *see* sin
Innocent I, Pope, 104, 122
intercession, *see* prayer
Irenaeus, St., 171n.21
Isaac (patriarch), 93
Isaiah (prophet), 59, 159, 161
Israelites, *see* Jews
Ithacius of Ossonumba, 107

Jacob (patriarch), 55, 93
Jambres (magician), 64
James (brother of Jesus), 159
James (Pelagian), 118n.14
Jannes (magician), 64

Jeremiah (prophet), 42, 159, 161
Jericho, 61, 62
Jerome, St., 109, 116; accusations against, 163n.288; Augustine and, 100, 101, 104n.31; Avitus of Braga and, 121n.24, 172n.27; on *Cervus*, 10n.30; *Contra Novatianos* and, 7, 11; Ctesiphon and, 117n.6; on Dexter, 5; Diospolis council and, 104; Jovinian and, 150n.203; letters of, 105; Orosius and, 99, 101, 118; on Pacian, 3, 4; pagan authors and, 12; on Paula, 80n.45; on Pelagius, 103, 119–20, 129, 130n.72, 161n.275; on Priscillianists, 171n.24
Jerusalem: Ark transported to, 77; conference in, 102–4, 108, 109, 118–22, 123; *coup d'état* in, 117; Pelagius in, 100–101, 116n.4; Spanish priest in, 107, 172; treachery in, 124, 125
Jesus Christ: Adam and, 167; apostles of (*see* apostles); authority of, 47; baptism into, 49; on binding/loosing, 51, 52; bishops and, 25, 26; body of, 173; Church of (*see* Catholic Church); as cornerstone, 68; cross of, 124; on darkness, 139; disciples of, 9; as foundation, 153; gifts from, 137, 138, 144; grace of (*see* grace); human ability and, 132; on John the Baptist, 145–46; judgment by, 133, 134, 140–41, 152; law of (*see* law); on love, 162; love of, 43–44; "Memoir of the Apostles" on, 171; mercy of, 62; miracles of, 126, 130; misguided love for, 148; Novatian and, 37, 39, 69; Origenism on, 107; parables of, 24, 53, 54; Pharisees and, 27; Priscillian on, 170; promises of, 127–28; rebuke by, 160–61; relief by, 23, 63; on repentance, 55; resistance to, 19; salvation by (*see* salvation); as shepherd, 71; sinlessness of, 136, 151; supplications of, 79; temptations of, 89–90, 135; testimony against, 123, 128; on unforgiveable sin, 56;

GENERAL INDEX

(Jesus Christ *continued*)
  unity in, 163; unrighteous and, 38; unworthiness for, 158; as vine, 57, 166; Zacchaeus and, 132
Jews: Ark of God and, 77; choosing of, 87; gentile believers and, 54; idolatry of, 65; of Minorca, 105; miracles and, 126; patriarchs of, 93, 107, 170; Philistines vs., 117; repentance by, 48, 49; sparing of, 66; *see also* Pharisees; Sadducees; scribes
Job (O.T. character): admonishment of, 146; character of, 144–45; deliverance of, 42, 65, 66; intercession by, 64; on man, 159; protection of, 143–44
Joel (prophet), 58
John of Jerusalem, Bishop, 100–102, 116n.4; accusation by, 104, 108, 109, 122–25, 141n.145; at conference, 102–4, 118–19, 120–22; oblique references to, 117n.6, 163n.286; relics and, 105n.32
John the Apostle, St.: on sin, 57, 75, 131, 159; on sons of God, 92; weeping of, 134; on Word, 151
John the Baptist, 138, 145–46
Jordan River, 126
Joseph (patriarch), 157
Jovinian (monk), 116, 150
Judah (patriarch), 170
Judas Iscariot, 135
Julian of Carthage, 110n.45
Julius Caesar, 101n.19
Jupiter (Roman deity), 29n.7

Kauer, Robert, 13
Kelly, J. N.D., 100n.17, 101

Lacedaemonians, 34
Lactantius, 12
Lampius, Bishop, 3
languages, 31, 32
Laodicean church, 24
lapsi, see apostates
Latin Christians: at Jerusalem conference, 102n.22, 103, 104; literary works of, 12; Pelagianism and, 108, 121
law: bearing of, 163, 164; Christ and, 155; death through, 88; divine power and, 126; eternity of, 75–76; gentiles and, 52; of love, 162; obedience to, 40, 167; Pelagius on, 102n.24, 103, 119, 128, 129, 136; redemption from, 74; repentance and, 48; restraint by, 152; severity of, 61–62, 73, 160, 161; subjects of, 54
Lazarus of Aix, 104
Lazarus of Bethany, 126
Lernaean Hydra, 18
Leto (classical mythology), 84n.64
Leucius, 18
Levi (patriarch), 170
loosing and binding, 25, 51, 52–53
Lot (son of Haran), 62
love, 36, 43–44, 60, 72, 162
Lucretius, 12
luxury, 81–82, 161

Magona, 105n.34
Manichaeism, 11, 107–8, 169, 171
Marcion of Pontus, 17, 21, 39n.5, 150n.204
Marcionites, 20
Martin of Tours, St., 80n.45
"Martyrdom of Novatian," 35n.46
martyrs, 55, 65
Mary, Virgin, 80, 91
matrimonial status, 150n.203
Maximilla, 18
Mediterranean area, 11
"Memoir of the Apostles," 171
Menander (heretic), 17
mercy: absence of, 76; awaiting of, 165; gratitude for, 140; hope for, 63, 163; law and, 161; promises of, 58, 86; truth and, 133
Meribah, 155n.228
Middle Ages, 111
Milan, 150n.203
Minorca, 105
Montanists, *see* Cataphrygians
Montanus (schismatic), 18, 20, 21
morality, 71, 72
Morin, Germain, 11
mortal sin: gravity of, 74–75; incidence of, 76; John the Apostle on, 57, 75; Novatianists on, 8, 38; unforgiveable, 56–57; unrepented

of, 77; *see also* fornication; idolatry; murder
Mosaic law, *see* law
Moses (confessor), 44–45
Moses (prophet), 87, 143; death of, 154–55; Egyptian magicians and, 64; on idolatrous loved ones, 58; intercession by, 37, 38, 65–66, 75; opposition to, 125
Mt. Aetna, 84
Mt. Dicte, 83
Mt. Vesuvius, 84
murder, 9, 75, 76, 78
Muses (classical mythology), 31–32

Naboth (Jezreelite), 125
Nadab (priest), 125
nature, 21, 88, 141–42, 152–53, 158
Nebuchadnezzar II, King of Babylon, 23, 33, 58, 81
Nicolaus of Antioch, 17
Nicostratus, 42, 61
Ninevites, 58
Noah (patriarch), 42, 64, 65, 66
North Africa, 100; Augustinianism in, 119; Orosius in, 98–99, 105; Pelagianism in, 102, 108, 118
Novatian (antipope), 40, 66; apostasy of, 29; on apostates, 41, 44–45; disciples of, 42; doctrines of, 38–39; harshness of, 60; impotence of, 69; name of, 20, 28, 30; personal attack on, 7, 8, 34–37; pretensions of, 46
Novatianists, 7, 11; "blamelessness" of, 62–63; as blemishes, 43; in Carthage, 20n.12, 40nn.10, 11; churches condemned by, 60; detachment of, 17, 42; doctrines of, 8, 38; "hangnails" of, 68; history of, 45–46; laws violated by, 61; name of, 20, 30; princes and, 33; self-satisfaction of, 56; Sozomen on, 135n.102; word struggles of, 69
Novatus (sectarian), 40; disciples of, 42; name of, 20; Novatian and, 35, 36, 38, 45–46; sins of, 29, 61

Origen, 116, 120, 155n.228
Origenism, 109; Augustine on, 108;

Orosius on, 100, 106, 172–74; Spanish Church and, 98, 107
original sin, 91, 109, 153
Orosius of Braga: *Book in Defense against the Pelagians*, 115–67; *Inquiry or Memorandum to Augustine on the Error of the Priscillianists and Origenists*, 168–74; life of, 97–111
Ovid, 12

Pacian of Barcelona: *Letter 1*, 17–26; *Letter 2*, 27–37; *Letter 3*, 38–70; life of, 3–13; *On Baptism*, 87–94; *On Penitents*, 71–86
pagan persons: binding/loosing of, 51, 52–53; divine power and, 126; instructions to, 74; justification of, 54; literary works of, 12, 111; persecution by, 32; repentance of, 48; salvation of, 50; *see also* Germanic invasions
pagan religion, 11, 87, 110; *see also* Fawn festival; idolatry
Palestine, 99, 101, 102, 120n.23, 121n.24
Palmer, L. R., 19n.11
Pamphilus (martyr), 5n.14
Paradise (Eden), 10, 89, 153, 167
pardon, *see* forgiveness
Pasiphaë (classical mythology), 81n.47
Passerius (priest), 103n.28, 121, 123
Paternus, Bishop, 97
patriarchs, 93, 107, 170
Paul, Bishop, 168
Paul, St.: affliction of, 132–33; on Antichrist, 155–56; on atonement, 151; on baptism, 49–50; on begetting, 92; on blamelessness, 145; on body, 42; on caution, 147; on charity, 36, 44; on contention, 19, 33; on correction, 62, 81; on death, 88, 90, 91, 93, 165; on divine wisdom, 35; on Eucharist, 78; on false gospels, 39; on flesh, 162; on forgiveness, 26, 60, 93; on fornicators, 75; on freedom, 74; on gentiles, 54; on invocation of, 153; on Jews, 48–49; on judgment, 84, 132, 140; on grace, 127, 137, 144, 159; on helpers, 47; intercession by, 66;

(St. Paul *continued*)
  kindred, 37, 38; on laying on hands, 61, 79; on love of Christ, 43–44; on penitent, 86; on philosophy, 32; on pleasing, 34; on reprobates, 64; on salvation, 154; on successors, 25; on teaching, 21; Timothy and, 55–56; on transgressions, 24; on unrepentant, 59; verse quotation of, 12, 31; on weakness, 164, 166; on willingness, 152
Paula (Roman widow), 80n.45
Paulus, Sergius, 33
pax (the word), 19n.11
Pelagianism, 101, 102–4, 108, 109, 115–67
Pelagius (heretic), 109, 149; apostolic refutation of, 153–54; Ctesiphon and, 117n.6; examination of, 102–4, 118–20, 121; on frailty, 160; "hissing" by, 116; on human ability, 127, 128, 130, 150–51; humble words of, 137; in Jerusalem, 100–101, 116n.4; presumption of, 134, 135–36, 140–41; silence imposed on, 122; stoutness of, 161–62; unseemly letter of, 157–58
penance, 71–86; appeals for, 24; authority for, 25; compulsion to, 47; heretics on, 18; necessity of, 22; Novatianists on, 7n.20, 8, 45; pain of, 49; public, 9–10; refusal of, 59; reluctance for, 65; Sympronian on, 37; *see also* forgiveness; repentance
Pergamum church, 24
Peter, St.: authorization of, 52; on "bishop," 26; invocation of, 153; on law, 161; misguided love of, 148; "one hundred and twenty" and, 31n.17; on prophecy, 139; rebuke of, 155; repentance of, 50; on salvation, 144, 154; Simon Magus and, 33; sin against, 53; on water, 126–27
Peyrot, Philippe Henri, 13n.39; on *estis*, 47n.56; gaps conjectured by, 18n.4, 76n.27; on *impium*, 54n.94; interrogatives supplied by, 30n.15, 32n.25, 39n.7; on *partibus*, 33n.34; quotation list of, 12n.35

Pharisees, 17, 27, 56, 90
Philip (deacon), 92
Philistines, 117
Philumene (prophetess), 39
Phinehas (son of Eli), 158
Phoenicians, 62
Phrygians, *see* Cataphrygians
physicians, 49, 55, 63, 79, 80
Plinval, Georges de, 117n.6
postbaptismal sin, 7, 22, 38
praefero (the word), 135n.101
Praetextatus, Bishop, 3, 4
praevaricante (the word), 135n.105
Praxeas (priest), 18
prayer: of Fathers, 116; for fertility, 142; hopeful, 131–32; for humbled souls, 63, 85; for multitudes, 66; penitential, 48, 65, 82, 148; for sinners, 37, 57, 66; in weakness, 164–65, 166; of widows, 83; *see also* confession
Priscilla (prophetess), 18
Priscillian, Bishop, 116
Priscillianism: Augustine on, 107–8; in Galicia, 97, 98; Orosius on, 100, 106, 107, 169–72; Pelagianism and, 109
Proculus, 18
prophets: false, 64; as foundation, 54, 67; inquiry by, 144; lamentations of, 159; law and, 161
Prudentius, 3, 90n.14
public penance, 9–10
publicans, 53, 54, 55

Quintilian, 108, 109

Rahab (harlot), 58, 62
reason, 21, 152, 174
rebuke, 72, 78
reconciliation, *see* forgiveness
Red Sea (Erythraean Sea), 101n.19, 126
redemption, *see* salvation
Rees, B. R., 103n.29, 130n.72, 162n.277
repentance: acceptance of, 23; of apostles, 50–51; divine goodness and, 84; fruits evidencing, 57; by Jews, 48, 49; law and, 48; laying on hands and, 61; lost opportunities

GENERAL INDEX

for, 85; mercy for, 58, 133; Novatianists on, 38; refusal of, 59, 65; rejoicing for, 55; sadness unto, 24, 132; *see also* penance
Reuben (patriarch), 170
ritual anointing, 10, 92
Roman de la Higuera, Jeronimo, 5n.12
Roman Empire, 11, 98, 110, 121, 129
Rome: Capitolium of, 29n.7; Christians of, 161n.275; clergy of, 41n.23; councils at, 150n.203; Novatus in, 46; rich citizens of, 163n.288; Spanish priest in, 107, 172
Rubio Fernández, Lisardo, 12n.35, 13, 18n.4, 84n.66; on *akrobystian*, 54n.95; on *Cervulus*, 10n.30; on *epotata*, 24n.34; on *est*, 47n.56; on *legatus*, 33n.32; on *liberorum*, 61n.144; on Pacian, 4–5; on *patribus*, 33n.34; on *peritomen*, 54n.94; on prelates, 3; on "seventy," 31n.17
Rufinus, Tyrannius, 5
rulers, 33

Sabellians, 171n.26
Sadducees, 17
saints, 73, 93
salvation: apostles on, 154; assurances of, 10, 50; basis for, 91–92; freedom in, 93–94; godly sorrow and, 24, 132; inquiry into, 144; law and, 74; of lowly persons, 68
Samuel (prophet), 53, 161
sanctity, *see* sinlessness
Sardica Council (342/343), 4n.6
Sardis church, 24
Satan, 10; as *accusator*, 132n.79; defeat of, 89–90, 135, 146; deliverance to, 59, 60, 81; fiery darts of, 83; forgiveness and, 26; limitations on, 50; lying by, 133; miracles attributed to, 56, 57; Peter as, 148; protection by, 144; renunciation of, 94; salvation of, 173; trickery of, 22; venom of, 23; visits by, 142–43; zodiac and, 170
Schepss, Georg, 172n.32
schisms, *see* heresies
scribes, 90, 130
second anointing, 92n.29

secret sin, 148–49
Segor (Zoar), 58
self-confidence, 162
self-indulgence, 81–82, 161
Serapeum, 101n.19
Sergius Paulus, 33
Severus (martyr), 3
sexual sin, *see* adultery; fornication
sexual status, 150n.203
Sicily, 102
sickness, 78, 79
silence, 139
Simon Magus, 17, 33
sin: absent faith and, 163; aggravation of, 80; avoidance of, 10; compensation for, 75; complaining as, 164; as darkness, 139; death and, 87–88, 90, 91, 93, 153, 165; degrees of, 72, 73, 173; denial of, 159; forsaken, 58, 92; free will and, 131, 152; loosing of, 25, 51, 52–53; original, 91, 109, 153; postbaptismal, 7, 22, 38; remission of (*see* forgiveness; repentance); repeated, 49; responsibility for, 42; return to, 94; secret, 148–49; silence on, 71; Stoic view of, 35n.41; unforgiveable, 56–57; *see also* mortal sin
sinlessness: alleged impossibility of, 104, 122, 124, 125, 156; blamelessness and, 145; of Christ, 151; claims of, 63, 166; divine power and, 130, 141; doctrinal condemnation of, 103, 119–20; immortality and, 165, 167; Latin term for, 135n.102; modified assertion of, 103–4, 121, 128, 129, 136; reaffirmation of, 102n.24, 119
sinners: correction of, 62; deception of, 83; devil and, 90; disciples as, 9; flattery of, 76; forgiveness for, 7, 58, 79; future of, 136; intercession for, 37, 57, 66; judgment of, 133; justification of, 50, 63–64; lamentation by, 55–56; mercy for, 62, 140; parables on, 53–54, 55; preservation of, 68; purification of, 173; reception of, 38; rejoicing over, 86; remedy refused by, 80, 81n.48; salvation of (*see* salvation);

(sinners *continued*)
  separation from, 60, 61; status of, 43; temptations of, 22; unforgiveness of, 8; unrepentant, 9–10, 59, 75, 77; *see also* apostates
Socrates Scholasticus, 35n.47
Sodomites, 62
Solomon, King, 62, 117, 149, 150, 155
Solon, 12, 71
Sozomen, 135n.102
Spanish Church, 98, 99–100, 107
Spirit of God, *see* Holy Spirit
spiritual equality, 150n.203
spiritual gifts, 25, 26, 137–38
Stephen, St., 104–5, 124, 172n.27
Stoics, 35n.41
Suevi, 97, 169n.9
Sulpicius Severus, 80n.45
Susanna (Apocrypha character), 125, 128
swallows, 83
Symposius, Bishop, 97
Sympronian (Novatianist), 6, 7, 11; schooling described to, 4; treatise from, 8; on Virgil, 12
Syria, 74

Tamar (wife of Onan), 62
Tartarus, 84, 90, 91, 125, 136
Taurus (zodiac), 170
teaching, 139
Temple of God (Jerusalem), 73, 149–50
Temple of Jupiter (Rome), 29n.7
temptation, 89–90, 135, 143
Tertullian, 8, 12; on forgiveness, 66; on Marcion, 150n.204; on Nebuchadnezzar, 81nn.46, 48; on penitence, 82n.55, 83n.56; on philosophers, 34n.40
Theodoret of Cyrrhus, 171n.21
Theodosius I, Emperor of Rome, 3, 4, 5
Theodotus the Gnostic, 18
Thomas, St., 50–51
Thyatira church, 24
Tillet, Jean du, 13
Timasius (Pelagian), 118n.14

Timothy, St., 55
Titus (companion of Paul), 31
Tityus (classical mythology), 84
torture, 85
Tranquillus, Gaius Suetonius, 5n.13
transgression, *see* sin
Trinity: baptism and, 51; creation and, 172; human ability and, 128; Priscillian on, 107, 171; undefiled persons and, 147; *see also* God; Holy Spirit; Jesus Christ

underworld, 84, 90, 91, 125, 136
unforgiveable sin, 56–57
Uzzah (son of Abinadab), 77

Valentinians, 28, 43
Valentinus (Gnostic), 17, 28
Vandals, 169n.9
vates (the word), 90n.14
Vesuvius (volcano), 84
vice, *see* sin
Victorinus, Marius, 11, 107, 171n.25, 172
Victorinus of Pettau, 172n.27
Virgil, 12, 30, 81n.47, 171n.24
Virgin Mary, 80, 91
virgins, 157n.240
visitatio (the word), 26n.50
Vitalis (priest), 103n.28, 123
Vulgate, 74n.17

Western European historiography, 111
wicked spirits, *see* devils
widows, 83
wild goats, 83
wine, 83n.58

Zacchaeus (tax collector), 132
Zangemeister, Karl, 111, 164n.291, 166n.305
Zechariah (father of John the Baptist), 120, 145, 147
Zechariah (prophet), 161
Zetus, Bishop, 40n.10
Zeus (Greek deity), 84n.64
zodiac, 170

INDEX OF HOLY SCRIPTURE

Old Testament

Genesis
1.11: 152
1.14: 152
1.16: 152
1.31: 158, 172
2.7: 92, 153
2.8: 153
2.23: 43(2)
3.17–19: 153
3.18: 42
3.19: 88
3.23–24: 153
4: 153
6.6: 153
6.18: 63
7.2–3: 63
7.7: 63
7.13: 63
8: 66
9.6: 75
9.22–27: 63
15.6: 147
16.9: 169
17.1: 120, 147
17.4–5: 147
18.14: 141
18.27: 127, 159
19.1–29: 62
19.20–22: 66
19.22–30 [LXX]: 58
22.17: 69
22.18: 69
38.6–30: 62
39: 157
47.9: 55

Exodus
6.23: 125
7:11: 64
7.22: 64
9.14: 174
14: 126
16.7–8: 73
19.5: 143
21.12: 75
24.1: 125
24.9: 125
28.1: 125
32: 65
32.11: 65
32.14: 66
32.32: 37, 38
32.33: 65, 75
35.2: 73
37.29: 137

Leviticus
7.19–20: 77
10.1–2: 125
11.1–23: 73
11.24–40: 72
13.47–59: 73
14.34–53: 73
19.18: 162

Numbers
3.2: 125
3.4: 125
16.1–33: 125
20.10–12: 155
26.9–10: 125
26.60–61: 125

Deuteronomy
5.17: 88
5.18: 88
5.21: 88
6.5: 162

11.6: 125
13.6: 58
13.8–9 [LXX]: 58
19.21: 61(2)
21.18–21: 62
24.14: 25
32.2: 120, 174
34.4: 155

Joshua
3: 126
6.17–27: 62
6.25: 58
7: 61
9.26: 58

Judges
6.36–40: 120
13.18: 28

1 Samuel
1, 2, 4: 158
2.25: 57
8.7: 53
13.14: 149
17.3: 117(2)
17.4–7: 117
17.8–10: 117
17.16: 117

2 Samuel
6.6–7: 77
12.13: 23
12.15–16: 80
15.16–17: 117
16.15: 117

1 Kings
21.1–16: 125

INDEX OF HOLY SCRIPTURE

2 Kings
  2.11: 126

1 Chronicles
  6.3: 125
  24.1–2: 125
  28.3: 149
  28.6: 149

Esther
  7.10: 32

2 Maccabees
  2.4–8: 169
  7.28: 172

Job
  1.7: 142
  1.8: 143, 145
  1.10: 143
  1.11: 142
  1.12: 143
  2.5: 142
  2.6: 144
  15.25–27: 162
  25.6: 159
  33.9: 122
  34.15: 127
  38.2–4 [LXX]: 146
  39.34 [LXX]: 146
  40.25 [40.20 Vulgate]: 120
  42.10: 66

Psalms
  6.5: 85
  6.6: 23, 26, 55, 82
  8.2–3: 90
  9.6: 173
  10.16: 173
  15.1–2: 133
  15.2: 134, 136
  15.2–3: 133
  16.10: 55, 91
  19.12: 148(2)
  19.12–13: 148
  24.1: 143
  32.1: 94
  32.5: 23(2)
  35.18: 69(2)
  45.12: 22, 40, 43, 66
  45.14: 22
  50.1: 69
  50.12: 143
  50.18: 60
  51.4: 90, 131
  62.9: 150
  63.7–8: 164
  68.18: 137
  89.11: 137, 143
  89.14: 133
  89.21–22: 148
  89.24: 149
  91.13 [LXX]: 75
  92.1: 59
  102.9: 55
  105.4: 164
  106.17: 125
  113.3: 69
  116.9: 158
  116.11: 150
  116.16–17: 94
  119.1: 147, 148
  120.7: 62
  123.2: 165
  128.3: 40, 43, 67
  141.3: 128
  141.5: 64
  143.1–2: 159
  146.7–8: 93

Proverbs
  9.8: 72
  18.19: 62
  20.9 [LXX]: 63
  28.13: 23

Ecclesiastes
  1.9–10: 149
  3.1–3: 155
  3.16–17: 155
  4.9: 69
  4.12: 69
  9.10: 85

Song of Songs
  1.3: 137
  4.12: 63
  6.8: 22, 40, 67
  6.9: 22, 40, 67

Wisdom
  1.13: 76
  2.23: 158
  12.18: 126

Sirach
  12.3: 49
  13.1: 60
  14.16–17: 85
  15.14: 158
  34.28: 117
  34.30: 64
  39.16: 158

Isaiah
  1.18: 59
  1.28: 59
  3.12: 76
  6.5: 159
  7.14–15: 89
  11.2–3: 134
  25.8: 165
  29.13: 129
  30.15 [LXX]: 48, 86
  40.1: 159
  40.5: 140
  40.6: 159
  40.8: 159
  45.23: 146
  53.7: 90, 151
  53.9: 89, 90, 151
  55.7: 23, 58
  64.4: 94
  65.5: 122
  66.2: 76

Jeremiah
  2.13: 41(2), 63
  8.4: 23, 86
  31.29–30: 42

Baruch
  3.1–2: 159

Ezekiel
  14.16: 42
  14.18: 42
  14.20: 42, 65, 66
  16.32: 64
  18.4: 42

INDEX OF HOLY SCRIPTURE

18.20: 42
18.23: 48, 85
18.24: 58
18.32: 48, 76, 85
33.11: 48, 76, 85

Daniel
  2: 66
  3: 130
  3.25: 82, 130
  3.29: 33
  4: 23
  4.28–33: 81
  4.34: 58

6.23–24: 32
9.5: 82
13 [*Historia Susannae*]: 125
13.42–43 [*Historia Susannae*]: 128
14.32–38 [Vulgate]: 126

Hosea
  13.14: 165

Joel
  2.12–13: 23, 80

2.12–14: 58
2.13: 23, 65, 85

Amos
  5.8: 142
  9.6: 142

Jonah
  3:10: 58

Habbakuk
  3.16 [LXX]: 159

New Testament

Matthew
  3.4: 145
  3.8: 57
  3.10: 167, 168
  3.12: 36, 42
  4.1–11: 135
  4.3: 89
  4.6: 89
  4.8–9: 89
  5.4: 55
  5.13: 47
  5.14: 138
  5.18: 76
  5.25: 85
  5.29–30: 58
  5.42: 138
  5.44: 27
  5.45: 141, 142
  6.23: 139
  7.3–5: 62
  7.13: 162
  7.13–14: 162
  7.15: 64
  7.16: 42
  7.19: 168
  7.22–23: 133
  8.2: 130
  8.23–27: 126
  8.25: 159
  8.29: 157
  9.2: 130
  9.12: 55
  9.28: 130

10.10: 25
10.33: 44, 47
12.24: 56
12.31–32: 56
12.32: 56
13.3: 171
13.3–5: 171
13.8: 169
13.12: 167
13.23: 169
13.25: 166
13.45–46: 169
14.25–32: 127
15.15: 168
16.9: 25
16.17: 148, 161
16.18: 148, 153, 161
16.18–19: 52
16.19: 51, 52, 53(2)
16.22: 148
16.23: 148
16.27: 133
17.3: 37
18.15: 53
18.18: 25, 51, 52, 53(2)
18.22: 53
18.23–33: 160
20.15: 56
22.32: 93
22.36–40: 162
24.22: 156
25.29: 167

25.33–34: 158
25.37: 141
26.14–15: 125
26.41: 159
26.47: 124
26.47–50: 124
26.52: 75
26.53–54: 155
26.57–68: 123
26.63: 151
26.69–75: 127
26.75: 50
27.26: 125
28.19: 51
28.20: 128, 164

Mark
  1.12–13: 135
  2.7: 130
  2.17: 55
  5.1–17: 157
  10.15: 163
  12.28–34: 162
  14.10–11: 125
  14.43: 124
  14.43–46: 124
  14.53–65: 123
  15.15: 125

Luke
  1.6: 120, 145
  1.20: 147
  1.22: 147

INDEX OF HOLY SCRIPTURE

(Luke *continued*)
3.17: 36, 42
4.1–13: 135
4.3: 89
4.5–7: 89
4.11: 89
4.13: 135
6.41–42: 62
7.33: 145
7.36–50: 62
8.26–37: 157
10.7: 25
10.25–28: 162
10.30–35: 24
10.30–37: 63
11.26: 94
12.10: 56
12.35: 139
13.24: 162
15: 53
15.4–6: 24
15.4–7: 86
15.7: 55
15.8–9: 24, 86
15.11–32: 24
15.15–16: 85, 87
15.18–19: 85
15.19: 169
15.20–22: 85
15.21: 169
15.32: 24
16.22: 147
18.27: 127
19.9: 132
20.38: 93
22.3–6: 125
22.47–48: 124
22.54: 123
22.63–71: 123

John
1.1–3: 151
1.3: 172
1.9: 138
1.12: 92
1.14: 151
1.16: 137
1.29: 135
1.29–34: 138
1.42: 161

3.33: 150
4.10–15: 63
5.14: 49
5.22: 134
5.43: 137
6.44: 127
6.60: 76
7.37–39: 63
8.1–11: 62
8.44: 133
9: 126
11: 126
11.25: 93
13.10: 50
14.30: 133
15.1–2: 57
15.5: 127, 166
16.7: 128
18.3–9: 124
18.11: 155
18.13–14: 123
18.19–24: 123
19.1: 125
20.23: 25, 51(2), 52, 53(2)
20.27: 51

Acts
1.7: 155
1.15: 31
1.25: 135
6.11–13: 124
8.9–24: 33
8.32: 90, 151
8.37: 92
9.15: 154
9.16: 132
13.6–12: 33
13.22: 149(2)
15.10: 61
15.10–11: 161
15.23–24: 74
15.28–29: 74
15.29: 74, 75
17.21: 32
17.28–29: 12, 31
20.29: 115
21–26: 33
25.10–11: 33
26.31–32: 33

27.21–25: 66

Romans
2.4–5: 84
3.3: 32
3.4: 150
3.19: 48, 54
3.25: 140
3.25–26: 151
3.26: 64
3.29–30: 54
3.30: 64
4.3: 147
4.17–18: 147
4.22–23: 147
5.1–2: 144
5.8–9: 50
5.12: 88, 91
5.13: 88
5.14: 87
5.19: 21, 91
5.21: 91
6.3–4: 50
6.4: 92
6.9: 50, 94
6.23: 93
7.24–25: 88, 159
8.20: 174
8.29: 137, 151
8.34: 50
9.1–2: 162
9.3: 37, 38, 62
9.20: 164
10.3: 35
11.16: 29
11.17: 54(2)
11.18: 166
11.24: 54
12.3: 137
13.3–4: 33
13.14: 162
14.4: 56, 86
14.10: 33, 140
14.11: 146
14.23: 163

1 Corinthians
1.4–7: 144
1.7–8: 145
1.21: 35

2.9: 94
3.3: 43
3.6-7: 47
3.6-8: 166
3.7: 142, 169
3.9: 47, 166
3.10: 25
3.11: 153
3.17: 75
4.5: 132
4.8: 56
4.15: 92
5.3-5: 59, 81
5.5: 47, 48, 49, 57
5.6: 78
5.11: 59
5.13: 59
6.7: 145
7.7: 67
7.28: 60
9.10: 142
9.17: 152
9.22: 62, 158
9.27: 147
10.1-4: 49
10.11: 54
10.12: 147
10.26: 143
10.33: 34
11.14: 21
11.16: 19, 33
11.27: 78
11.29-32: 78
12.4-6: 138
12.8-10: 138
12.11: 138
12.12-30: 138
12.14: 42
13.2-3: 36
13.7: 44
15.10: 127
15.19: 93
15.45: 92
15.47: 92
15.49: 92
15.54-56: 165
15.56: 90

2 Corinthians
2.6-8: 60

2.9: 21
2.10-11: 26, 60
4.11: 158
5.6-7: 93
5.7: 148
5.9-10: 140
6.14-15: 60
7.9: 24
7.10: 24
11.10: 162, 174
11.29: 44
12.2: 37
12.9: 164, 166
12.10: 164
12.21: 24

Galatians
1.8: 39
3.6: 147
3.15: 51
3.28: 54
4.4: 155
4.9: 94
5.9: 78
5.13: 74
5.16: 162
6.1: 24
6.1-2: 62
6.2: 167

Ephesians
1.3-10: 154
2.3: 140
2.20: 40, 54, 68
3.20-21: 165
4.2-3: 44
4.7: 137
4.8: 137, 151
5.25: 44
5.27: 40, 43
5.30: 40, 43
5.31-32: 91

Philippians
1.21: 93
1.23: 93
2.9: 136
2.10: 140
2.11: 140, 146
2.25: 25

4.6-7: 164

Colossians
1.16: 173
2.3: 138
2.8: 32
2.9: 138, 151
2.13-15: 93
2.14: 170
2.14-15: 90
2.18: 94
3.2-4: 165

2 Thessalonians
2.3-4: 134
2.5-6: 156
2.10-11: 83

1 Timothy
2.5: 151
3.15: 40
5.18: 25, 43
5.22: 61, 79
6.16: 151

2 Timothy
1.4: 55
2.13: 19
2.17: 43, 147
2.20: 40, 43, 68
3.8-9: 64
4.1: 133

Titus
1.7: 145
1.10-11: 34
1.12-13: 31
3:10: 19

Hebrews
10.1: 54

James
2.23: 147
3.2: 159

1 Peter
1.3-5: 154
1.9-10: 144
2.22: 89, 90, 151

(1 Peter *continued*)
  2.25: 26
  3.20: 63

2 Peter
  1.19: 139(2)
  2.17: 63(2)
  3.9: 85
  3.10: 133

1 John
  1.8: 159
  2.1: 50
  3.8: 133

  5.16: 57, 75
  5.20: 138

Jude
  12: 63

Revelation
  2.5: 48, 86
  2.17: 169
  2–3: 24

  3.17: 161
  3.19: 72
  5.2–3: 134
  5.5: 134
  5.6: 134(2), 135
  13.10: 75
  18.7: 84
  20.11: 133
  20.12: 131

www.ingramcontent.com/pod-product-compliance
Lightning Source LLC
Chambersburg PA
CBHW032037290426
44110CB00012B/837